SIEGE: Malta

Other Books by Ernle Bradford

The Story of the *Mary Rose*
The Mighty *Hood*
The Great Siege
Ulysses Found
Three Centuries of Sailing
The Companion Guide to the Greek Islands
The Mediterranean: Portrait of a Sea
The Shield and the Sword: the Knights of St. John
The Sword and the Scimitar: the Saga of the Crusades
The Year of Thermopylae

Biographies

Southward the Caravels: the story of Henry the Navigator
Drake
The Sultan's Admiral: the life of Barbarossa
Christopher Columbus
Nelson
Hannibal
Julius Caesar: the pursuit of power

SIEGE: Malta 1940-1943

Ernle Bradford

PEN & SWORD MILITARY CLASSICS

First published in 1985 by Hamish Hamilton Limited
Published in 2003, in this format, by
PEN & SWORD MILITARY CLASSICS
an imprint of
Pen & Sword Books Limited
47, Church Street
Barnsley
S. Yorkshire
S70 2AS

© Ernle Bradford, 1985, 2003

ISBN 0 85052 930 1

A CIP record for this book is
available from the British Library

Printed in England by
CPI UK

Contents

'If the Turks should prevail against the Isle of Malta it is uncertain what further peril might follow to the rest of Christendom.'

Queen Elizabeth I. 1565.

'To Honour her brave people I award the George Cross to the Island Fortress of Malta to bear witness to a Heroism and Devotion that will long be famous in History.'

King George VI. 1942.

Illustrations

Maps

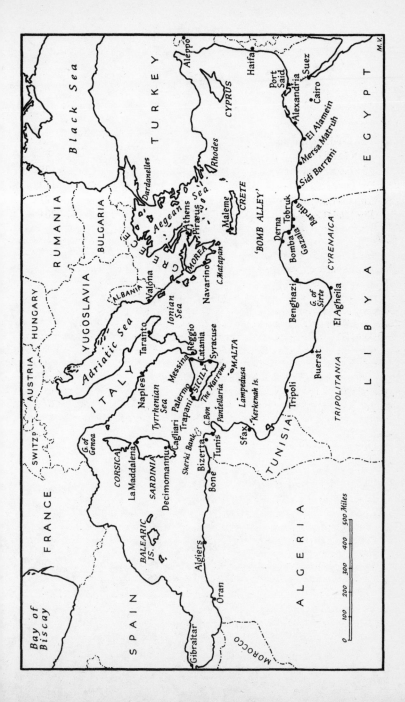

Author's Foreword

I first saw Malta as navigating officer of a destroyer in July 1943. I was on the bridge at dawn, and I remember when the sun rose how the low tawny coast showed up on our port bow as we made our landfall, slightly to the south of Grand Harbour and the island's capital, Valletta. Six months after the siege had ended the waters around the island were still dangerous from mines of every type, and we were very careful to stay well within the swept channel as we made our approach to the harbour entrance.

Malta had haunted me – and I suppose all others in the Mediterranean fleet – ever since I had first arrived in this sea at the age of nineteen in 1941. It was a name famous throughout the world, but also a name of ill-omen and foreboding. How often had I seen merchant ships loading in Alexandria, destroyers alongside jetties taking on stores, and barges going out to capital ships deep-laden with ammunition and stores of every kind – all for Malta. Twice I had been destined for the island myself on what was euphemistically called 'the Malta run'. Once, the ship in which I was serving had been torpedoed; the second time, in another ship, our convoy had been turned back to Alexandria because too many merchantmen had been lost to make it worth proceeding. In any case, we were less than half way there and most of the escorting ships had almost run out of anti-aircraft ammunition. The violence of the action during that convoy, in the sinister area south of Crete known as 'Bomb Alley', had stayed in my mind as nightmarishly as the battle of Crete itself. So, to see Malta at long last from a destroyer's bridge, unbombed and untorpedoed, seemed a kind of achievement.

To enter Grand Harbour, with the long defences of Fort Ricasoli on the port hand and bomb-battered Fort St Elmo (a legend in itself) to starboard, was to sail into history. Some of my friends and many wartime acquaintances had died in or off this island, and many more had failed to reach it or never succeeded in getting back to Alexandria. Malta was no enchanted place that lured men towards it with siren voices but, rather, a Medusa that killed with a glance. I was vaguely aware that it had an ancient and remarkable history, but young men who are in the thick of modern history have little or no time for the past. In any case, as I saw the moment that

xiii

we entered Grand Harbour, a new part of Malta's amazing story was unfolding.

That great inlet of sea had probably never before been so full of ships in all its long maritime life: battleships and aircraft carriers (cruisers were almost commonplace) and – as for destroyers, mine-sweepers and lesser fry – their masts, guns and radar antennae bristled above every dusty stretch of quayside or landing stage. Hardly had we ourselves secured in our appointed berth – outboard of two others – than an American destroyer came in alongside us. (I have long forgotten her name or number, but I remember that her first lieutenant was one of President Roosevelt's sons, for we became acquainted later over a drink in our wardroom.) Every one of the harbours and creeks of Malta – even those rarely used – was as thick with ships as Grand Harbour itself. Operation Husky, the assault on Sicily, was due to start in three days' time.

To say I saw nothing of Malta during the war may sound absurd since I revisited the island on at least a dozen occasions, but all I remember is trudging ashore occasionally through dust and ruined buildings on some official business connected with the ship. There was little enough to go ashore for 'on pleasure bent', and the war in the Mediterranean was now elsewhere: first Sicily, then Italy and the Salerno landings, and finally Anzio. To Malta our ship returned to revictual, reammunition, refuel, and on one occasion to have some shell damage repaired – from, of all unlikely things, a German Tiger tank in Sicily's Augusta harbour. A friend, who was in Hal Far for over a year during the siege, remembers nothing but his flying operations and a few parties in the mess; another, who was in one of the cruisers of Force H, remembers, apart from the air raids, the joy of coming back after one successful operation and finding the whole of Grand Harbour lined with cheering people. For myself, when I finally left, posted to the Home Fleet and Russian convoys, I never expected nor particularly wanted to see the island again.

I returned to Malta, this time of my own volition, in 1951 at the helm of my own small sailing boat. During the following three years I used Malta as my base for expeditions to Greece and the Aegean islands and as many other places in the central and eastern Mediterranean as I could find time for.

It was during the months spent in Malta, wintering or refitting after some cruise, that I really got to know something of its people and its strange, intense quality. By that time most of the damage from the war had been made good, although work would still go on for years, and the authorities were being wise enough in almost all places to restore rather than rebuild in the usual post-war fashion. I spent one whole winter in the small boat harbour originally designed for the galleys of the Knights of St John that lies between Fort St Angelo and the old city of Vittoriosa. In the narrow twisting alleys (heavily bombed during the war) vivid now with life, where carved coats-of-arms in stone and elaborate windows and doorways still spoke of the sixteenth century, I did my daily shopping. Boat trips by *dghaisa* across Grand Harbour brought me to the restored grandeur of Valletta, and many expeditions into the countryside began to uncover for me something of the extraordinary complexity of this island. Smaller than Britain's Isle of Wight, it contains in its onion-skin towns and villages layer upon layer of ancient life and cultures, while parts of the barren and scarcely visited ridge-land to the west speak of an unfathomable past, older even than the great neolithic and copper age temples that are one of Malta's gifts to the world.

During those years and subsequently I have been to most of the islands in the Mediterranean, from the Balearics in the west to Cyprus in the east, to the far north of the Aegean and to sun-blinded Jerba in the south, yet for some curious reason I have found nowhere that detained me as did Malta and its smaller sister-island, Gozo. They held me so much, indeed, that I lived there for more than ten years. And yet the islands have none of the conventional beauty that draws visitors to so many others in this sea. It was perhaps the rich layers of visible history, going back over thousands of years, that attracted me; but even more than that it was the nature of the people. They had an outward warmth that was not unusual in the Mediterranean, but their friendship once given was totally enduring, and they were endowed with a rock-like strength of character. Something of this I have attempted to show under the terrible conditions of adversity during the siege of 1940–1943.

I went back to the island in 1960 intent on writing a history of that other siege – by the Ottomans in 1565 – of which Voltaire had said, 'Nothing is better known than the siege of Malta,' but of which practically nothing had been written in English. It was while I was working on this book that a friend who had been in the island throughout the Second World War, and had married and settled there, remarked that he thought my subject had been much written about during the war itself. I realised we were talking at cross purposes and explained that the siege I was trying to explore and describe was not the recent one. Thinking about it, I reckoned I was lucky to be dealing with such old material, since reputations were inviolate and even the effects of the whole action had long since ceased to have much bearing on modern times. The recent siege would, I thought, prove much more difficult: over-documented and laden with pit-falls.

I considered then that fifty years would need to pass, before enough dust had settled, for the Second World War 'Great Siege of Malta' to be viewed in anything like perspective. It is a few years less that that, but I have now attempted it. The survivors, even in the island, are relatively few – for many Maltese have emigrated in the past forty years – and the passions and sadnesses of those days have largely faded or been burned away by many subsequent summer suns. The ships are all gone under the sea and most of the men with them. Grand Harbour, though merchantmen still call and cruise liners visit, is largely a place of peace and silence now. Manoel Island in Marsamuscetto, the former submarine headquarters, provides berths for a multitude of yachts, of all shapes and sizes under the flags of all nations. Luqa airport, vastly extended since those days, roars only with jet airliners, full of businessmen and tourists, coming and going. (They provide those peaceful flashes in the sky.) Malta is an independent Republic, although its flag is still the same half white, half red, that has flown for centuries, and English is still the second language.

After so many years living in the island, ten of them in a house on Kalkara Creek, seeing Grand Harbour under my eyes every day, I found that the second siege would not leave me alone. I had written about the first, and a history of the Knights, but the ghosts of my contemporaries encountered on early morning or evening walks beside the still waters of the harbour seemed to represent something of a reproach. How distant does history have to be before you can write about it? It has not been any easier than I estimated it would be – a quarter of a century ago.

Ernle Bradford
London, 1985

xvi

CHAPTER ONE

A Distant Day

Over dinner on 11 June 1940, Hitler heard that the Italians had just bombed Malta. He was at his temporary headquarters in a deserted village in southern Belgium, and the second half of his campaign against France, Operation 'Red', was proceeding as smoothly as was the whole German war machine. France, weak within and without, was collapsing according to plan, and almost on schedule — something that hadn't been achieved by the invading armies of the Kaiser in the First World War. These were the golden hours of Hitler's life, and it might have been expected that his Italian partner would manage to inject the only note of discord.

Mussolini had served a formal declaration of war on Britain and France the previous day, provoking his ally's contempt. Hitler held that such things belonged with the Middle Ages and were no more than a hypocritical pretence that the Age of Chivalry was not dead. He believed in striking first, and let the scream of the dive-bombers and the grinding clatter of the tanks be the declaration of war. Over dinner the select group of a dozen or so who attended on the Führer discussed the Italian action. They agreed it was no more than a gesture of course, for it was no secret that the British Mediterranean fleet had withdrawn from Malta to Alexandria; Mussolini with Latin grandiosity was serving notice on nothing of importance. It was over an empty harbour, old buildings and sun-stunned peasants, that the Regia Aeronautica triumphantly rode the air-waves of the sky. The Germans already doubted whether his fleet would do the same upon the sea and, if they really meant business, why were the Italians not already bombarding Malta's Grand Harbour prior to a seaborne invasion? It should have been possible, for the modern Caesar laid claim to the Middle Sea in true Roman fashion as 'Mare Nostrum'.

Embittered by the fact that Italy had not clearly associated herself with Germany in the autumn of the previous year, Hitler (who had known about this impending declaration of war for several days) was not prepared to pull the Italian chestnuts out of the fire — and they were already asking for help. They urgently needed formations from the Luftwaffe to assist their drive into France through the Alps, but none could or would be spared until the battle for France was over.

He had tried to persuade the Duce to withhold his entry into the war at this moment but, eager to lay his hands upon the spoils, the other partner in the Axis had determined to rush in as soon as it was clear that France was falling.[1]

Hitler little knew at that time how often over the years to come he would be called to the assistance of his ally in the south, nor how much the weaknesses which would develop in that quarter would later distract him from other all-important theatres of the war. While the British mocked and compared the Italian dictator's activities to a jackal's, the Germans cynically nicknamed their allies 'the harvest hands' for their entry upon the field at such a moment. Over the Mediterranean, which had hardly yet become a theatre of war, the seeds of distrust between the Axis partners were already sown.

It was at five minutes to seven on that blue June morning when the first of thousands of air raid warnings sounded over the island of Malta. They had long been expected, and indeed Malta had held practice blackouts years before they became a part of life in the western world, for the island had been anticipating war ever since the Italian-Abyssinian crisis of 1935. A shadow of terror, arising from the First World War, was the expectation that in any subsequent conflict poison gas would be used — dropped from aircraft this time not, as before, released from canisters on the ground. Although it was highly unlikely that gas would be effective on a small island where, even in an apparent calm, some light airs were always stirring, almost the only preparations that had been made, and instructions given to the civilian population, were anti-gas. High-explosive and incendiary bombs had hardly been taken into account. As early as October 1935 the first mock air raid had been carried out on Malta's capital, Valletta, with dummy explosions, church bells ringing as a warning, and public utilities turned off. The explosions, very similar to the petards that the Maltese loved to fire during their many religious festas, had brought cheering people out on to the streets.[2] It was very different in 1940, and it would be years before the bells would call to church or the fireworks of peace explode.

The great island of Sicily was only sixty miles to the north and, even without the early radar which had been installed on Malta, the enemy raiders would soon have been spotted in that clear summer sky. Two small groups — ten planes in all — of Savoia Marchetti trimotor bombers were escorted by nine Macchi fighters. Little enough in itself for the first raid of the war, they were more like the gauntlet flung down to confirm the high words of their leader on the previous day. They came over at about 20,000 feet in the conventional high-level bombing technique of the time — one that the Germans had already discounted, having proved over Europe that it

2

was low-level dive-bombing tactics that were accurate and at the same time instilled the maximum amount of terror.

The sun flashes on their silver fuselages, the rumble of their engines, these inspired an unknown fear among the watching population. Like so many in those distant days, the Maltese who looked skyward knew only by picture and report of the devastation caused by bombing, in countries that seemed to them very far away. Anticipation of pain, injury, loss and death is often worse than the reality which, when it occurs, must be borne and somehow or other endured. Then from far up, the high-whistling, thin-screaming of the falling bombs began, and the sound of the anti-aircraft barrage — mute indeed compared with what it would become — reinforced by the guns of the old monitor, *Terror*, and two 'China river gunboats', *Aphis* and *Lady Bird*, moored in the harbour to aid the shore defences, thundered on eardrums used only to the sounds of island life. It had begun. Like random dabs of shaving soap the first shells burst against the sky below the high-flying silver fish that seemed so inhuman, but in which young Italians also endured their baptism of fire and felt for the first time the great lift of bursting air below them that told of a fearful hostility equal to their own.[3]

An island is always besieged by the surrounding sea. Its inhabitants throw up the defences of breakwaters and harbour walls, which must constantly be defended and repaired, while in the surge and thunder of bad weather the natural defences of cliff and headland are always under assault. Unlike the inhabitants of large countries, islanders are accustomed to the feeling of being on their own; independent people, but dependent for any connection with the outside world upon the estranging sea that only unites through boat or ship. The intensification of this eternal siege by an act of war is not so grave a shock then as is similar violence to the inhabitants of an inland city in a large landmass. The islanders are accustomed in any case to foreign intrusion — commercial, friendly or hostile. Deep in their racial memory lie the necessary responses designed to cope with the arrival of a strange race by sea, a different language used by visiting traders, or the knowledge that some alteration in the balance of power among the distant, invisible nations will inevitably mean a change in their own lives. People who live on small islands do not expect to be able to alter things; theirs is the acceptance world.

On that first day of their war there were eight air raids on their homeland. In the later raids of the afternoon and early evening thirty-eight bombers escorted by twelve fighters returned.[4] The last raid was the most unpleasant, but all of them were primarily designed to demoralize the population as well as cause damage to the dockyard installations and the airforce bases. That there was no

3

force of fighters to rise to meet the raiders, or to be destroyed on the ground, was due to a decision taken long ago by the Royal Air Force that Malta was indefensible in the event of war. Only three old Gloster Gladiator fighters had clattered up from Hal Far airstrip — to the surprise of many of the defenders who did not even know of their existence, and to the alarm of the attackers who had been incorrectly informed that no fighters were to be expected.

The casualties were heavy, almost all civilian — indeed only a few soldiers were killed at their posts and no guns were knocked out. They were mostly among the families which lived in the small cube-shaped houses around the dockyard. This was inevitable under high-level bombing attack — inaccurate as it was at that time — and the fact that Malta, and particularly its dockyard area, was one of the most densely-populated areas in Europe.

No one had visualised the scenes of a modern air raid in which civilian men, women and children would die under bomb-blast or be razored by flying glass and metal or crushed under falling walls. Violent death was something that was associated in the island principally with sailors in the great warships, or with airmen up in the remote sky, or perhaps with gunners at their posts, but very few had any idea of what it meant. Even the warships with their ominous long guns, sleeping like peaceful whales in Grand Harbour and the adjacent creeks of the island throughout the summers of the interwar years, had been regarded on the whole with affection, as a source of revenue. The distant thunder of the guns on practice shoots off the island had been no more disturbing than the familiar rumble of electric storms over the Mediterranean — part of the pattern of life. Their real purpose and that of the aircraft, hitherto regarded as pretty and eccentric new toys of the island's rulers, was not fully revealed.

Things can be anticipated but not really understood, and certainly the reality of unknown things can never be fully imagined. About thirty civilians killed and more wounded was something immediately felt throughout a population of 250,000 of closely-knit families, where at some point or another it would often seem in conversation that everyone was related to everyone else.[5] One thing that was quickly established in those first raids was that the solid limestone blocks with which most of the houses were built, combined with their flat roofs of stone, made them almost impervious to incendiary bombs and highly resistant even to high-explosive. The island itself was little more than a huge block of limestone rising out of the sea, and it was this geological fact that was to contribute to its defensibility under horrific bombardment. That the stone could be easily quarried meant that hundreds of tunnels would soon shelter

4

its people, resulting in a casualty rate almost unbelievably low when measured against the thousands of tons of explosives that would be rained down upon the island.

The long embattled history of the Mediterranean has witnessed innumerable sieges. There is hardly a city on a headland, hardly an island out of the hundreds in the sea, that at some time or other has not been the subject of a siege, great or small.

Standing at the crossroads of the sea, Malta had inevitably been involved in previous sieges. Indeed, until 1940, the Great Siege of Malta in 1565 had been one of the most famous in recorded history. Then, the Ottoman Empire under Suleiman the Magnificent had attacked this outlying bastion of Christendom — and been defeated. Of this savage epic Voltaire had said, 'Nothing is better known than the siege of Malta.' In the Wars of Religion Malta, as the fortress home of the Knights of St John, had played a major part in the Marches of the West. So famous had the island become after 1565 that the oldest Order of Chivalry in existence, and the third oldest religious Order in Christendom, had become known simply throughout the world as 'The Knights of Malta'.[6] In the many accounts in almost every known European language of the Knights and their deeds — particularly during that Great Siege — one thing had largely escaped the attention of biographers and historians — the people of Malta themselves. Now, as the first day of the twentieth century siege ended, they started a new phase in their lives — most in their familiar small homes near the harbours but many, resuming a trek that had begun with the outbreak of war, to friends, relatives or acquaintances in outlying villages.

On the following day, 12 June 1940, one Italian reconnaissance aircraft flew over from Sicily to assess the damage caused by the first acts of war. It was shot down.

5

CHAPTER TWO

Islanded in Time

At the cross roads of the Mediterranean, almost equidistant from Gibraltar on the one hand and Cyprus on the other, the small Maltese archipelago commands the trade routes not only between East and West, but between North and South. Sicily lies sixty miles to the north and Tripoli in Africa is just over two hundred miles to the south. Gibraltar and Cyprus (or Port Said for the Suez Canal) are each about one thousand miles away. In the siege of 1565 the Sultan Suleiman had been interested in Malta as a stepping stone to Sicily and Italy for the expansion of his empire into Europe. Over two centuries later, Napoleon had seized the island in 1798 on his way from Europe for the conquest of Egypt and the East. In this new siege that was beginning it was the north-south axis that interested Mussolini, since this was the main sea-route between Italy and Sicily and the Italian colony of Tripolitania to the south.

As in 1565, Malta was the focus of attention for the warring powers upon this sea because the island possessed in its Grand Harbour and other ancillary harbours and anchorages the finest fleet base in the central Mediterranean. The accident of nature that had carved Grand Harbour with its attendant creeks out of Malta's north-eastern coast into a deepwater basin that could easily accommodate the draughts of modern battleships and aircraft carriers and their attendant deep-laden tankers had made its acquisition important even in the days of comparatively shallow-draught warships and merchantmen. A natural harbour, standing in the centre of the sea, it was unique.

It was small wonder that Malta had featured in Mediterranean history long before history was even written. The Neolithic and Copper Age temples to be found in greater profusion and sophistication than anywhere else in the world made the island unique again. After these unknown temple builders had died out or departed, the Phoenicians trading with Spain in the far west for tin and other metals had been the first to use the island's harbours and, since they had no need for deep water but only a place to drag their boats ashore for repair and security, had made their settlement at Marsaxlokk, the shallow Southern Harbour. Their descendants, the Carthaginians, had found the island a useful stepping-stone to their

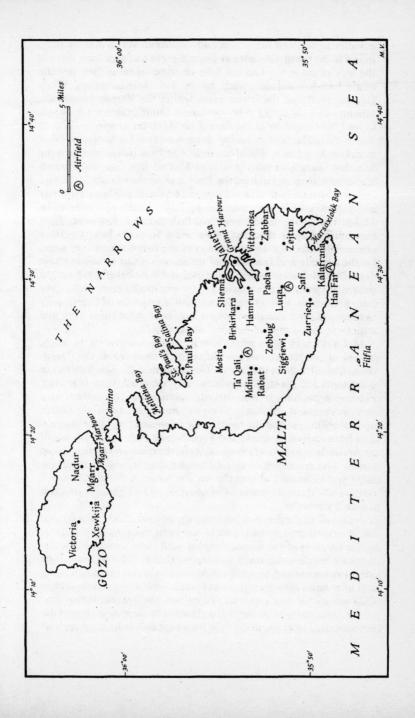

colonies in western Sicily and had colonized Malta and its sister island to the north, Ghaudex or Gozo. Greeks had also come there in the way of trade but had left little imprint, whereas their Semitic rivals had left not only their tombs but their language. When Carthage fell and the island came within the Roman empire the inhabitants were found to be speaking a Semitic dialect, which was to lead the chronicler of the Acts of the Apostles to refer to them as 'barbaroi', barbarians, meaning those who spoke a language other than Greek or Latin. The shipwreck of St Paul (traditionally in the bay that bears his name) produced Malta's first Christian church leader or bishop in Publius, the head man of the island.

The Christian faith then is a very old tradition in Malta. However much it may have been overlaid by Islam in the centuries when Malta, like Sicily, was subject to Moslem rule it has never been extinguished since the visit of the Apostle. This fact is neither obscure nor irrelevant to the history of the twentieth century siege, for the attitude and behaviour of the islanders can to some certain degree be attributed to their deep faith, and their belief that from the time of St Paul's visit they have come under special protection. They have a more real and traceable link with the founder of Christianity than any of the subsequent nobles who have ruled them have had with their so-called blue-blooded ancestors.

Malta is a slate upon which is written and overwritten the whole history of the Mediterranean.[1] After the Romans came the Byzantines, and after them the Arabs. The latter in their two centuries of occupation left the most significant imprint of all, their language. Finding a population who already spoke some old version of a Semitic tongue it was not difficult to impress their Islamic Arabic upon the Maltese and the modern language, despite all its borrowings from Italian, Spanish, and French (and later, English), is still an Arabic language in grammar and construction and in all its basic words. The possession of this distinctive tongue, and their attachment to the Roman Catholic church, has served to sustain this small community through centuries of occupation and given them their national character.

Although in the decades following the Second World War Malta, like every other western country, has been changed by the internationalization of the world, coupled with some decline in simple religious belief, it still keeps a character that is different from all its Mediterranean neighbours. Since Malta is only seventeen miles long and nine miles across at its widest point, with a population that in 1939 was a little over a quarter of a million, the fact that throughout all the vicissitudes of history it has retained its identity is close to the miraculous. The key to this is to be found not only in its language and

8

churches but in its villages and countryside. Many British servicemen billeted in remote parts of the island during the last siege stumbled upon this secret Malta with some surprise (as is recorded in published books and records and private diaries that have survived). It might have been with Malta in mind that Virginia Woolf wrote: 'The peasants are the great sanctuary of sanity, the country the last stronghold of happiness. When they disappear there is no hope for the race.'

After the Arabic centuries came the Norman conquest, restoring the Church which had greatly declined (since those who did not accept Islam paid a heavy tax for the privilege) and, although rulers rather than colonizers, the Normans brought the island back once again within the European fold. This process was further strengthened by the Aragonese who, with their controlling interest in Sicily, introduced some aspects of Spanish life and culture as well as reinforcing its Catholic ties. When the island was finally given by the Emperor Charles V to the homeless Knights of St John in 1530 the period of its greatest fame and prosperity was at hand. The Knights were members of the oldest and richest families in Europe and the fame which Malta acquired in the Great Siege of 1565 resulted in an influx of money as well as making it from then on a focus of international interest. During the centuries to come, through their organized and 'official' piracy of the Moslem shipping lanes, the Order and with it the island prospered. From this period date the innumerable fortifications which protect and embellish its rocky shores as well as the magnificent palaces, churches, and the great cathedral of St John; many of these buildings were of course badly damaged or destroyed in the Second World War.

By the end of the eighteenth century the Order had become an anachronism in the new nationalistic Europe and its rule over Malta collapsed with hardly a sign before the armada of Napoleon on its way to pursue his imperialistic ambitions in the East. It was now that the Maltese, not for the first time in their long history, displayed that dogged and resolute character which was to be so marked a feature of the years between 1940 and 1943. They may well have been tired of the Knights, who had become not only decadent but inefficient in their later years, but they were not prepared to accept the arrogance and the atheism displayed by the revolutionary French. More than anything else it was the wanton defacement and vandalizing of their beloved churches — the heart of every village and the cornerstone of their lives — which drove them to revolt against the French garrison imposed upon them by the departing Napoleon.

This spirited reaction of an illiterate peasantry, led by their priests

9

and a handful of educated people, against the conquerors of Europe, the all-powerful French, was very significant. At that time no country except Britain withstood the triumphant armies of Napoleon, yet now, in the middle of the Mediterranean Sea, the people of a little island had had the temerity to reject him, his soldiers, and his revolutionary doctrines. With the assistance of British troops and the Royal Navy the Maltese proceeded to conduct a siege of their own capital, Valletta, where the French had taken refuge. By the autumn of 1800, after an occupation of just over two years, the French were forced to capitulate and leave the island. 'Brave Maltese', said a British colonel who had served with the Anglo-Maltese land forces, 'you have rendered yourselves interesting and conspicuous to the world. History affords no more striking example.'

In the maelstrom of the war that engulfed Europe the Maltese now sought for protection within the British Empire. But the British curiously enough were reluctant at this time to add the island to their many other charges. Even Nelson, whose victory at the Battle of the Nile had largely led to the French capitulation in Valletta, did not at first see the importance of Malta's position in the Mediterranean. Napoleon on the other hand had never been in any doubt, declaring: 'Peace or war depends upon Malta.... I would put you in possession of the Faubourg Saint Antoine rather than of Malta.'

By the time the long Anglo-Napoleonic war had come to an end the British had had time to realise the significant role that Malta played in the control and administration of the Mediterranean, as well as commanding the sea route to the East. In 1814, and confirmed a year later at the Congress of Vienna, the Maltese islands came under the British Crown. Below the Royal Arms on the Main Guard in the Palace Square of Valletta are engraved in Latin the words: 'To Great and Unconquered Britain the Love of the Maltese and the Voice of Europe Confirms these Islands AD 1814.' This then was a colony unusual among all the many in the British Empire in that the protection of Great Britain had been sought by the inhabitants at all levels, and that both Maltese and British had fought together to restore the island's freedom against an unwanted conquering power. The intervening hundred and twenty-five years had cemented this union between a small island race of basically Semitic blood, situated between the two worlds of Europe and Africa, and the northern island race whose Mediterranean fleet had come to form the mainstay of Malta's economy. The island could never feed itself, had always been dependent upon grain imports, and especially so since the great expansion in population from the nineteenth century onward. There had been much intermarriage

10

and, although there had been a number of differences on matters of internal politics, the soldiers and sailors of all ranks and classes had got on well with the Maltese islanders, above all perhaps because they shared a coarse and earthy sense of humour.

Malta, despite the Great Depression of the thirties, was affluent compared to most Mediterranean countries. Visitors during the inter-war years might have echoed the remarks of the eighteenth century traveller Patrick Brydone[2] who visited Sicily and Malta in 1770: 'on getting on shore [Valletta] we found ourselves in a new world indeed. The streets crowded with well-dressed people, who have all the appearance of health and affluence; whereas at Syracuse there was scarce a creature to be seen; and even those few had the appearance of disease and wretchedness.... [We found] an inn, which had more the appearance of a palace. We have had an excellent supper, and good Burgundy.... We are now going into clean, comfortable beds, in expectation of the sweetest of slumbers.'

Malta's sister island Gozo lies across a narrow strait a few miles to the north-west. About half the size and without harbours, Gozo was untouched by the Great Siege of 1565 and relatively little affected during the greater siege that was about to start. True, a few bombers would offload unused bombs on Gozo if fleeing back to the north, or machine-gun fishing boats or people on the roads, but Gozo remained, as it had always been, the farm and vegetable garden for the larger island. In the channel between the two was the small island of Comino, inhabited by a few peasant families, and an uninhabited islet, Cominotto. Just off the south coast of Malta was Filfla, another uninhabited island, and there was yet another on the east coast surmounted by a statue of St Paul, marking the entrance to the bay where the Apostle was reputed to have been shipwrecked. Such was the totality of the Maltese archipelago upon which all the efforts of the Axis partners were to be directed in an attempt to neutralize it by siege. This, although predominantly carried out by air, would also entail the mining by submarine and surface craft of all the approaches to it, and the destruction by submarine, surface warships and bombers of any convoy that endeavoured to break a blockade which for long periods, not of weeks but of months, seemed to present a complete ring of steel.

It was this apparent indefensibility of Malta in the event of a war involving Italy that had led the British Army and particularly the Royal Air Force to conclude that, in view of the proximity of seemingly overwhelming air power which could be deployed by Italy's Regia Aeronautica from its bases in Sicily, Malta would be untenable. The Navy did not share this opinion. That the British Mediterranean Fleet had now withdrawn to Alexandria, and that the Italian navy could match it ship for ship, and with a greater number of submarines, and that most of the Italian battlefleet was completely modern as compared with the ageing British capital ships, all seemed to argue that the pessimistic view of Malta's future was the correct one.

CHAPTER THREE

The Divided Sea

In the early summer of 1940 the Mediterranean seemed relatively quiet. The eastern end was dominated by the British from their fleet base at Alexandria, while the western basin was in the hands of the French from their harbours in North Africa and the South of France. In the centre, however, the young but powerful navy of Italy's Duce posed a threat to both the older established powers. With the fall of France the whole balance of sea power suddenly and drastically altered.

'Graver and graver became the news from France,' wrote Admiral Cunningham, recalling those days when he was Commander-in-Chief of the Mediterranean fleet, 'until, on 24 June, we heard that she had capitulated to Germany and Italy.' He himself had never been in any doubt about the importance of Malta to the control of the Mediterranean. It was he who had given the authority for the four Gloster Gladiators to be uncrated from boxes where they had been found on the island and which were to provide the only fighter coverage (and a remarkable deterrent they proved) in those early days.[1] One of these was destroyed in the first day's engagement, but for some time to come the other three were to furnish a morale booster to the islanders and to the men on the guns. There were few enough guns — sufficient for shore defence against the anticipated landings that never came, but there was a great shortage of anti-aircraft guns. There would be just enough to keep the Regia Aeronautica on high and imperfect courses for the moment, during which time convoys would bring into the island sufficient guns of heavy and light calibre to stand up under the thunderous Wagnerian onslaught that was to come.

With the fall of France the Mediterranean was left in a state of vacuum — one which by reason of their geographical position the Italian navy should have found it easy to fill. Their fast modern ships, their preponderance of submarines, and their recently modernized harbours and port installations at Taranto on the heel of Italy, and in Sicily and the coast of the Italian peninsula, in theory dominated all but the eastern Mediterranean now that the French fleet was out of the war. Many factors, however, militated against the triumph that should have been theirs (including the reduction of the small island of Malta). It was not lack of courage as British propaganda was to maintain at the time, for courage — particularly of an individual character — was something the Italians were to display at sea over and over again in later actions during the war. Morale was another matter. At a lower-deck level, among sailors less well-educated and less well-trained than their British counterparts, this essential canvas of a navy was too light to withstand the storm of war. Sailors, to be of use in a modern battle fleet, were hardly to be found among the fishermen and merchant seamen raised in the waters of the Mediterranean. Coming from bad housing, underpaid and poorly educated, they were often regarded by their superior officers as little more than seagoing peasants. If officers were something of a superior class in the British navy, they were a whole gulf of culture and breeding apart from their sailors in the Italian. The officers in the imposing Marine Militare of the Duce were, as they demonstrated in small boat exploits and in mini-submarines, capable of that passionate bravery — especially of a quixotic kind — which is almost a hallmark of the Latin races. The long and boring endurance of modern warfare, however, calls for a slower and more dour kind of courage. Among many officers, moreover, and particularly the more senior, there was always a feeling that their loyalties were to old-fashioned values, to noble blood, and to the royal family. The Duce, it could not be disguised, was a common fellow. (Many German officers felt this also about their Führer, but he at least had proved his brilliance, and had shown a grasp of strategy far in advance of anything that the well-bred military *ancien régime* of Germany had demonstrated in the Kaiser's war.)

The Italian navy had good ships, good guns, good torpedoes, and flashless ammunition — but they lacked radar, which was as yet far from universal in the British fleet. At all levels, however, and this of course mattered most at the top, they lacked confidence. The age-old reputation of the Royal Navy overawed them, and they lived and fought in the sea over which the shadow of Nelson lay like a great cloak. An anecdote in Admiral Cunningham's autobiography points this up in his pawky Scots way.[2] In 1938 two of the Italian battleships that now confronted him, the *Giulio Cesare* and the *Conte di Cavour*, had paid a courtesy visit to Malta. Admiral Riccardi, now Chief of the Italian Naval Staff, was at that time flying his flag in the *Conte di Cavour* and had entertained Cunningham on board. 'We lunched on board the *Conte di Cavour* with Admiral Riccardi, and came to the conclusion that he must have embarked the whole catering staff and band from one of the best hotels in Rome, so distinguished was his entertainment. Afterwards he took us round his palatial and highly decorated private apartments, and took some

14

pride in pointing out a book, *The Life of Nelson*, which always lay on a table by his bedside. His subsequent actions during the war showed that he had not greatly profited by his nightly reading.'

Throughout the war the Italian navy suffered always from the most crippling of constraints — shortage of oil fuel. Whereas the British had full access to the oil of the Persian Gulf, Italy was dependent upon the generosity of her German partner and the oil fields of the Balkans. As German fortunes waxed or waned in later years during their drive into Russia and their pursuit of oil in the east, so did their controlling hands upon the levers that could release oil from Rumania to the fleet of their Italian ally. Without oil and without coal, Italy was always condemned to the role of jackal when her German partner carved up the feast of Europe.

Another major failing in the Italian fleet, accounting to some degree for its indifferent showing during the war, was its complete lack of battle experience; and this is not only an acquired but an inherited characteristic. Lacking a tradition of naval warfare (and few but the Genoese could point back to Andrea Doria with any real confidence) their senior officers could only be fired by the feeling that the Mediterranean was justifiably *their* sea upon which the Anglo-Saxons were trespassing. A colony of these foreigners mingled with semi-Arabs — their Maltese peasants — situated on an unattractive rock to the south of Sicily was a very natural affront of their pride. These sentiments were not enough to produce a necessary fire in the belly. There were other practical matters, their complete lack of training, and therefore skill, in the difficult technique of night fighting. 'They had not', says Cunningham 'visualized a night action between heavy ships and did not keep their heavy guns manned [during the dark hours] ... they were no further advanced than we had been at Jutland twenty-five years before.'[3] These were but some of the reasons why the Italians, with what was on the surface a superb navy, could not keep the British with their fleet of ageing capital ships bottled up in Alexandria — if not destroyed in one great action.

Early sweeps carried out by Cunningham from Alexandria served to confirm the Italian naval command in its sense of inferiority, and increased in the British an inherited self-confidence, which was soon to be eroded when it became evident that it was the power of shore-based aircraft that was to dominate the actions at sea. For the moment both fleets were ill-served by their long range reconnaissance air arm, the Italians being dependent upon single-engined Cant seaplanes which came under their Air Force command, and the British on a handful of flying boats totally incapable of operating within range of shore-based fighter aircraft. Admiral Cunningham

15

had, however, one asset which was never available to the Italians — an aircraft carrier. This was the *Eagle* (originally a battleship built for the Chilean navy, and converted shortly after the 1914-18 war to be one of the first aircraft carriers in the world). Until finally sunk, on one of her many runs to Malta, she carried 17 Swordfish biplanes, designed for reconnaissance and torpedo-carrying. These, slow though they were, proved themselves time and again incomparable in their dual role, while as torpedo-carriers they were to inflict a strike upon the Italian fleet which changed not only the balance of power in the Mediterranean but the whole history of warfare at sea. Flying out of Malta in the years to come Swordfish aircraft were also to inflict grave losses on the Italian shipping fleet as it moved its cargoes of men and material between Europe and North Africa. Highly manoeuvrable, their very slowness was sardonically rated by some pilots as an asset in itself, since enemy fighters and anti-aircraft gunners, they said, could not credit it and missed them accordingly. Nine of these aircraft had reached Malta shortly before the fall of France.

Doubts, which had always existed in London about the British ability to hold Malta in the event of war, were redoubled after the French collapse and the isolation of the British Mediterranean fleet at its port in Egypt. The pre-war policies which had denied Malta its proper complement of anti-aircraft, its fighter squadrons, and its proposed submarine pens cut out of the rock (all subjects which had been discussed and then put aside, partly through ill-reasoned argument and partly through financial stringencies) now seemed to many of those in authority to have been justified; the island was untenable.

It is interesting to note that in the councils of the Knights prior to the Great Siege of 1565 very similar arguments had been advanced against spending money on forts and fortifications as a precaution against attack by the Ottoman Empire. It was Grand Master La Vallette who had then said that there could be no withdrawal and that it was the fate of the Order 'to defend the bare rock to the end', and it was Winston Churchill who now maintained that Malta must be held at all costs or the road to the East would be open to the Axis forces. In this view he was fully supported by his admiral, for Cunningham had never had the slightest doubt about the small island's importance in any conflict that might take place in the Mediterranean. Fortunately for Malta, Hitler was considerably less percipient than his predecessor Napoleon. An early German strike with their immense preponderance of air power against the poorly-equipped island might well have succeeded, and the face of history would indeed have been changed. Malta was a diarchy in theory,

16

with legislative and executive powers divided between the British Governor and the representatives of the Maltese people. This complicated system never worked very effectively and, while it had always been agreed that Imperial strategic interest came first, on other matters there had been some friction. Throughout the whole period of the siege, however, the politics of the island were more or less in abeyance and the Governor was in effective control. One point rarely enough made in official accounts and personal records of these years is that, if the Maltese people had not willingly and fully participated in the defence of their island, the position would indeed have been completely untenable. This is a fact which was constantly ignored by historians of the first great siege, but it should never be forgotten in accounts of the second.

Throughout the pre-war years the Italians had made great efforts through cultural and educational links with the island, as well as more flagrant devices such as promoting the Fascist Youth party, to infiltrate the social structure and to subvert the Maltese from their old allegiance and into some form of union with Italy.[4] It was natural enough for geographic and mercantile reasons that Malta should feel a close affinity with Italy, added to which was the fact that Italian was the accepted cultural language among many of the upper classes. Until 1934 it had indeed been the language of the courts, with English or Maltese used as second languages. But, as only about fifteen per cent of the population spoke Italian (and almost none of the working classes), this anomaly was removed when it was decided that proceedings must be conducted in Maltese, since 'it is the national language of the Island, and the one which every Maltese speaks' ...'[5] This official recognition of Maltese as a written language with the full authority of the law did much to strengthen the people's sense of national identity. It was, as Sir Harry Luke put it, 'its elevation from the kitchen to the Courts.'[6] A comparatively small handful of people — about seventy — whose dedication to Italy, if not to the Duce, made them necessarily suspect to the authorities were detained, most of them being transferred to Kenya in 1942; although there was never any evidence that any of them was liable to emulate Norway's Quisling.

One of the strange things about the siege that was about to develop was the way in which the island sank back almost into its medieval past. The small archipelago had never really become involved with the Renaissance: this had been something that had no part in the consciousness of the ruling Knights and, insofar as it had, it was something to be distrusted. The later developments of Europe were perfectly reflected in the magnificence of the Italo-Spanish baroque which fashioned the palaces, churches and the auberges of the Knights, and the very latest in fortress architecture had always been evident in the immense stone walls, scarps and counterscarps, bastions and demibastions which frowned over Grand Harbour or encircled the dockyard cities on the southern side. This mania for increasing the fortifications of the island was carried on even into the nineteenth century by the British in the Victoria Lines. These spread right across Malta at the geological line known as the Great Fault, and were designed to secure the harbours and populous areas against an improbable French landing. Intellectually, however, as is shown by the contents of the library of the Knights, Malta had been somewhat (some would say deliberately) cut off from the mainstream of European thought. Here the Counter-Reformation had triumphed. The militant catholicism displayed by the Knights of St John, long after the Crusades had become but a distant memory to the new nations of Europe, had become absorbed into the very fabric of the island. The brief French episode and the new spirit of revolutionary France, far from being accepted, had been the principal cause for the Maltese revolt. It is significant that the priests had been foremost among their leaders, and vengeance for their vandalized churches had lit the torch for their liberation from French rule. The British army and navy, governors, civil servants and others who had taken the place of the Knights, were conservative by nature and had been careful not to affront Catholic susceptibilities. Inevitably there had been some incidents involving ardent Protestants attempting to wean Maltese away from Rome, but one of the least successful Governors had been an Irish Anglo-Catholic, and the general policy had always been to leave the clergy to organize the lives and the education of the islanders. Despite all the social and other changes of the inter-war years this policy had remained very much unaltered, with the result that in Malta there was to be found a socio-religious pattern of life that seemed cut off from the modern world. Of Valletta, far more accurately than of Oxford, Matthew Arnold could have written: 'Beautiful city! so venerable, so lovely, so unravaged by the fierce intellectual life of our century, so serene! ... whispering from her towers the last enchantments of the Middle Age.'

The early Italian bombing raids aroused a deep feeling of anger and affront. Apart from the death and wounding of members of the family, relatives and friends, the devastation of churches and familiar landmarks was felt far more deeply by a small race, interconnected, intermarried, and insular in almost every respect of the word. Furthermore, the Maltese, quite unlike their Latin neighbours, although volatile enough in sport and politics, had a distinctly dour strain. It was to serve them in good stead when the regular pattern of air attack from the north continued by day and by night — when,

18

because of the technical limitations of the time, it was inevitably indiscriminate. To the surprise of the population however the long-anticipated gas attacks never occurred, nor did the invasion by sea for which the gunners of the Royal Malta artillery and the British Royal Artillery had prepared in their gun positions around the coast. The island, which the British had always been happy to keep relatively uninfluenced by the modern world (rejected by most pre-war travellers or cruise liners as an army garrison, a fleet-base, not scenically attractive, and somehow secretive), now became completely 'Fortress Malta'.

CHAPTER FOUR

Thunder Afar

Thunder echoes all round the islands on heavy summer nights, and sometimes at the beginning of the first heavy rainfalls in September; from June 1940 its man-made counterfeit would only be absent for a day or two at a time over a period of years. At first, however, the normal processes of life continued almost unchanged: bars, cafés and restaurants (Malta boasted few of the latter) remained open and, if business was not as usual because of air raids, it was superficially little changed. The reason for this was the nature of the island itself. Malta, as the Knights had found out centuries ago, was an ideal fortress because the limestone was so easily quarryable, and within a comparatively short space of time the butter-yellow blocks developed a hard exterior face due to the briny salt wind which is always present, even on hot seemingly airless days. An old railway tunnel outside Valletta was reopened and turned into an immense dormitory that served many of the capital's inhabitants and those of its suburb Floriana in the years to come. Tunnels were also dug out of the solid rock, and some within the dense fortifications left by the Knights. People armed with pickaxes excavated others; caves outside the cities in many parts of the rocky islands were reoccupied for the first time since prehistory; the ghosts of Phoenicians were disturbed in their urn-burial grounds by new families; Mass was celebrated throughout the island in catacombs and communal shelters, as a new persecution of Christians roared overhead. It was like the dawn of Malta's second Neolithic Age.[1]

Eager to test the Italian fleet and the striking power of the Duce's airforce Cunningham had earlier provoked them as much as possible by fleet raids along the North African coast but, apart from the loss of an old light cruiser *Calypso* to an Italian submarine, these assays had done no more than show that the Italians seemed unprepared to defend the ports and installations of their North African colony by bringing their battlefleet to sea. It was used, however, to cover their convoys transporting men and munitions from Italy to Libya and in the second month of Italy's war one such convoy provided an occasion for a trial of strength between the two fleets.

The Italian fleet was out covering an important convoy southward bound for Benghazi, but it was two convoys from Malta which fortuitously had the British fleet at sea on the same date. The Malta convoys, one fast and one slow, were bound for Alexandria. One was carrying naval stores, the other civilians, including the wives and children of service personnel, some of whom were now in Egypt while others were scattered throughout the world in the great dispersion of war. Their departure from the island seemed to many of the defenders to mark the real opening of the siege. It had always been the practice in the past to remove as many noncombatants as possible before the gates closed and the real trial began; but in this case the children and old people among the islanders could not be taken to safety, since such an exodus would have required a vast assembly of merchant ships. Even as it was, one of the only ships available in Malta for this operation was an Italian prize, the *Rodi*. This had been loaded with Italian prisoners of war, who had already reached the island and were the first of the many thousands who, captured in later desert campaigns, would have to be sent on to East Africa and elsewhere. When these prisoners left the island, the Duce's voice was loud in Italy, the legions under the fasces of old Rome marched in parade before him, the Regia Aeronautica proudly rode the skies, and the noble great ships of their navy seemed to dominate the central Mediterranean.

Cunningham, steaming westward in his flagship, *Warspite*, accompanied by two other older battleships and his aircraft carrier *Eagle*, five cruisers and accompanying destroyers, was not only covering these two convoys from surface attack but hoping to provoke the Italian commander, Admiral Inigo Campioni, to a trial of strength. Ashore in Malta the defenders might later become almost indifferent to Italian bombing (secure as most were by then in shelters of their native rock), but at sea Cunningham was soon to discover that the Italian airforce had squadrons specially trained in high-level attack on shipping; operating out of Rhodes (once the home of the Knights of St John) and the other islands of the Dodecanese, the Italian bombers soon proved that they were in no way to be despised. At that time few sailors in the British fleet had had any real experience of bombing — of the high-screaming, ear-piercing whistle of the bombs' descent or the sight of those dark shapes swiftly falling, every one conveying the illusion that it was directed at the individual onlooker. Over and over again as the ships thudded and pounded to the shout of their own guns (comparatively few light anti-aircraft in those days as compared with later), the staccato yammer of the pom-poms, the hard crack of four-inchers, ships were hidden from one another by high-rising curtains of water from near misses. (Dark they seemed against the brightness of sky and sea.) Exploding fragments hammered against steel hulls or

21

swept through sides never designed to ward off high-velocity fragments.

Coming in on a level course at about 12,000 feet, regardless it seemed of the bursting fire around them, their bomb bays opening, their patterned clusters falling, the Italian aircraft presented something completely new and chilling to the British, indeed to any, fleet. Up until now, though the range had increased as technology developed, naval engagements had followed the same basic pattern over the centuries, even when the high explosive shell replaced the cannonball. It was a comfort to remember, remarked Admiral Cunningham, 'that there was always more water than ship' — but not very much, for a ship stood up huge, bare, and exposed above the absorbing flat acres of the sea. Years later he was to write: 'It is not too much to say of those early months that the Italian high-level bombing was the best I have ever seen, far better than the German. . . . I shall always remember it with respect.'

The astonishing thing about that first meeting of the new force from the air and the old force on the sea was that the cruiser *Gloucester* was the only ship to receive a direct hit, though there were dozens of near misses. A bomb exploded on the bridge; the captain was killed, so were six other officers and eleven ratings, while a number of others were wounded. Modern lightly-built ships dependent on the immense complexity of their electrical and communication systems would probably have succumbed; but *Gloucester* had been designed for more old-fashioned actions involving bursting shells (speaking tubes and hand communications if all else failed) and she did not burn disastrously. Within a short space of time she was brought under control, being steered from her aft position, and although reduced in speed resumed her place in the line.

Admiral Cunningham had by now confirmed the information that he had earlier in the day received from the submarine *Phoenix*: an Italian fleet including two battleships was at sea, two hundred miles east of Malta heading south. In the afternoon of 8 July, a flying boat, also out of Malta, old and unsuited for modern warfare but containing trained eyes, sent a further report. There were two battleships at sea, six cruisers and seven destroyers. Clearly they must be covering some important convoy, and the reason for the day's heavy bombing of the British fleet became apparent: it was to deny them use of the central Mediterranean. It was clearly vital to strike towards the heart of the sea and if possible cut off the Italian fleet from its base. Cunningham turned his ships towards Taranto.

The action, in which both battle fleets were covering important 'soft' convoys of merchantmen — out of sight and unharmed in both cases — was in itself the justification for such fleets, though of

Cunningham's three battleships only *Warspite* had recently been modernized, *Malaya* and *Royal Sovereign* were both slow, the latter notoriously so.

Across the summer sea of the central Mediterranean, broomed by the light but steady north-westerly common to those months, the two fleets drew together, the one anxious to provoke an action, the other to avoid it. Admiral Campioni, having covered his convoy to a position north-west of Benghazi, had turned north again. He had been expressly directed by his High Command to keep well to the westward so as not to risk an engagement until noon the following day, by which time his fleet would have come under air cover from Sicily and the Italian mainland.

It was a flying boat out of Malta that once again was the first to report the Italian fleet — about one-hundred and forty-five miles to the westward of Cunningham at 7.30 a.m. next morning. This was soon confirmed by reconnaissance aircraft flown off from the *Eagle*. Admiral Campioni, who should have been informed of the position of the British fleet, was badly let down by his air force: an argument not only in favour of fleets having aircraft carriers with them, but of shore-based aircraft operating with ships being trained by, and coming under the control of the commanding officers afloat. Indeed it was not until nearly noon, when the fleets were some eighty miles apart, that the Italians located the British by means of an aircraft catapulted off Campioni's flagship, the *Giulio Cesare*. He was only about fifty miles from Cape Spartivento at the toe of Italy, close to the Messina Straits, and had every reason to expect that his opponents would by now have come under heavy air attack from shorebased aircraft of the Regia Aeronautica. Nothing. Nevertheless he had many more destroyers than the British, and twelve cruisers altogether — six of them heavy cruisers — against Cunningham's five light cruisers (one of which, *Gloucester*, being damaged, was held back in support of *Eagle*.) His two battleships were considerably faster and recently modernized, and could outrange the British battleships with the sole exception of the *Warspite*. The odds were more than favourable, particularly since every mile he steamed he was drawing more and more under the protection of his own air cover.

The Italians were both dismayed and infuriated by the lack of cooperation from their air force; the British were to be disappointed on this occasion by the performance of their own torpedo-carrying Swordfish. Two attacks were launched from the *Eagle* during the day, the first shortly before noon and the second four hours later, but neither scored any hits. They too were learning as they went along; but their very presence contributed to an increased nervousness and some loss of morale on the part of their opponents. The threat implicit in those torpedo-carrying biplanes was worth more than if the British had had a further new fifteen-inch gun battleship.

'The breeze was in the north-west, with a slight sea and a sky dappled with thin cloud. The visibility was fifteen to twenty miles when, between 2.52 and 3 p.m. the *Orion* and *Neptune* sighted enemy destroyers and cruisers.'[2]

These two cruisers, together with *Liverpool* and *Sydney*, were fulfilling a classic function — spread on a line of bearing about ten miles ahead of Cunningham's flagship and designed to locate the opposing fleet. A few minutes after three in the afternoon Captain Rory O'Connor in *Neptune* had the privilege of making the signal 'Enemy battle fleet in sight' — the first time that this had been seen in the Mediterranean since the days of Nelson. Such high moments are few and far between in naval history; often, because of their rarity, eclipsing all the long hard-slogging times of convoy duties or the harsh moments of action itself when the guns crash and the wounds are given and received.

Six minutes later four Italian heavy cruisers, also outriders of their fleet, opened fire with their 8-inch guns. Outranged and outgunned, the smaller British cruisers replied, but only the fact that *Warspite* had drawn far ahead of the two other battleships, *Malaya* and *Royal Sovereign*, could prevent Cunningham's cruisers, well-handled though they were, from receiving a mauling. At an extreme range for his 15-inch guns of 26,400 yards, *Warspite* opened fire on the Italian cruisers. For the first time in the Mediterranean Sea, outside of practice shoots, the summer air was now rent by the long rumble of those great cordite explosions, followed by a noise, like a giant sheet being torn, of the shells' swift passage. Menaced from afar, the Italian cruisers prudently withdrew under cover of a smokescreen. During the ensuing lull *Warspite* was turned through 360° to allow her slower-steaming partners to catch up. She was travelling at her maximum speed of 24.5 knots, and this necessary turn (to bring the full fire-power of the British battleships into line ahead) provided an opportunity for two of the Italian heavy cruisers to attempt a cast to the east, with a view of getting at *Eagle*. A few salvoes of 15-inch shells dissuaded them. Then — at 3.53 p.m. — the opposing battleships were in sight of one another, the *Warspite* opening fire at 26,000 yards. The two Italian battleships replied, both sides shooting well even at this great range and straddling their targets almost at once. Seven minutes after the action began Cunningham, who had been watching the splashes of 'our 15-inches salvoes straddling the target' saw, at exactly 4 p.m., 'the great orange-coloured flash of a heavy explosion at the base of the enemy flagship's funnels'. Smoke

24

rose as fires broke out below decks in the *Giulio Cesare*, and the Italian fleet turned away under cover of smoke. Admiral Campioni's flagship had been hit at a range of thirteen miles.

With the smokescreen lying heavy and greasy over the sea, rolling slowly under the summer wind, a confused action took place with cruisers and destroyers on both sides looming or jinking out of the dark veils. Unwilling to risk what might well be a trap (submarines lying in wait for him in defence of their fleet), Cunningham took his own ships round to the north of the smoke. His opponents in any case had the legs of him and were away for the Messina Straits and the supposed safety of their air cover. The Regia Aeronautica did at last appear in large numbers and made a concerted attack, mainly on *Warspite* and *Eagle*. Once again, despite their comparative accuracy, they were not accurate enough and their ground control was obviously in some state of confusion. *Warspite's* own aircraft, which had been flown off during the action and had kept up a running commentary throughout the brief engagement, was happy to report that Admiral Campioni's fleet was now being bombed by his own air force.[3]

Although damaged, Admiral Campioni's flagship's speed was not impaired and, although outraged by the criminal efficiency of his air command, he could return to harbour with the knowledge that his important convoy had been passed through safely to the army in Libya. Although engaged by the prestigious Royal Navy, his fleet had not disgraced itself at what came to be called the battle of Calabria. It had also proved to the Italian High Command that nothing was to be gained by the fleet attempting to provoke a major action. They could pass their convoys to and from North Africa without any such risk, so long as the British fleet was based far away at Alexandria, and so long as the island of Malta did not possess sufficient offensive power by air or sea to threaten this lifeline.

Cunningham's fleet, heavily but again ineffectively bombed on their return voyage, had received a boost to morale by the enemy's evident unwillingness to face them, but they had been somewhat shaken by their new experience of air attack. The tendency, however, was to draw a wrong conclusion from the events of the past few days — that they could command the Mediterranean from the Egyptian base and that bombing, although very unpleasant, was acceptable. Even their admiral had not as yet appreciated the true situation, for he was to write: 'It must have shown the Italians clearly that their Air Force and submarines cannot stop our Fleet penetrating into the Central Mediterranean and that only their main Fleet can seriously interfere with our operating there.'

The arrival in due course of the Luftwaffe with their highly-trained divebomber squadrons, and then — as and when they could be spared from the main Battle of the Atlantic — the incursion of German U-boats, with their skilled captains and their hardy crews, was to change things totally. But it was hardly surprising that the wrong conclusions were indeed drawn in these early days, for they were based on the indifferent performance of the Italian air and submarine arm.

At the heart of the matter was the fact that Mussolini was an opportunist, who had no real long-term plans for the war on which he had embarked. With the fall of France he had anticipated an early British withdrawal from the war and some form of patched-up peace to ensue, which would enable him to continue with the expansion of his North African empire. He was aware that Hitler had no wish for a war with Britain; and indeed the German dictator was to make many peace proposals through every avenue available to him throughout 1940 and well into 1941. Unknown to Mussolini, Hitler's real aims and ambitions were always directed towards Russia. He considered the war, as it developed in the Mediterranean, no more than a sideshow. It was something that might certainly be useful if Egypt and the Suez Canal could be brought under Axis control, but the maps that revolved constantly in his head consisted of the frontiers of Prussia and the lands that lay beyond. A small island to the south of Sicily called Malta had probably hardly penetrated his consciousness until that day when his ally had first bombed it.

This encounter between the two battlefleets was to be the only one of the war in which the main units were ever to engage one another. When it was known about in Malta it was seen as proof of the fact that the British still ruled the sea — even if they no longer did so from their principal base, the Grand Harbour of the island.

26

CHAPTER FIVE

Parochial and Other Matters

This was the summer and the autumn in which the fate of the western world was being decided in the Battle of Britain; irrevocably, the whole pattern which the war would follow over the succeeding years was being shaped by a handful of young men. Few indeed — like those in the Pass of Thermopylae — 'their shoulders held the sky suspended.'[1] It was hardly surprising that when the fate of Britain itself was in the balance little enough could be spared for that other island far away, and now under a similar threat. Indeed it was remarkable that anything could be spared at all, yet in August an old aircraft carrier, *Argus*, covered by a powerful striking force which had been assembled at Gibraltar (Force H), flew off twelve Hurricane fighters for the relief of Malta from a position off southern Sardinia — right in the heartland of the Middle Sea. That fighter aircraft could be spared at such a moment in Britain's history was evidence that Churchill had convinced certain reluctant quarters of the essential importance of holding Malta at whatever cost. It is a fact that not so very long before this a department of the Admiralty in London had sent an indignant signal to Malta demanding to know why Fleet Air Arm property (the four Gloster Gladiator biplanes) had been handed over to the RAF — whose pilots were now flying the three of them that were left, in the teeth of overwhelming Italian fighter and bomber superiority![2] At this moment in its history the mood of the island was largely expressed, and to some degree determined, by the Governor — a man who deserves to go down in history with his name bracketed with that of La Valette, that supreme Grand Master of the Knights who had defied the overwhelming might of the Ottoman Empire at the height of its military power. His name was William Dobbie, a lieutenant-general in the British Army (later to be knighted for his services in Malta), a Scot and — rare among Scots and rarer among soldiers — a Plymouth Brother. Nothing could have been further from the somewhat baroque catholicism of the Maltese than this austere form of protestantism, nor more remote from the almost medieval power of the priesthood on the island than the Brethrens' belief that official ministry is a denial of the spiritual priesthood of all believers and of the guidance of the Holy Spirit. Yet Dobbie, who conducted family

27

prayers every evening and to whom his own household accorded such respect that his wife and daughter would rise to their feet when he entered a room, was a man whom the Maltese took to their hearts. Admiral Cunningham rightly assessed what it was about this soldier which so appealed to the Mediterranean islanders. '[He was] an Ironside of a man. His profound faith in the justice of our cause made a great impression upon the religious Maltese. The complete and calm faith shown in the broadcasts he made nearly every evening contributed immensely towards keeping up the morale of the people.'[3] On the day that Italy had declared war, Dobbie's first act as commander-in-chief had been to issue a special Order of the Day to the British and Maltese garrison:

> The decision of His Majesty's Government to fight until our enemies are defeated will be heard with the greatest satisfaction by all ranks of the Garrison of Malta.
>
> It may be that hard times lie ahead of us, but I know that however hard they may be, the courage and determination of all ranks will not falter, and that with God's help we will maintain the security of this fortress.
>
> I call on all officers and other ranks humbly to seek God's help, and then in reliance on Him to do their duty unflinchingly.

Read many years later such words sound like a call from a past that seems far distant indeed.

The refugee problem (later to engulf the whole of Europe) was the most pressing one for the authorities on the island. After the first bombing raids the flood of families out of the capital and its suburb Floriana (and especially out of the Three Cities that held the heart of the dockyard communities) into houses, schools and other institutions in other townships and small villages led to inevitable complications with landlords and other authorities. The areas that were left behind, part abandoned or almost totally so, teemed with dogs and cats, so much so that at various times over the years these descendants of former domestic pets had to be ruthlessly culled. Drainage and sanitation problems which were to remain a permanent hazard of the siege showed themselves from the earliest stages. The abandoned central areas were on main drainage systems, but most of the outlying villages into which families now poured were dependent on cesspits. The emptying of these with inadequate equipment to meet the demand, and later the shortage of transport, meant that for many months the medical authorities were on tenterhooks about the possible outbreak of virulent diseases. But the islanders enjoyed certain great benefits unknown to the crowded industrial cities of

28

northern countries like those of Britain and Germany when these came under heavy attack — the sea air penetrated even the underground shelters where so many thousands were to make their troglodytic homes.

After the first months when it had become obvious, even to those in Whitehall who had had earlier discarded Malta as indefensible, that the weight of the Italian attack by air was something that the island, almost unprotected as it was, could endure and the concept of Malta as a dagger pointing at the heart of Italy was better understood. Churchill, Cunningham and a number of others had long recognized this, and now with the flying-in of further Hurricanes (making the Regia Aeronautica even more disinclined to offensive action over the island, at any rate by day) and some torpedo-carrying Swordfish for strikes against Italian shipping, together with the arrival of further stores and military supplies, passed through in convoys from both east and west. The submarines which in later days were to have so devastating an effect on the Italy – Libya shipping route had as yet played little part. Those which were on the island when Mussolini declared war were large boats that had formerly been stationed in the Far East and were particularly vulnerable in the pellucid waters of the Mediterranean. It was not until the arrival of the smaller U class from Britain via Gibraltar that their lethal potential began to be fully exploited. *Kalafrana*, the flying boat base in Marsaxlokk Bay, received the welcome addition of Sunderland flying boats from Alexandria which, vulnerable though they were to modern fighter aircraft, were efficient enough for reconnaissance and for the detection and destruction of enemy submarines. In September four Marylands were flown in to provide additional air reconnaissance, shortly to be followed by Wellington bombers — an efficient striking arm that was to pound enemy ports and harbours and shipping for the duration of the war, increasing in fury as the years went by and their numbers increased.

Marooned on what Churchill was to call 'that unsinkable aircraft carrier', a strange transformation affected the people. For one thing, difficult though it may be for those to understand who live in large countries with modern transportation systems, Maltese society had remained almost medieval — and this meant that people rarely travelled. Until the war the inhabitants of the dockyard area, familiar with ships and the sea and the rough manners and *mores* of British and other foreign sailors, were very distinct in their outlook from country people no more than three miles away. The early exodus from harbour towns and settlements meant a return to peasant roots of a semi-sophisticated people and the encounter for men and women who lived entirely within a circumscribed village (church, social club, bar and store, plough and horse) with their cousins from the early twentieth century. For, despite the date, it was still only the early twentieth century even in the waterfront world of Malta. One British army officer wrote: 'When the Hampshires [his regiment] arrived in Malta early in 1941, after settling in and getting to know the people, we felt that we had somehow slipped back in time; that everything about us was some twenty-five years behind our known civilization, our thinking and our normal everyday struggle for existence. For one thing there was not the same struggle to achieve and we discovered the "not to worry, Joe" attitude which in the Maltese produced a happier, easier way of life.'[4] Dr Jeremy Boissevain in a monograph on Maltese social anthropology has commented: 'The war itself was a major force in the same direction [social integration], for British troops and people from the urban areas were evacuated to the country to escape the bombing attacks, and so shared the life of their rural neighbours. All learned a good deal from one another. It is not surprising, therefore, that many Maltese, especially in the villages, regard the last war as a social milestone, a dividing line between past dependence upon agriculture and present wage labour, between poverty and relative prosperity.'[5] War is always a disastrous and malevolent force, but the changes effected by it are not always so.

Towards the end of 1940, the giant pattern in the desert campaign took a dramatic shift. In the early months of the war the Italian army, overwhelming in numbers but ill-equipped and low in morale (few wanted to be in any desert to start with and all sensibly regretted leaving home), had advanced against the thin line of the British army and had prodded forward into Egypt. The Suez canal and the route to the oil of the Persian Gulf were the objects, but these were little understood by the sweating soldiers and sailors, who as always had to endure the death and havoc initiated by their remote masters.

Prior to the long prepared offensive of the British army against the Italian forces in the Western Desert the most momentous event of the early sea war had already taken place. This was the British air attack on the Italian fleet in their base at Taranto, an attack carried out by torpedo-carrying Swordfish aircraft from HMS *Illustrious*. HMS *Eagle* was also to have taken part but had developed too many defects caused by near misses from high-level bombing attacks during recent months. *Illustrious*, a modern carrier with an armoured flight deck, had been sent out to join Admiral Cunningham's fleet — proof that his needs in the Mediterranean were understood and that the importance of the air arm in the landlocked sea had not gone unremarked in London, even though it had been somewhat played down by Cunningham himself. This brilliant example of the use of sea-air power (acutely observed at the time by the Japanese) changed the balance in the Mediterranean, restoring to the British, even if only momentarily, the confidence that had been theirs before the fall of France. From the moment that *Illustrious* had arrived with the fleet in Alexandria, plans had been afoot to launch an airborne attack with torpedo-carrying Swordfish on the Italian battle fleet in Taranto. Since it seemed impossible to force a fleet action upon them the only thing was for the air arm to effect the same damage or worse upon the Italians as might have been achieved in a major engagement at sea. Taranto was of course very heavily defended, and only a night attack from some distance away (which might normally be considered as out of range for planes from an aircraft carrier) could achieve this. But *Illustrious* had brought out with her from Britain just such long-range tanks for the aircraft to make this feasible. At a time when Maryland reconnaissance planes out of Malta showed that all the Italian major fleet units were present in the port, and using as 'cover' for the presence of the British fleet at sea the passage of a convoy to Malta, the planes were launched from the vicinity of the Greek island of Cephalonia on the night of 11th November. The attack was overwhelmingly successful and deservedly ranks in the annals of the Royal Navy with Trafalgar.[6]

At one blow the strength of the Italian battlefleet was reduced by three battleships, the *Littorio* and the *Duilio* both being out of action for months, and the *Cavour* beached and out of the war for good. Only the *Vittorio Veneto* and the *Cesare* escaped. The aircraft carrier had shown itself to be the most potent weapon of war at sea, and the battleship had joined the long ranks of ships which had once dominated the oceans and whose day was over. The withdrawal of the Italian fleet to Naples out of reach of Fleet Air Arm attacks and the exultant improvement in morale in the British fleet due to Taranto obscured at the time the real facts of this victory — the dominance of the air over the sea. So long as the Italian air force remained inefficient and ill-directed the British could feel that they had secured control of the central Mediterranean, as well as the eastern end of the sea. Two convoys, one from Alexandria and one from Gibraltar, were passed through to Malta, both covered by battleships and aircraft carriers (the *Ark Royal*, so often 'sunk' in German broadcasts, being with the western convoy). Despite a threat by the Italian fleet from Naples — wisely withdrawn when the composition of the western convoy became known to Admiral Campioni — both arrived unscathed in the island.

Additional troops for the military garrison, stores, motor transport, guns and ammunition all served to confirm a confidence that had been growing ever since Cunningham's first action against the Italian fleet and which had been immensely reinforced by Taranto. 'Life,' wrote a British artillery officer, 'was not very different from normal. Still no mails arrived and so there were no home papers, but food and drink were to be had in plenty provided you could get them — transport was very scarce. Dances were held once a week at the Club; women wore their evening dresses and many officers changed into their "blues" at night.'[7] The amateur dramatic society flourished, and regular concert parties toured the outlying posts where groups of soldiers waited at their guns for assault from the sea.

Small though it is, Malta has the ability to evoke immense depth out of less than one hundred square miles. The whole group of islands is smaller than the Isle of Wight, and yet it gives the sense of extraordinary complexity and density, something reinforced by the onion-skin pattern of its old townships and villages. Once away from the areas of dense population on the east coast the biblical landscape unfolds. Few trees break its sun-varnished canvas, a scattering here and there of olives, the lonely and very ancient carob, small fields contained against the wind and the winter rains by drystone walls, remote farm buildings often seeming to slump back out of the rock from which they were built, and at night a profound and dense darkness. There were hardly any good roads on the island, the best being the military road on the east coast and one between Valletta and the ancient inland capital of Mdina. Once away from these the roads became dust and dirt tracks, fading away in veinlets that wandered off between rocks and prickly pear and scattered tumbles of stone, where walls had been abandoned and never repaired. Along most of the coastal areas, and particularly on the west where the high cliffs stoop into the sea the paths became little more than goat tracks. In this countryside, at carefully selected points, the soldiers had built gun emplacements and machine-gun posts, where the dimmed blue flicker of a kerosene lamp or the high buzz of a Primus cooker were all that revealed their presence against the dark and ancient rocks. Bare, steepsided limestone ridges, uninhabited at any time since the islands rose from the sea, yielding little even for goats, now sometimes echoed to the tang of soldiers' metalled boots or equipment. Those who spent weeks or months on patrol in these lonely places did not escape the immense weight of time which seems to engulf the Maltese islands more deeply than any others in this sea. On moonlit nights the neolithic temples threw their profound shadows, and the remains of Roman buildings in comfortable valleys seemed almost modern. For the soldiers the daytime advent of a concert party, carried about in a horse-drawn cart, was an event of far greater significance than the weekly visit to the cinema in their distant home towns had ever been.

Malta lies well south of the latitude of Tunis. Its climate is North African, and in summer reaches over ninety degrees Fahrenheit. The land wakes only with the first rains of late September or early October — rains of a type as unfamiliar to the northerner as the enemy sun of summer. Heavy as monsoon weather the island steams and roars under them, as the water pours down cart tracks and roads and pathways in sudden rivers of mud. Seen from the air, as the Italians now knew it, the island spreads around it at those times a khaki stain in the clear blue sea. But if the summer was to try those unused to its oven heat and harsh aridity the winter, even after the rains had stopped, was not without its discomforts. Although the temperature rarely fell below fifty degrees Fahrenheit, the wind off the snow-capped mountains of Sicily and great Etna to the north blew down piercing cold, and the island — once its rains had been absorbed — became damp and draughty like an old stone corridor. The people in their shelters and the wireless operators, coders and cypher officers, deep down under fortresses like St Angelo and Lascaris, badly needed then the kerosene that recent convoys had brought in. If summer meant the minimum of clothes — shorts and steel helmets at gun positions — winter meant the same level of clothing as if the British had been back in their native country.

It was against a winter background that the news reached them all of the British advances in the Western Desert. The Italian army under Marshal Graziani was expelled from its foothold in Egypt by General Wavell's Army of the Nile, some 30,000 prisoners being taken almost immediately. Meanwhile Mussolini's misguided attack on Greece, with its inevitable demands upon the Italian air force, meant an even further easing of the pressure on Malta. Unfortunately, the attention of the German dictator had now inevitably been drawn by the misfortunes and incompetence of his ally to the Mediterranean and its potential importance as a theatre of war. His immense successes on the continent, eclipsing by far those of any previous European warlord, had hitherto prevented him from paying much attention to the sea to the south and the adventures of his partner in the Axis. While the year drew to a close in Malta with the happy feeling that the Royal Navy had proved itself master of the sea yet again, and the British and allied forces were routing the Italian military in the desert, and the threat from the air had diminished and dwindled, many began to return to their houses and abandon their shelter life. Food seemed relatively plentiful, bars that had been closed opened their old-fashioned swinging doors again, schools in the threatened areas began to be reopened, and soldiers, sailors and civilians alike began to hope that the threat by air from the north had been endured and outlasted.

As if to crown this feeling of optimism the watchers on the defences and the people of Valletta received a surprising Christmas gift from the sea. In the early afternoon of 20 December Admiral Cunningham's flagship *Warspite* and a destroyer escort hove into sight off the eastern coast. She and the battleship *Valiant* had just been helping Britain's Greek allies by bombarding the Albanian city of Valona, the main port for the Italian army in that area, while other fleet units were sweeping for enemy convoys off the Tunisian coast. Cunningham wrote: 'We then went on to Malta, and as things had been very quiet for some time I decided to take the *Warspite* into Grand Harbour for a night or two while the destroyers refuelled. . . . It was our first visit since May, and news of our arrival had been spread abroad. As we moved in with our bands playing and guard paraded, the Barracas and other points of vantage were black with wildly-cheering Maltese. Our reception was touchingly overwhelming.

> I went round seeing all our friends in the intervals of more official visits. Admiralty House looked very stripped and deserted, and in the hall I was met by my bandmaster and our two Maltese maids, both the latter weeping with emotion and asking if I could not persuade my wife to return.
>
> I went all over the dockyard next morning with the Vice-Admiral [Sir Wilbraham Ford] and was mobbed by crowds of excited workmen singing 'God Save the King' and 'Rule Britannia'. I had difficulty in preventing myself from being carried around, and had to make more than a dozen impromptu speeches telling all and sundry how greatly the fleet still depended upon them, and congratulating them on the fine way they were working under incessant attack and great difficulties. It was a very moving experience, and once again I realized what a great acquisition we had in Sir Wilbraham Ford. I had several meetings with the Governor, Lieutenant-General William Dobbie, another fine man and a tower of strength. My staff discussed the supply situation. We stayed in Malta about forty hours completely undisturbed by any air attack. It was a most useful visit.[8]

When *Warspite* steamed out of Grand Harbour again, the destroyers weaving and jinking around her on the winter-blue sea, those who watched her go hoped that she was the harbinger of happy days, when the great grey ships would once more dominate the harbours and the clouds of lesser vessels infest the creeks and inlets. Hitler, however, had decided that the actions of his Axis partner — first over Malta itself (which he had expected to be invaded long ago), then in the Western Desert, and now in Greece — could no longer be dismissed as incompetent buffoonery. They represented a real threat to the New Order in Europe. The continent was conquered, and for the first time he could spare for the Mediterranean theatre the kind of planes that were unsuited for the Battle of Britain, but ideal for the reduction of civilian city areas where there was little or no air defence. During December Fliegerkorps X began its transference from Norway down through Europe, to airfields in southern Italy and Sicily.

CHAPTER SIX

The Germans Intervene

Fliegerkorps X, commanded by General Geissler, was a crack unit which had been seasoned during the Norwegian campaign and in later attacks on England. The cream of the Luftwaffe, it had been specially trained in anti-shipping tactics and was composed of divebombers — the 'pure' divebombers, the Stuka 87, and the shallow divebombers, the twin-engined Junkers 88. They spearheaded the arrival of some three-hundred and fifty other Heinkel and Junkers bombers together with an escort of Messerchmitt fighters, the latter more than a match for the few Hurricanes on Malta. The German High Command, seeing the weaknesses of the Regia Aeronautica and the success that the British had achieved by the use of *Illustrious* as well as the other two aircraft carriers, had drawn up a list of priorities — to which the Italians had happily agreed — for Fliegerkorps X upon its arrival in the Mediterranean. It was to act in collaboration with the Italians in attacking enemy maritime units at sea, to put the bases at Malta and Alexandria out of commission, and to mine the Suez canal as well as the approaches to all ports and harbours in enemy hands. At the top of the list was simply 'Sink *Illustrious*.'

Christmas 1940 in Malta, despite the blackout and the permanent state of readiness, had almost something peacetime in its quality. True, the illuminated crib could not appear in the doorways of churches, or the Christmas-scene figures in the windows of private houses and the traditional Christmas Midnight Mass could not be held, but throughout the island the liturgy was celebrated on Christmas Eve afternoon. Servicemen organized their own celebrations, but the Maltese whose homes had been destroyed and who had moved into shelters or out into the evacuee centres away from the harbour areas were not forgotten. Air Raid wardens and members of the Special Constabulary clubbed together and gave Christmas parties for the children. Joseph Micalleff records how at Cottonera, in the heart of the dockyard area, after Mass and Communion, 'during the day men enjoyed themselves singing and playing string instruments.'[1]

Most of the cinemas reopened some time before Christmas, encouraged by the lull in the bombing (there had been two-hundred air raids by the end of the year), and cinema shows were often given three times daily to meet the demands of the throngs of British and Maltese servicemen, while newsreels of the distant war in the Atlantic and elsewhere received in recent convoys served to remind the besieged that they were not alone in their struggle. The Royal Opera House in Valletta opened a Christmas series of entertainments, starting with a comic opera in Maltese. Air raid shelters were decorated with festoons and flags, military bands enlivened the holiday, football matches were held, and civilian and military teams played one another in the Empire Stadium. (The Maltese, many years before Europe and the rest of the world, had developed a passionate enthusiasm for this British sport.) The Italians, true to their own old traditions, kept the Christmas peace and the Regia Aeronautica was grounded over the week. At Catania and Comiso airfields in Sicily the Luftwaffe was settling in.

It was a hard, cold winter over all of Europe and everywhere the conquered learned to adjust themselves to their new status. The cold to the north of the island — snow on the Madonie and Nebrodi ranges of Sicily as well as Etna and its foothills — effected one of those little miracles that happen in Malta once or twice only in a generation. On the morning of 17 December flurries of snow fell over the old walled capital Mdina and its suburb Rabat. Snow is so rare in Malta[2] that people called their children out from their homes and held up babies to see the brief swirls of evanescent 'mystery stuff'. . . . Meanwhile at Luqa air base and at other military bases and camps throughout the island thousands of Maltese children were entertained with parties and presents.

The jinx-winged, wheel-spatted Stuka 87s meanwhile began practising concerted attacks off the Sicilian coast on a mock-up target representing the flight deck of an aircraft carrier.

Operation 'Excess', the passage of two important convoys through the Mediterranean, one from Gibraltar and the other from Alexandria, had been planned to take place early in December. This date had been scrapped because of disruption caused in the Atlantic by the German cruiser *Hipper* and held back until early January 1941. Four large merchantmen under Admiral Somerville's Force H out of Gibraltar were to be passed through to the central Mediterranean, three of them destined for the Piraeus to aid Britain's Greek allies and one for Malta with 4,000 tons of ammunition and — almost as important — 3000 tons of seed potatoes. At the same time from the east Admiral Cunningham aimed to pass an oiler to Suda Bay in the island of Crete and two merchant vessels with general supplies, oil fuel and petrol to Malta. Empty merchantmen waiting in Malta would then be escorted back to Alexandria. The threat still posed by the Italian battleships in the area was almost eliminated on the night of 8 January when Wellington bombers operating out of Malta raided Naples, now the headquarters of the Italian fleet, and badly damaged the battleship *Giulio Cesare*, with the result that both she and the *Vittorio Veneto* were hastily withdrawn to Genoa in the north. The island was proving already how much it could affect the issues of the war.

With little threat of intervention by Italian surface forces it now looked as if the complicated operation of moving these two convoys through the Mediterranean was going to proceed without a hitch. Two Italian destroyers covering a convoy were unfortunate enough to run into the British cruiser *Bonaventure* and the destroyer *Hereward*, one being sunk and the other escaping damaged. The only British casualty so far was the destroyer *Gallant* which fell foul of the minefield off the Italian fortress-island of Pantellaria and had her bows blown off. Taken in tow by the stern she was despatched with escorting cruisers to Malta (where along with other casualties of the war she was to be beached for years to come). On the morning of 9 January the convoy and escort from Gibraltar were attacked by ten Savoia bombers in the usual high-level — ineffective even if alarming — fashion. The battleship *Malaya* and the cruiser *Gloucester* were straddled but survived intact, while Fulmar fighters from the *Ark Royal* clawed two of the bombers out of the sky. Meanwhile Cunningham's force advancing from the east was preparing to cover Somerville's convoy once Force H turned back to Gibraltar.

Cunningham's main force now consisted of *Warspite*, the battleship *Valiant*, the carrier *Illustrious* and an escort of five destroyers. They were reported by shadowing aircraft, one of which was brought down by fighters from *Illustrious*. Although the position of the British fleet had been known to the Axis air forces for some time, a number of bombers looking for the fleet from Alexandria had failed to find them on the previous day. By 10 January it was clear that they were pinpointed and the Fulmar fighters had to be constantly aloft on the watch for further planes. It was a clear almost windless day with that wintry clarity in the air often found in the Mediterranean. The fleet was on alert, expecting high level attacks or torpedo-carrying aircraft — all things to which they had become accustomed during recent months. At 12.20, coming in low over the sea, a pair of Savoia torpedo bombers drew everyone's attention down to their attack — clearly designed for *Illustrious* — and the patrolling fighters, seeing the gunfire from the fleet, at once began to descend. The Savoias, having loosed their torpedoes (missing the aircraft carrier, which had wheeled to comb their tracks but passing narrowly astern of *Valiant*), made off for Sicily low over the water. The fighters followed.

It was 12.28, an attack had been repelled, the Fulmars which had been on patrol were in pursuit of the Italians, and the sky was empty. Another flight of Fulmars was due to take off at 12.35.

At 12.30 a jagged thickening on the screen of the early radar aboard *Illustrious* indicated a large group of aircraft to the north of the fleet. Neither officers nor operators in those days aboard the ship had ever seen anything quite like it before. Usually a few 'indentations', as it were, would disclose the arrival of a reconnaissance plane or — as recently — the approach of a few bombers. This was something different; a large group of aircraft was on its way down from Sicily. Captain Boyd of *Illustrious* had just made the customary signal to his commander-in-chief asking for permission to turn into the wind so that his next flight of Fulmars could take off at 12.35; suddenly, and clearly visible to everyone on the upper decks of all the ships, a darkening mass of aircraft came into sight. These were the Junkers 87s, Stukas, forty in all, with behind them a further wave of Junkers 88s; Fliegerkorps X had arrived over the Mediterranean.

The attack that followed was, as Ian Cameron wrote, 'one of the great flying achievements of the war (comparable with the crippling of the Italian fleet at Taranto; Guy Gibson's breaking of the Mohne dam; the Mosquito bombing of Amsterdam gaol; and the Air Arm's Barracuda attack on the *Tirpitz*.'[3] Disregarding the intense barrage put up by the fleet, they approached at 12,000 feet and then broke up into two formations, one of thirty planes concentrating entirely on *Illustrious* while the other ten broke away to attack the two battleships.

For the first time in war the vulnerability of sea to the new air power was made evident. Everything was suddenly changed. There have been other such moments when, in the long violent history of man, a flight of arrows directed against armoured knights or the thunder of an early siege gun against stone walls, have transformed for ever the whole technique of war. This was one of those, and even the threatened spectators could only marvel: 'We could not but admire the skill and precision of it all. The attacks were pressed home to point-blank range, and as they pulled out of their dives some of them were seen to fly along the flight deck of the *Illustrious* below the level of her funnel.'[4] Admiral Cunningham was so engrossed that he hardly seemed to notice when a thousand-pound bomb hurtled over his own bridge and, missing the foredeck, struck the fluke of the battleship's starboard bow anchor.

Some of the attackers dived in from the full 12,000 feet at which they had approached, others dived to about half their approach height, checked with a neat twist and then turned into their bombing dive. The angles at which they finally dived varied slightly pilot by pilot but some were as steep as eighty degrees before, using their airbrakes, they flattened out after releasing their bomb load. The screaming siren sound of a Stuka's dive, its guns flashing, and the knowledge of the hurling death it carried, was something that those who were beneath it would never forget, even amid all the other terrors of war.

The attack had begun at 12.38 and six and a half minutes later it was all over, with the Stukas zig-zagging away at sea level in the direction of Sicily. The earlier flight of Fulmars which had been lured away in pursuit of the Italian torpedo bombers had never been able to regain height before the real attack started, and the relief flight had only just got airborne. Caught completely unawares, and below instead of above the attackers, they fought desperately to catch the bombers in their downward plunge. Five of the dive bombers were shot down and the last ten to attack had their bombing run severely disrupted by the wheeling, spitting fighters. One thing was immediately clear to the *Illustrious* pilots — they would not be returning to their mothership.

Had it not been for the desperate efforts of her own aircraft, it is doubtful if the *Illustrious* would have survived at all. As it was, in those six and a half minutes when General Geissler's crack team displayed their skill, she had sustained such severe damage that she would be out of the war for many months — if indeed she survived at all to make it back to a repair yard. Her only destination now could be Malta.

The presence of the Luftwaffe in Sicily had been known from reconnaissance flights made from the island. What some of those involved, both civilians and military, noted as a 'singular feeling of unease' had no doubt been communicated to them by the silence of their senior officers, who knew but were not telling. The success in Europe of the cataclysmic bombing of cities was fully appreciated by all those who had to consider Malta's place in this Mediterranean war, which was now fast becoming the only battleground where the opponents could get at each other. If the full weight of the German might was to fall upon the small island could the people endure it? It is very doubtful if at that moment the moral question was ever raised in the minds of Britain's war leaders — should they be asked to endure it? Would they, or could they — that was the question. It was to be answered by the response given to the arrival of *HMS Illustrious* in the Grand Harbour of the small colony. It was true that the people of Malta had asked to become a British colony, but that had been in a very different century, and although the Maltese men had constantly exposed themselves to French fire during the siege of Valletta they were always secure that their women and children were safe at home in their villages.

The flight of Fulmars which was taking off when the attack started actually flew through the fountains of water raised by near misses of one-thousand-pound bombs. If they had not managed to get airborne there can be no doubt that *Illustrious* would have been hit even more than she was, very possibly sunk. Only her armoured flight deck saved her from this fate and, although hit by six thousand pounders, she staggered on. Her steering gear had been put out of action, bombs had fallen down the flight lifts that took the aircraft up and down from the deck below, giant fires fuelled by aviation spirit roared through the hold, some fifty per cent of her 4.5 inch anti-aircraft guns were knocked out, fuel tanks and ammunition were exploding, and her human casualties were heavy. The one all-important thing was that, despite the vast damage, the ship's main engines were still working and she was able to steam at nearly twenty knots. For some time she circled out of control. With her steering gear gone, the only way of making for Malta was by jamming the rudder amidships and varying the revolutions on the main engines to maintain a more or less steady course.

For hour after hour the fight to save her went on, stokers fainting in the boiler rooms from the intense heat, and the captain permanently in anguish in case the magazines went up (he did not flood them for fear of further attacks and the necessity of using what was left of his fire power). His decision was proved right, for they came back.

First there was an attack by Savoia bombers, but as usual they did not descend to face the gunfire of the fleet and, again as usual, their high-level attacks were unsuccessful. Then, shortly after 1600, the Stukas returned, only fifteen of them this time, but with an escort of Messerschmitt fighters. The Fulmars, which had earlier flown on to Malta to refuel and rearm, were waiting for them, high up and prepared. Although the Fulmar was a slow-climbing aircraft and hardly a match for the Messerschmitt they still managed to break up the attack, several Stukas being shot down and others damaged. It was the kind of novel dogfight over the fleet that raised the morale of the British, badly shaken by the first evidence (hardly yet absorbed) that efficient land-based dive bombers were almost unstoppable. If the attack on Taranto had signalled the end of the battleship as the most powerful vessel afloat, the attack on *Illustrious* heralded the ultimate demise of the aircraft carrier — certainly in a land-locked sea like the Mediterranean.

Listing heavily, with thousands of tons of water sluicing about inside the ship, with some fires still out of control, and with many dead and dying aboard, *Illustrious* was about fifteen miles off Malta at

41

sunset. In the last Stuka attack only one bomber had got through, but its one-thousand pounder almost sounded the ship's death knell, falling near the after lift, penetrating the armour plate and bursting within. The moon was up and the great ship, still steering under engines alone, was heading for the swept channel off Grand Harbour when the last attack of the day came — torpedo bombers. Beaten off by the anti-aircraft barrage they failed in their mission — one torpedo strike would almost certainly have sent her to the bottom. It was a radio signal from Malta advising that torpedo bombers were approaching the island which had alerted the carrier and her destroyer escorts to the last attack.

Throughout the day the whole progress of events had been plotted in operations rooms deep below the rock of Malta, and at the Fleet Air Arm base of Hal Far the Fulmar pilots as they arrived to fuel and ammunition had told their story. But even in the remotest villages the sound of the action, the thunder of the guns over the now darkened sea, had alerted the islanders to the fact that some naval battle was taking place in the region of Malta. The flights of Fulmars coming and going during the day had hardly escaped the eyes of country farmers used over the years to gazing skywards in spring and autumn for the annual migration of birds between Africa and Europe, before reaching for their shot guns.

The cargo ships, for which the whole action had been fought, had already reached Grand Harbour safely. The unloading of vital equipment, of ammunition and of stores, had begun. At ten o'clock that night, with powerful side-paddle tugs assisting her, *Illustrious* came darkly down the harbour like an exhausted gladiator and was secured to Parlatorio Wharf in French Creek. Smoke still rose from her, she stank of burning cordite, of aviation fuel and oil and blood and tired sweat. So the very face of war was seen in the heart of the island.

CHAPTER SEVEN

Full Fury

Upon the old and indomitable fortress of the Knights of St John there was to fall the weight of an attack far heavier than the Grand Turk at the peak of the Ottoman Empire's power could have conceived. But first there was a lull. It was as if even the conquerors of Europe had been momentarily disturbed by the losses that their crack squadrons had sustained from the gunfire of the fleet. Their principal target, as they knew from reconnaissance on 11 January, remained obstinately afloat at the far end of Grand Harbour, and reports from their allies of the density of anti-aircraft fire over the area (doubtless somewhat magnified to excuse the ineffectuality of their own bombing of the island) prompted some cautious preparation in the attack that must certainly follow. In the meantime they had other successes to report.

The two British cruisers which had escorted the damaged destroyer *Gallant* into Malta were withdrawing to rejoin the fleet when they were attacked by dive bombers coming in out of the sun — a classic tactic, which proved effective since neither ship was fitted with radar. The *Gloucester* was struck on the bridge by a bomb that went down into the bowels of the ship but failed to explode, but the cruiser *Southampton* was hit twice, so badly that she had to be abandoned and sunk by torpedo. The arrival of the Luftwaffe in the Mediterranean had abruptly changed the whole balance of power.

There could be no question of repairing *Illustrious* in Malta even if there had been no threat from the air. All that could be done, even if there was enough respite from attack to permit anything, was to patch her up temporarily to make her fit for sea. It was clear that she would have to run the gauntlet yet again (if she got to sea at all) and make for Alexandria. It was fortunate that early in the New Year a very experienced artillery officer, Brigadier Sadler, had arrived in Malta to take charge of the anti-aircraft defences, for he had previously served in Dover during the Battle of Britain in a similar command — the guns of Dover during that period having been credited with ninety planes destroyed. Malta had hitherto been unfamiliar with dive-bombing tactics but now that they might be expected Sadler had immediately set in train the preparation of a box barrage to cover the whole area of Grand Harbour. The details

43

of such a barrage, designed to cover French Creek where *Illustrious* lay, had hardly been completed before the first attack came. There had just been time for the coordinates of fire to be worked out, more guns brought from other positions to saturate the area at fixed angles, and heights of shellburst determined so that, as one gunner put it, 'no gaps should be left through which the Stukas could bomb with comparative immunity'.[1]

Meanwhile, from the moment of her arrival, the work on the ship had gone on relentlessly. When the dead, the dying and the wounded had been taken ashore, the latter to be transported to the large hospital at Mtarfa on its high ridge near the old city Mdina, the work on the ship had never ceased. Throughout that first night, with dockyard hoses playing on still smouldering fires and surgeons and medical orderlies attending the wounded, constructors and engineers were aboard to take survey of the damage. The final assessment by the ship's Engineer Commander was: 'Her engines are not too bad, we'll get her away all right.'[2]

Night and day, during that almost unbelievable lull when the ship and her crew enjoyed the breathing space to prepare, the ship echoed to the sound of workmen. 'At first light on the morning of the 11th the Maltese dockyard workers took over. Their specific orders were not to deal with the smashed deck and twisted alleyways, and anything else above the waterline, but to attend only to the bare essentials that would make it possible for the ship to go out to sea and quickly. Divers went down to examine the bottom, the fitters invaded the engine room, and the welders began to take out the wooden pegs in her punctured hull and to weld the holes. . . . That morning the news had flashed all over the island and onlookers began to appear over the bastions and in boats outside the creek to see the fantastic ship that had withstood so much, so that Malta could have her convoy.'[3]

The writer, who was a boy at the time, goes on to tell how five days later, on Thursday 16 January, his father who was himself one of the workmen aboard *Illustrious* asked him to collect a cap for him and bring it down to the dockyard. He was thus one of those who without being in any way involved in the action that followed fortuitously witnessed the arrival of the force sent to ensure that *Illustrious* never again haunted the sea lanes of the Mediterranean. Others who were engaged at the guns, including one British artillery officer, have also left us their record of the attack, still remembered by old men in the island as they sit in peace at home or in the dark caverns of local bars.

> 'Old men forget; yet all shall be forgot,
> But he'll remember, with advantages,
> What feats he did that day.'

44

At a quarter past twelve noon on 16 January a special announcement was made throughout the island over the cable radio system that, in the event of an air raid, all civilians must immediately take cover and go into shelters as a new form of air defence tactics was about to be employed. The reason for the announcement was that in the recent past, after the alarm at the first air raids had given way to something of a contempt for the high-flying raiders, many of the Maltese living and working around Grand Harbour had got in the habit of collecting on the high vantage points of Valletta or in the Three Cities on their own roof tops to watch the defending fighters rise up and the ensuing dog fights, as if it was all some spectacular opera. This time it was known that it would be Fliegerkorps X coming over, and that the box barrage would be of such density that any watchers were as likely to be killed by falling shrapnel as by the enemy.

At 13.55 the radar plot darkened. 'It was the largest that had ever been recorded in Malta till then. . . .' All those who were watching the sky recorded the same impression of a multitude of dark dots approaching, 'wave after wave of them'.[4] The air raid warning sirens wailed over the island and the red flags went up. Everywhere the people scurried for shelter. All round the harbour, all along the mile after mile of the strange configurations of its indented creeks, the mouths of guns lifted, light anti aircraft, heavy anti aircraft, pom-poms, machine guns, and 4.5 inch. Even some of the heavy guns in the forts, hitherto unused because valueless against high-level bombers, swivelled and turned to provide massive death-dealing blasts in the air at the height where divebombers might be expected to level off.

Brilliantly directed, bravely sustained, the attack when it came was something in the nature of another charge of the Light Brigade — but more effective. Messerschmitt fighters and Italian Fiat and Macchi fighters hung like a swarm of gnats above the darker approaching cloud of bombers. That day there were only four Hurricanes and three Fulmars and two of the old original Gladiators in serviceable condition to rise against them. They were ordered to patrol outside the Harbour area and pick off stragglers or damaged planes as they emerged from the bursting forest that was shortly to grow over the sheltered water. (Not all of them, as will be seen, obeyed.)

The attack came in two main waves — first of all, the shallow-dive twin-engined Junkers 88, and then in the second and larger wave, the Stukas — over seventy bombers in all. The barrage that rose up to meet them was universally described as 'hell let loose', beating on the eardrums in such waves of sound that some of those who heard it felt as if they were going mad. Apart from all the shore defences and

45

anti-aircraft guns guarding the area, every ship in the harbour as well as *Illustrious* herself opened fire, the thunder clamouring round and round the stony heights above the harbour, while the ramparts and fortresses of the Knights reverberated like a great drum. Joseph Attard remembers '... the shaking of the shelter as bombs were hitting the Dockyard part which was beneath the bastion where the shelter stood, only fifty yards away. I felt the strong wave of blast in the shelter and pressed myself to the wall in the first cavity I found. Women and men alike, screaming prayers, were toppled on each other.... Children began to cry while the shattering noise outside continued, with more diving, whistling bombs, explosions, blocks of concrete that were lifted from the dockyard below and smashed against the face of the shelter, and of course the never-ending gunfire. It looked as if the world had come to an end and no one would live.'[5]

Illustrious was at times completely hidden from view by the fountains of bomb splashes and exploding near misses and yet, despite the great bravery (which all accounts acclaim) with which the pilots pressed home their attack, they only managed to score one direct hit on the carrier — on the quarterdeck and causing relatively minor damage. An eyewitness described the ship at that moment: 'HMS *Illustrious* herself struck me as being rather like a great cat at bay. She had her back arched up against the walls of the cliffs rising sheer from the docks and her guns were spitting back defiance at any and every target that came within range.'[6] The Island rocked to the shock of the battle and the Three Cities rumbled and roared with the weight of exploding bombs and the crash of heavy masonry as stone ramparts and walls came thundering down.

An officer of the Royal Artillery watched one fighter disregard the orders to stay outside the area of the box barrage: 'I was on a light-aircraft gun position in the harbour area for one of these attacks, and I can still see clearly a German bomber diving through that terrific curtain of steel, followed by a Fulmar, release his bomb almost at the last moment and then turn and fly out only a few feet above the water and turn right-handed towards the entrance of the harbour. He was so low that he had to rise to clear the breakwater, which is only some fifteen feet high. As the Stuka rose to clear the mole the Fulmar pilot shot him down into the sea on the far side. He later landed at Hal Far remarking that he didn't think much of Malta's bloody barrage! However, he never flew that particular plane again, so badly was it damaged.[7]

Lying on the opposite side of the creek from the *Illustrious* was a merchantman from the convoy, the *Essex*, which was hit by a heavy bomb in the engine room with a loss of thirty-eight dead and wounded. Fortunately for everyone in the area the bulkheads of the engine room contained the explosion — for the holds of the ship were loaded with four thousand tons of ammunition and torpedoes. Had these gone up, the whole creek and everything in it would have been destroyed.

One Stuka hit in the barrage released its bombload over Valletta before crashing into the sea beyond Fort St Elmo. The bombs brought down a high block of flats in the city's Old Mint Street. Everywhere the men of the Passive Defence Services were rushing to the rescue of victims trapped inside shattered houses, beneath shelters and in cellars. After the second wave of the attack had passed and the gunfire ceased, a sudden silence was remarked — a silence that seemed to be compounded by the crash of buildings still falling. Over the whole harbour area there hung a thick pall of smoke and yellow limestone dust, turning and eddying in the blue air.

Many people were killed or wounded that day. Buildings were demolished not only in Valletta, but most widely throughout the Three Cities surrounding the dockyard, the peninsula of Senglea faring the worst with over three hundred houses badly damaged or destroyed. Streets were blocked by fallen masonry, and through the ruins moved the ambulance men and mobile squads of rescue and demolition workers. The yellow limestone blocks that formed the houses, churches, ramparts and indeed almost every building in Malta, had proved how effective they were against incendiary bombs and how well they could withstand the blast from high explosives, but direct hits were another matter; shifting the blocks as quickly as possible to get at survivors buried beneath them was a herculean task. (The lack of relief squads to carry on this work when the first workers were exhausted was something that had to be corrected before further raids.) After this first day's attack the inhabitants of the Three Cities immediately took up the great exodus which had practically reversed during recent months. It was quite clear, now the Luftwaffe had arrived, that houses must be abandoned and families must either move to outlying districts or deep shelters must be sought within walking distance of the dockyard. It was Malta's main source of employment and there was nothing else for its workmen to do out in the countryside, where already there was a surplus of idle men whose shops or small businesses had been forced to close down.

During the raid of 16 January ten of the attackers were shot down, five by fighters and five by the anti-aircraft defences. Others were badly damaged, and the command in Sicily decided to give their squadrons a rest over the next day. The work on *Illustrious* continued, fitters and welders and construction officers working ceaselessly to

47

get her to sea before a further raid came. This took place on the 18th; but the German plan had changed — the aim now was to eliminate the airfields from which the fighter opposition came. Luqa and Hal Far were heavily attacked by eighty raiders, the former being so badly cratered that for a time it became unserviceable.

If fighter opposition could be eliminated the German Command reckoned that a further attack on *Illustrious* would be successful. But the word had inevitably gone round the pilots, even of General Geissler's crack formation, that the harbour of Malta was a kind of hell such as had not been encountered before during the course of the war. The fact was that the Stuka, still to sink many ships and damage the morale of many a sailor during the next few years, was obsolescent: terrifying in its dive, and accurate enough against the gunfire of a single ship, it was too slow in flight against modern fighters or the concentrated barrage of a fleet. It depended very largely upon the nerve and skill of its pilots, and as crack pilots were lost or wounded and less experienced hands took control the impact of the Stuka declined. In due course the arrival of Spitfires in the Mediterranean theatre would signal its demise, although the dour courage of the Germans kept it flying successfully for some years to come.

Despite the weight of the attack on the airfields Fliegerkorps X suffered badly, seven falling to the British fighters and four to the guns.

The last raid launched against the aircraft carrier itself came on Sunday 19 January. A colour sergeant of the Royal Marines manning one of the guns on top of Fort St Angelo (La Valette's headquarters in the Great Siege of 1565) described how: 'Bombs were dropped in and around all the creeks, causing terrific clouds of dust, flying masonry and iron. Although I did not see it myself, it was stated that a motor car went sailing over the top of us. The dust and spray often blinded our view, but the dive bombers always came on. As they broke through the dust they seemed like hawks looking for their prey.' He added: 'You lose all sense of fear and self-preservation while it lasts. You get the same feeling as being at a football final.'[8] A curious touch!

Six Hurricanes, one Fulmar, and one of the old Gladiators were up that day and accounted for eleven of the raiders, the guns bringing down another eight. This was reckoned to be about one quarter of the attacking force — sufficient deterrent in itself, especially since later Italian reports revealed a number of funerals taking place in Sicily for Luftwaffe aircrews and a Red Cross Italian seaplane was spotted assiduously searching the Malta-Sicily channel, presumably for aircraft that had failed to reach home. *Illustrious* received no direct hits but suffered underwater damage through the mining effect of

48

near misses which exploded beneath her on the bottom of the creek. Teams of technicians and welders and divers set to work on her again. There were no further air raids, for the rate of loss borne by the Luftwaffe could no longer be sustained. Preparations were indeed being made for a further attack, but early on the night of 23 January the great ship slipped away and headed east for Alexandria, gradually working up speed until she was making over twenty knots. Ian Cameron wrote: '. . . no warship of any Navy ever lived through such punishment — eight direct hits (at least five of them with 1000-pounders) with seven fractional misses.'[9] It was a tribute to the ship's constructors, the crew, and the dockyard staff of Malta, that she ever sailed again. So fast did she move during that night that the cruiser squadron which had been sent to escort her back missed her, underestimating her speed, and were themselves heavily bombed. She reached Alexandria safely and after further temporary repairs went on to Norfolk, Virginia, for a complete refit. Her place in the Mediterranean was taken two months later by another carrier with an armoured flight-deck, the *Formidable*.

The '*Illustrious* blitz' as it came to be known among the besieged was recognized by everyone as the beginning of a new phase in the history through which all were living. Two days after the first attack on the aircraft carrier the Government ordered the evacuation of the Three Cities. All available transport was ordered to the area, and soon army trucks, private cars, buses and horse-drawn carts were raising clouds of dust along the roads. Festooned with people (reminiscent of the sticky paper which hung from summer ceilings to catch flies) piled high with furniture and family treasures, the stream of transport made for outlying townships and villages. It was clear that so long as the harbour remained in use — which meant so long as Malta was not conquered — the whole area must be vacated except for people who from the safety of deep-tunnelled shelters could remain close to their source of work. Housing the refugees was one problem, but almost as difficult was feeding and clothing them. In January the rocky island is cold, damp and windy, and depots distributing clothing and blankets were immediately opened to try to meet their needs, while communal feeding centres and the first mobile canteens began to distribute food and hot drinks at minimal prices.

The Maltese, as befitted a Mediterranean island race, were both hardy and frugal: these were virtues that were to be tested almost to destruction in the months to come. As in all communities under similar pressures, however, not only does the good become evident but the bad thrives. The black market in every kind of commodity would continue to grow, and the abandoned cities around Grand

Harbour would hardly escape the looter. Archbishop Caruana might condemn this as 'a very grave sin' but even in Most Catholic Malta there were many sinners, and in dockyard areas rats thrive. The simpler rodents were kept down by the dogs and cats which, abandoned yet again, haunted the tumbled buildings and the empty streets.

CHAPTER EIGHT

Island, Desert and Sea

That same January 1941 the British army attacked in North Africa. The Italians were rolled back and the borders of Egypt were left far behind as General Wavell's troops advanced. Moving rapidly into Cyrenaica up that desert road, which was to become so sadly familiar to the soldiers during the years to come, the army took Bardia (yielding some 45,000 prisoners), and then the useful deep-water port of Tobruk — a name to be familiar in world headlines when it later became a solitary garrison in enemy-held territory. By 6 February the Italian forces had been driven right out of Cyrenaica, thus securing the safety of Egypt and producing — for the time being at any rate — a useful buffer state between the Canal Zone and Italian-held Tripolitania. There was no doubt that at that moment Wavell's army could have pushed right on to Tripoli itself and the desert war might have been over before ever the Germans got involved in it. But Churchill already had his eye on Greece and was pressing the Greek government to accept British tanks and weaponry and troops to aid them in their successful stand against the Italian invasion of their country. So, at a moment when the Axis forces might have been thrown out of North Africa for good, Wavell was compelled to start dividing his troops to go to the aid of Greece.

Hitler, alarmed by the collapse of his ally in the desert, was already ordering the transference of nearly half of Fliegerkorps X to Tripoli to stiffen the Italian resistance, which in its turn meant that the scale of the air attack on Malta began to decline. Luckily for the island this happened just when a series of day and night raids had begun to tell on the defenders. Apart from attacks on the air fields a new technique was the dropping of parachute mines over the land; their blast effect was enormous, shattering houses and nerves equally. At the same time, the systematic mining of the approaches to Malta, as well as the creeks and harbours, by magnetic mines was beginning to increase the hazards to the island and contribute to the sense of isolation from the outside world. Dive bombers escorted by fighters continued to attack by day, while the nights were rendered sleepless by the incursion of high-flying raiders, some bombing and others mining. Throughout January, February and March the attacks continued.

51

The principal aim of these raids was to wear down the resistance of the defence and at the same time to occupy the energy and the attention of everyone in Malta. For Hitler had already decided that his ally must be reinforced in North Africa and the crumbling resistance must be stiffened by an injection of German troops. The first advance guard of the Afrika Korps began to reach Tripoli in January, no more than a light motorized division at first, but soon to be followed by a complete armoured division, the 15th Panzer. On 12 February General Erwin Rommel arrived in Tripoli to command the Deutsches Afrika Korps. When combined with units of Fliegerkorps X and able also to call on long-range aircraft from Sicily, the general would have at his disposal a really efficient fighting force which, though still unskilled in the ways of desert warfare, would inflict grave losses on the extended line of British troops, soon to be depleted through the demands imposed by their leaders' commitment to Greece.

The weakness of Malta as an offensive base was shown by the fact that the Afrika Korps reached its destination with scarcely any losses. Shortage of aircraft and for some time a shortage of suitable submarines meant that the Italian navy was able to transport men and material comparatively unscathed, thus facilitating the establishment in the desert of a fighting force that would put paid to the British gains made early in the year. The arrival on the island in February of the first of a new class of submarines, the 'U' Class, was the beginning of a change in Malta's position. As a further number of these deservedly famous 'boats' reached Malta the attacks on Italian shipping would grow and grow, until the island dealt out more damage to the Axis war effort than ever it received itself. Yet even in this early spring of 1941 Wellington bombers were attacking the airfields of Sicily, while the few Swordfish available, acting in concert with the Sunderlands for air reconnaissance, were displaying the first evidence of Malta's potential against the Axis lifeline between Italy and Africa. Fortunately for the islanders this was so slight as yet that it did not provoke an immediate response — invasion.

Even at this moment it is doubtful if an invasion could have succeeded. The Italians had long possessed a plan for the invasion of Malta, but anyone may plan something, it is the carrying of it out that counts. And the Italian High Command had suspected all along that this Plan 'Operazione C3: Malta'[1] was little more than a pipe-dream. It called for some forty-thousand trained troops, landing craft, paratroops, an aircover of five-hundred planes, and — for the time that it took to establish troops successfully ashore — naval superiority in the area. Exercises had indeed been held with the relatively few motorised barges that existed and a limited number of troops — but these were more in the nature of a propaganda act for visiting dignitaries. It was all so much opera bouffe, and while the Germans had indeed expected something in the nature of an invasion to take place within days or hours of Italy entering the war, no one in the know in the Italian High Command ever imagined that such a thing was possible. For one thing the difficulty of landing troops on the rocky island of Malta was heightened by the fact that there were very few beaches of any size where troops could be put ashore from flat-bottomed barges.

'Malta lies in the sea like the deck of a sinking aircraft carrier, with the side to the southwest high out of the water, sloping towards the north and east, with the deck awash at several points. To the west, with the exception of the mouths of some water courses and of the main valleys which traverse the Island at three points, the cliffs are sheer and high and the beaches narrow.'[2] The only suitable places for landing were on the north-east coast in the areas of Mellieha and St Paul's Bay, and these were so well defended that it would have been suicide for any craft to try and approach by day or night. Paratroopers would hardly have had more success against Malta for, as Hitler was perspicacious enough to point out at a later date, the miniature fields, each bounded by irregular drystone walls, were obstacle enough in themselves and death to gliders.

Malta was hard. The bony island frame, which the Knights of St John had at first despaired of when coming here after their home in fertile and gracious Rhodes, made it a natural fortress. The only other place where a landing might have been attempted (and here the Italian plan was for a diversionary thrust) was in the big open bay of Marsaxlokk in the south. This 'South Harbour', with its sloping ledges of rock surrounded by immediately rising ground, would have been another death trap. The defenders' task was made the easier by the intractable nature of the island, and the Italian (and later German) staff officers who contemplated relief maps and models shook their heads in some despair. To neutralize Malta by such a weight of bombing, coupled with mining of the approaches, so that no aircraft could rise from its airfields in defence or offence, and no shipping could get through to relieve it, would be seen as the only answer to the problem. This neutralization of Malta would be tried in 1942.

Despite their new commitments in North Africa the Luftwaffe kept up pressure on the island. Determined to establish air superiority and wear out the pilots and the aircraft of the small core of defending Hurricanes, sweeps of Messerschmitt 109 fighters were sent over Malta in daylight. By the close of February these daylight raids were almost routine and, quite apart from their numbers, the Messerschmitts were more than a match for the Mark One Hurricanes. The watchers on the ground, who in the early days of the island's aerial warfare had been happy to see how a handful of fighters would spring up like the knights in their old tales of chivalry, putting to flight large numbers of the enemy, now grew sadly used to seeing the parachutes of their defenders opening over the barren hills and the patchwork green of the small fields. Sometimes Luqa airport would be rendered completely unserviceable by a Stuka raid. The accompanying fighters seemed to fly with easy insolence lower and lower overhead, spraying anything that moved on road or dusty track. The Wellington bombers, which had managed to make Naples unsafe for heavy units of the Italian fleet and had closed Sicilian ports and raided that island's airfields, were caught on the ground, some of them burned out and others badly damaged.

While far more ominous signs were visible in other parts of the Mediterranean theatre — the Afrika Korps making ready for the desert, and the Germans poised to invade Greece — the linchpin of the sea was itself being eroded. 'A blitz raid of several formations,' was reported, 'totalling no less than one hundred aircraft.... Sixty bombers attacked Hal Far.' The seaplane base at Kalafrana was also bombed and machine-gunned. To repulse this last attack every serviceable Hurricane and every available pilot was put into the air. There were no reserves left of aircraft or of men. A few days prior to this the main air base at Luqa had been equally heavily attacked, the old village from which the base takes its name receiving the residue of bombs dropped by pilots unwilling to face the lightning storm of air bursts over the airfield itself.

The *Times of Malta*, that remarkable newspaper which never ceased publication on any day throughout the war, sent a reporter to the scene: 'There is hardly a street without a demolished house or one seriously damaged or shaken.... The villagers told me that tons of bombs have fallen in or about the village. There were signs of destruction everywhere. Seventy-seven houses have been completely demolished, 25 others seriously damaged and uninhabitable, and it is reckoned that only about 25 per cent of the homes there have so far escaped completely unscathed. So many bombs — some of the biggest ever dropped — have fallen all round that village ... that almost all houses and farms on the outskirts facing the fields bear marks of the shrapnel, which bit holes into the walls.... These people, most of them miners, stone cutters and farmers, are among the most courageous and confident one can be privileged to meet. They have dug shelters, carried away to other villages the most valuable portions of their furniture and household goods, and they continue to live and work there, notwithstanding the severe punishment the village has had to submit to at the hands of the enemy.'[3] So well had the Maltese stone cutters dug shelters for their wives and families and fellow villagers that in the thunder of this raid, the collapse of houses and the bursting of walls and splintering of great stones, there was only one casualty.

At the beginning the attackers had concentrated on the harbour and any shipping in it as well as the all-important dockyard, then it had been the turn of the airfields, but now — during the raids in the clear spring nights — the indiscriminate bombing of residential areas, familiar in London and other British cities, became common in the miniature world of Malta. It had been the residents of the dockyard area who had suffered worst in the *Illustrious* blitz, but now the well-to-do Sliema — a seaside suburb bearing a marked resemblance to similar Victorian outcrops along the shores of Britain — learned the anguish of total war. Twenty-two were killed and thirty-six injured in one raid alone in March — small figures compared to those in Britain and Europe but in view of the size of the island and population heavy enough. A survivor recalled the aftermath of this raid: 'The bright moonlight bathed the scene of utter devastation, the acrid reek of explosive filled the cool night air. The uncanny silence was broken only by muffled groans and long drawn sighs. Husky and terse remarks from men who were looking for signs of humanity, accentuated the grim poignancy of the disaster.'[4]

Throughout the months following the arrival of the Luftwaffe in Sicily only a handful of individual merchant ships (their crews chancing their arm with old-fashioned blockade-runner's panache) had managed to reach the island with stores and weaponry. The first convoy proper of the year consisting of four merchantment, escorted by the battlefleet and the new aircraft carrier *Formidable* from Alexandria, reached Grand Harbour unobserved early on 23 March. But reconnaissance from Sicily immediately spotted the new arrivals, and two of the merchantmen were sunk at their moorings before they could even be unloaded. This disclosed a dangerous weakness in port arrangements for cargo handling, which was not to be properly dealt with until further losses of this kind had made such an overhaul tragically imperative.

It was towards the end of March that the British Mediterranean fleet managed to reassert itself — for the only time for many months; after this one success it would be the Luftwaffe which would dominate the inland sea. During the course of the month prior to the arrival of this convoy Admiral Cunningham, who never wearied of reminding London of the importance of Malta, had received something of a rebuff from the First Sea Lord, Admiral Sir Dudley Pound.

The latter pointed out that the Battle of the Atlantic transcended all other commitments, but that it was still hoped to pass some more Hurricanes through to Malta by carrier from Gibraltar as soon as circumstances permitted. In his reply Cunningham once again stressed the alarming condition of the island since the arrival of the Luftwaffe: 'The most drastic and early measures are needed to restore the situation at Malta, which alarms me seriously. Enemy air forces operate over the island as they please.'

The fleet action in March, which came to be known as the Battle of Cape Matapan, served to confirm the supremacy of the air arm at sea. In so far as it had any major bearing on the course of the Mediterranean war and Malta's part in it, Matapan served to confirm the superiority of the British over the Italian fleet, strengthening the latter's High Command in their reluctance to engage in any major actions. When it came to further assessments being made as to the feasibility of invading Malta (with the necessity of having naval superiority, even if only temporary in the area) Matapan played its part in deterring any such considerations.

While the Germans had congratulated the Italians on their successful convoying of the Afrika Korps to Libya with scarcely any loss, they were now extremely disturbed by the ease with which British convoys were making their way to Greece laden with supplies and troops, on the very eve of the German invasion. Pressure was accordingly brought to bear upon the Italians from the highest level to use their fleet to disrupt this supply line. Hitler, with his eyes obsessively fixed upon his major ambition, the invasion of Soviet Russia, did not want to get heavily embroiled in Balkan enterprises. He had already come to his partner's aid in the desert war and he was prepared to save Mussolini's face once again by sending troops to Greece. He wished to cover his southern flank before his major enterprise, but for him all these Mediterranean adventures were only a sideshow. Despite the objections which Admirals Riccardi and Iachino had already raised to any fleet ventures into the eastern Mediterranean, pleading accurately enough the superiority of British naval and land-based air reconnaissance in that area, they were at last compelled to take some action. They were promised the full cooperation of the Luftwaffe together with the Regia Aeronautica from its bases in the Dodecanese. After his previous experience off Cape Spartivento of the inefficiency of his own air force, Admiral Iachino may well have hesitated, but the promise of the Luftwaffe's support, combined with the fact that these orders came from the very top, gave him no option.

Flying his flag in the *Vittorio Veneto*, he passed through the Messina Straits early on 27 March in company with four escorting destroyers and preceded by the heavy cruisers *Trieste, Trento* and *Bolzano* together with their destroyer screen. East of Sicily they were met by three further heavy cruisers, *Zara, Pola* and *Fiume* from Taranto, and two light cruisers from Brindisi, all with their attendant destroyer screens. The object of this fleet was to position itself in the area south of Crete near Gavdo Island and intercept merchant traffic northward bound for Greece from Alexandria. Admiral Iachino's fears about the cooperation that he might expect from the air were sadly confirmed: neither the Regia Aeronautica nor, even more disappointing, the Luftwaffe made their anticipated appearance to protect him from being observed by British reconnaissance. Sure enough, a Sunderland flying-boat out of Malta sighted one of the cruiser divisions steering south-east in the direction of Crete.

This report alerted Admiral Cunningham who had already become suspicious of some major move by the Italian fleet by an increase in enemy air reconnaissance over Alexandria. Putting to sea overnight (Alexandria was full of prying eyes) in *Warspite*, along with the battleships *Barham* and *Valiant*, and the aircraft carrier *Formidable* and escorting destroyers, he too steered for the same position south of Crete towards which the Italian fleet was heading. In the battle which followed the collision of these two fleets, the battleships of neither side ever came within fighting range of one another. This was fortunate for the Italian admiral in any case since he was heavily outnumbered, while the possession of the aircraft carrier by the British made the whole difference to the engagement. Without the benefit of air reconnaissance Admiral Iachino was at the gravest disadvantage, being ignorant of what enemy forces were opposing him and of their position. His own ships were soon under attack from Royal Air Force bombers and then from *Formidable*'s planes, the cruiser *Pola* being hit and immobilized in a torpedo attack by Swordfish. Left behind as the Italian squadron turned about, she later provided the unintentional bait whereby Admiral Iachino, having misjudged the position of the British battlefleet and believing them to be far from the scene, sent back the two other heavy cruisers from her squadron together with escorting destroyers, either to take survivors off the *Pola* and sink her or tow her back to safety. Unfortunately on the night of 28 March this rescue mission fell right into the path of Cunningham's battle fleet in pursuit of the withdrawing *Vittorio Veneto*, which had also been damaged in a torpedo attack. The two cruisers and two of the destroyers were blown to pieces and the *Pola* was sunk at leisure. The British picked up what survivors they could but, on the morning of the 29th after saving some 900 men, were compelled to leave the scene by the arrival of the Luftwaffe. A message was sent to the Italian Admiralty giving the exact position of the survivors and a hospital ship was despatched to them. Other survivors were also picked up by a Greek destroyer flotilla which arrived on the scene.[5]

The Italians were without radar and untrained in night fighting, two fatal deficiences which led to their being overwhelmed. They were fortunate in one respect only, that the torpedo strike on Admiral Iachino's flagship was insufficient to slow her down so that she along with the other vessels were able to withdraw at high speed to their home bases. Matapan, a fleet action in which the battleships never sighted one another and in which the air arm dominated, was conclusive in the history of war.

Italian naval morale was naturally even further depressed by this action, while that of the British fleet, which had been shaken by the constant bombing they had to endure every time they went to sea, was correspondingly improved. They would need all the morale that they could call upon in the weeks that lay ahead.

CHAPTER NINE

Voices

In ancient sieges a dramatic keynote of the whole story is often the moment when a well wisher among the besieging army, or a spy who has managed to infiltrate it, shoots an arrow over the walls bearing, say, the word 'TOMORROW', thus ensuring that the besieged are all prepared when the great attack is launched. Something of this sort had happened at a crucial moment in the Great Siege of 1565. In the complexity of a modern siege such messages still arrived — and indeed still by air, but crossing not only the walls of the besieged fortress but often many miles of ocean. Malta throughout the siege was not only the recipient of innumerable messages by day and night, but was also a central distribution point for information throughout the Mediterranean, as well as back to Britain.

The island had long had a primary function not only as a fleet base but as a main headquarters for the reception of intelligence gleaned from Axis Europe and distributed to the allied forces. The threat that Malta posed to the lifeline of convoys between Italy and North Africa through its aircraft, submarines and surface forces, made its reduction all important to the German and Italian leaders, but this was not its only importance to the British. It was Malta as an intelligence centre, listening in to occupied Europe from Greece and the Balkans throughout the whole of the southern part of the continent, that made it so deadly. Army, navy and air force, all had their W/T (wireless telegraphy) and R/T (radio telegraphy) stations scanning the air waves twenty-four hours out of twenty-four. From the capital Valletta itself, to Fort St Angelo, to airfields and remote parts of the countryside, the island bristled with radio masts. Malta was a giant ear in the Mediterranean.

So far the story of the siege has been told following the traditional manner in which it has been presented in the many accounts of those days. Soldier, sailor or airman, whether of flag rank, junior officer or rating, have given their account of the siege, the air battles, and the relief convoys as these were seen in terms of action and events. There was another side. There was, as it were, a fourth dimension to the story of the siege, just as there was to the whole war. Very few of those involved ever knew of this other dimension, and even the few who did were constrained by their obligations of official secrecy never to reveal it. Thus, Admiral Cunningham in his autobiography published in 1951 maintains that it was a combination of 'unusual Italian wireless activity', coupled with the sighting of an Italian cruiser squadron by an aircraft flown off *Formidable*, that put him in a position to bring about the action known as the battle of Cape Matapan. Both these facts were true, but what was omitted was the fact that Cunningham, prior to taking his ships to sea from Alexandria, had already received the information from London that the Italian fleet was about to move against the convoys to Greece off the island of Crete.

The astonishing story of how at Bletchley Park in England the theoretically unbreakable German cyphering machine called Enigma had been cracked could not be told before 1974.[1] The incredibly valuable intelligence service that was called *Ultra* had sprung out of this achievement. 'A decisive factor in the allied victory,' General Eisenhower was to call it years later and, as everywhere else in the course of the long European war, it played an incalculable part in the Mediterranean. One of the two main centres for the reception of Ultra information was the island of Malta, the other was Cairo. Throughout the war, while many of the enemy's top secret messages were being read, the information contained in them was being assessed, classified, checked and put together by the brilliant team assembled at Bletchley Park. The sum total of this was then transmitted to Special Liaison Units (SLU) for the attention of commanders-in-chief and a selected handful of senior officers. One of the largest Special Liaison Units anywhere was in Malta. Also installed in Malta was the new RAF Type X machine cypher which had been carefully developed after the breaking of the German Enigma machine, thus putting it far in advance of that used by the Germans. Type X machines were only installed in main head-quarters which served two of the services. Malta served all three. Dozens of men and women passed the whole war in Malta with earphones clamped to their heads listening in at the intercept stations, striving to catch on whatever waveband signals that were being transmitted by the forces ranged against them.

The Y services (as they were known) of the army, navy and air force worked long hours — six hour watches were common — inconspicuously and indeed completely unknown to the men at the guns, the pilots, or the men in the ships. Their working conditions in Malta would hardly have been tolerated by any civilian in whatever form of employment, for many of them worked deep underground in limestone tunnels carved out beneath the immense Lascaris Bastion in the walls of Valletta. The naval operations room had been moved to this deep bomb-proof heart after Fort St Angelo had received too great attention from the enemy, standing up as it did conspicuously across the waters of Grand Harbour and inevitably becoming a focus for the bombers. Despite the fact that this old headquarters of the Knights of Malta received over sixty direct hits during the siege the great walls, bastions and cavaliers nevertheless withstood the impact of so many tons of high explosive — proof indeed that in the centuries for which it had been designed it would have been impregnable. Even as it was, deep below its battered ramparts men and women were also cyphering and coding, decyphering and decoding. They were working in what had originally been the tunnels excavated to make the quarters for the galley slaves in the days of the Knights. This area, like that below Lascaris Bastion, had been considerably enlarged by further tunnelling to accommodate these new citizens who, however remote their work from that of the slaves who had preceded them, was as arduous in its different way, and the circumstances almost equally disagreeable.

The benefits of air conditioning were unknown in the Malta of World War II and the air that filtered through these tunnels (into which box-like offices had been built) was inevitably hot, humid and dusty.[2] Limestone is quite easy to cut, but equally — until it develops a hard skin after length of exposure to the briny sea air — it crumbles easily. Both here and elsewhere in the island, where new tunnels had been dug, roof falls were not uncommon and the freshly-cut stone sweated with damp. In Malta, when the hot and damp sirocco blows — mostly in spring and autumn — the outside walls of buildings often stream with moisture as if after rain. In the tunnels of Lascaris and St Angelo, where so much of the island's vital work was carried out, clothing would grow mould within a day or so and a film of moisture often lay over everything. The porosity of the limestone, which had allowed the great underwater lakes to form beneath the island (from which Malta drew much of its water), was sadly in evidence in the tunnels during the rainy season. Pools of water formed in the passages and sea boots were often the rig-of-the-day. It is hardly surprising that chest and lung ailments were found among the operators who spent long working hours down there. These were circumstances that were peculiar to Malta, but something else which is hardly mentioned in accounts of the eavesdropping intelligence services during the war was the stress of the work itself. The island was under siege but so were the nerves of radio operators at all times — merely from the nature of their work. This was noted even in the comparative peace of Bletchley Park. Listening out intently for long periods in total concentration is a great strain in itself, and there are physical strains too; *tinnitus*, a constant buzzing in the ears, being an affliction among operators. But these,

61

and other centres like them, were the brains that helped to direct the war and Malta, unlike other places such as Cairo, was in the heart of the war itself.

When the action was fiercest during the long months of the siege — particularly in 1942 when the island was almost cut off — the only communication with the outside world was over the air waves. The wireless telegraphy for which the operators listened out was mostly on medium or high frequencies and on these emanated traffic from the Italians and the Germans in a number of codes and cyphers, including the all-important Enigma, and even *en clair*. Radio telephony was mostly employed by aircraft, usually fighter pilots in their single-engined machines, talking with fellow pilots or responding to their ground controller. These were conducted on very high frequencies which meant that the range of communication was short — but then it was only sixty miles from Malta to Sicily. Whether by day or by night the approach of the attackers could be recorded, the raid reaching its crescendo when the air was also filled by the voices of the defenders rising to meet them. R/T was also used by the Italian high speed motorboats, and, when they later reached the Mediterranean, the German E-boats. The torpedo boats usually came into action against convoys striving to reach Malta from the west during the height of the siege. Their main operating ground was in The Narrows between Sicily and Tunisia, where the Italian fortress island Pantellaria and the lesser islands of Lampedusa and Linosa barred the channel.

Intercept stations apart from Malta were at Gibraltar and Alexandria, and there were others too — from Baghdad to Aden — listening for traffic from all over the Middle East, from North Africa, and as far afield as the Balkans. Sailings from Italian and Greek ports were monitored in Malta among other places, and Italian naval cyphers read as well as German Luftwaffe traffic on Enigma, the whole being put together at Bletchley Park whence the intelligence picture was transmitted to the commanders-in-chief.

It was known, for instance, that Fliegerkorps X was moving down through Europe to Sicily at the time that it did. (This fact does not appear in earlier accounts because the existence of Enigma and Ultra was not known to the authors or, in the case of the few senior officers who did know about it, they could not reveal their source.) If this was so, it may be asked, why did the subsequent deadly attacks on HMS *Illustrious* and the blitz on Grand Harbour take place? The answer is that it is one thing to have advance secret intelligence, but quite another to be able to act upon it. Action demands resources and at this stage in the war these were spread so thin as to be almost minimal in places. Malta had to receive its convoy, and *Illustrious* was the only aircraft carrier available for escort. The deadly efficiency of Fliegerkorps X in their divebombing attacks might have been anticipated but could hardly have been obviated. On the other hand, the reception that the Luftwaffe got when it arrived over Grand Harbour to finish off the aircraft carrier, as it thought, was a deadly surprise. The air defences of the island which had been in action previously against the Italians had given nobody an inkling of what had been prepared for their allies. The losses sustained by the Luftwaffe during those attacks from the newly-installed box barrage proved unacceptable, and the escape of *Illustrious*, even given some element of luck, was made possible.

In this case, as throughout the war, Ultra information was acted upon *where resources permitted* and often enabled commanders in the field — particularly in the Western Desert — to 'box canny' and make the greatest use of what they had at a time when the Axis force possessed considerable superiority. On the other hand it was understood that where Ultra was used, it must always be in such a way that the Germans would never suspect that their signals were being read. This often entailed cover plans to make it appear as if the action that was subsequently taken had been due to ordinary reconnaissance which had, by no more than chance as it were, stumbled upon the passage of a convoy or the movement of an Afrika Korps section through the desert. If there was any chance of the Germans suspecting that some particular move could only have been due to Enigma cyphers being read, then no action could be taken. This was an obligation of the utmost stringency that was laid upon all commanders-in-chief since, so valuable was Ultra information, losses had to be accepted if it looked as if this great secret might otherwise be compromised.[3]

Apart from the reception of Ultra information from Bletchley Park and the routine eavesdropping on the air, one of the functions of the Y service in Malta, as elsewhere, was direction-finding (D/F), or taking bearings upon enemy transmissions so that, for instance, the movements of ships could be plotted. Wireless silence at sea was of course the general rule but submarines still had to report and there are always indiscretions. The operations room could use every scrap of information out of which, like many bits from a jigsaw puzzle, a picture could be formed. Quite apart from this, such things as an increased volume in activity from some known port or area could provide a hint of troop movements or indicate the preparation of a convoy preparing to leave, or of major fleet units gathering to cover it. Of Malta during those years it could well be said, echoing *The Tempest*, that 'the isle is full noises' and 'a thousand twangling instruments'.

CHAPTER TEN

Spring '41

The Battle of Matapan had been fought because the Italian navy, relinquishing its sensible policy of avoiding action and remaining a fleet in being, had been compelled to strike at the British convoys making their way with troops and material between Egypt and Greece. Just as these intentions had been revealed by Ultra so the very convoys that lured it into the eastern Mediterranean had been prompted by Ultra information. Early in 1941 the build up of German forces in southern Rumania had become known, and further signals had shown that Hitler's aim was for his forces to move through Bulgaria and attack Greece. The British decision to go to the aid of Greece, which was quite contrary to the wishes of General Wavell, was a political one. A similar political decision, when the British forces had in due course to be withdrawn from Greece, to try and hold the great island of Crete in the face of overwhelming German airpower, was to lead to such heavy losses in the Mediterranean fleet that the whole naval position in the sea was changed and the achievements of Spartivento, Taranto and Matapan were largely nullified. Just as Ultra information had led to the British reinforcement of Greece so it had forewarned of the later German intention to attack Crete. Winston Churchill became particularly impressed at this time with the efficiency and accuracy of Ultra, but the resultant usage of this information remained a political judgement. To attempt to hold the Germans in Greece via a supply line to the British forces running back to Egypt (and subsequently all the way round the Cape of Good Hope) was illogical. Similarly, so was the attempt to hold Crete against overwhelming German air power.

During that bad spring which was to lead to an even worse summer — the nadir, so it seemed, of Britain's fortunes during World War II — it was evidence of the understanding of the true importance of Malta in the war that, despite the situation in Britain, twelve Hurricane Mark IIAs, reckoned to be more than a match for the Messerschmitt 109s, were put aboard the carrier *Argus* for transference at Gibralter to the *Ark Royal*. Even the old mark of Hurricanes that had seen such service in Malta had shown what a toll they could take of the invaders. In March that year a convoy of four merchant ships had been passed through to the island (in the subsequent air attacks on it in harbour two were damaged) bringing supplies and reinforcements to the garrison. During the air attacks Malta's Hurricanes had shot down nine dive bombers, the guns taking a further four. The addition of some of the new Hurricanes to the island's defence was as appreciated as it was important at the time. Later in that month a further twenty-three Hurricanes were transferred from Britain by the same means, being flown off the *Ark Royal* from a point south of the great island of Sardinia.[1]

Despite the reduction in daylight air attacks due to the movement of part of Fliegerkorps X to North Africa the grip of the siege upon the island began to tighten. In February 1941 a law was passed giving the authorities the right to call up all able-bodied men between the ages of 16 and 56 for military service. Government employees, dockyard workers, farmers, quarry men and stonecutters were exempted, but by the end of the year nearly 4000 men in the 19-29 age groups had been conscripted. Other evidences of war were to be found in the increasing shortage of food stuffs: sugar, coffee, tea, margarine, matches, lard and rice, were all rationed, as was household soap.[2] There was goats' milk available, but cows had not then been introduced to the island and one of the staple requirements was tinned milk, also rationed. Tea and coffee, particularly tea — with tinned milk, heavily sweetened, and drunk out of glasses — had long been a pleasure to the islanders, and its increasing unavailability was to be one of the sorest trials as the siege developed. Olive oil and bread, baked in ovens fired by wood, formed the basis of the island diet, and these were as yet untouched. The introduction of conscription was a reminder of distant days; the last time it had happened was in 1792 when the islanders were besieging the French locked in Valletta. Now it was they themselves who were besieged.

Early in April that year the islanders rejoiced to see four of the most powerful new fleet destroyers arrive in Malta — *Mohawk* and *Nubian* of the Tribal class and *Jervis* and *Janus* of the J class. The choice of such a time to reinforce the island with a powerful stri'' force was clear enough in the context of the presence in North of the Afrika Korps; it would mean increased demands on t' supply line between Italy and Tripoli. Rommel's arrival h known since February and the fact that throughout t' campaigns his headquarters sent a situation report every almost the same time on a known frequency and fro location was a great bonus to intelligence. Because of from their main headquarters in Europe, German co with their forces in North Africa were all-important of their requirements (read by Ultra) led to ant' convoys being run to meet them. The German buil' interfered with while Malta was barren of fighting ships, short of aircraft, and without an efficient submarine force, but all these defects now began to be remedied. A flotilla of the small 'U' class submarines had been assembled. These submarines were to prove immensely effective in future months and their activities were in evidence from the very beginning.

Early that year Field Marshal Kesselring, airman turned soldier, had been sent to Rome to coordinate both air and land forces, for it was clear that, although ostensible deference must be paid to the Italian High Command, in the end the Germans would have to look after more than their own. For the moment the existence of a German army assisting the Italians in North Africa called for a high-ranking officer to coordinate Luftwaffe and Afrika Korps. He informed Rommel by signal that he and an Italian general would be visiting him in mid July. Hero though he was later to become (almost as much admired by his enemies as by his own troops) Rommel did not command such confidence in the German high command. He was deeply patriotic, but had the reputation of acting independently and without consultation with the OKW (Supreme Command of the Armed Forces). At the far end of a communications link with Germany the desert might suit Rommel well, but his superiors mistrusted his impetuosity. General Franz Halder, army chief of staff, was one of those who suspected that Rommel might take the bit between his teeth unless suitably restrained, and so towards the end of April that year he despatched his deputy, General Friedrich Paulus, to check on Rommel's intentions and discuss the whole desert campaign with him. After discussions in depth, and a two week visit to North Africa, General Paulus sent a lengthy signal to Berlin detailing the strategy which he and Rommel had together agreed to pursue in the desert. Curiously enough, seeing that it dealt almost exclusively with military matters, this important signal was sent in the cypher used by the Luftwaffe, and this was one which had been most satisfactorily broken at Bletchley Park, while German army cyphers proved more difficult. The British commanders now had a complete picture of the overall strategy which the Germans intended to pursue. While it could in no way prevent their forces having to retreat in the face of superior arms, it meant that the retreat was conducted without the disaster that might otherwise have occurred.

The reading of German Luftwaffe Enigma traffic and Italian cyphers was an intelligence operation coordinated back in and but it was then transmitted directly to the Commander-in-Mediterranean. Sailings from Italian ports were known about ian cyphers and details of air escorts provided for convoys from Enigma — something that accounts for some of the surprisingly accurate attacks made by surface craft and submarines in those early days. Later on in the war contacts made with Italian convoys could often be ascribed to radar as well as to highly developed air reconnaissance — and certainly radar would confirm the presence of the enemy when the attacking ships or aircraft were within radar range — but it must be noted that the four destroyers which had just reached Malta to form an attacking force were not yet fitted with radar. Nevertheless, on 15 April a convoy of five ships escorted by three destroyers was located by the 14th Flotilla (*Mohawk, Nubian, Jervis* and *Janus*) off the Tunisian coast. In the ensuing action all five transports, laden with troops and supplies for the Afrika Korps, were sunk as well as two of the destroyers, the third being put out of action and drifting onto the Kerkenah Bank (later to be salvaged). In the last stage of this action the Italian destroyer *Tarigo*, with her captain mortally wounded and with his ship hit time and again, yet managed to lay herself between the attackers and their prey and launch three torpedoes which sank the *Mohawk*. As later events in the war would show, particularly in escort work and small boat actions, the Italians could show a spirit second to none. The stories of cowardice carried in the British press were designed for home consumption.

The source of the British knowledge of likely convoy sailing times and routes was a secret kept from all but a very small selected handful and so no mention is made in any post-war books on the siege of the reason why aircraft or ships were sent in particular directions to intercept convoys.

April showed the island most clearly in its dual role — attacked and attacker. Malta was somewhat like an old counter-puncher in the boxing ring, who, although battered and bloody, still comes forward with blows that make his apparently superior opponent hesitate and then reel back. Swordfish and Wellingtons operating from the island served in a co-ordinated attack with Cunningham's battlefleet on the main Libyan port and capital of Tripoli on 20 April at the same time as a convoy was passed through to Malta and empty merchant ships taken out. That night RAF bombers and the Fleet Air Arm attacked the port first so that, when the three battleships *Warspite, Barham* and *Valiant* and the heavy cruiser *Gloucester* arrived on the scene with their destroyer escort, complete surprise was achieved. The defenders of Tripoli were disorientated by the air attack and totally surprised by this sudden whistling thunder from the sea. From the beginning of the year up to the end of April submarines sank ten ships: this was just an earnest of what they would do later.

Throughout the Mediterranean T.S. Eliot's 'cruellest month',

April, was about to justify the poet's epithet in the activities of man, but from the beginning of the month all the islands were, as always, peacefully crowned with wild flowers. Nowhere was this more true than in the Maltese archipelago where, apart from the hundreds of indigenous species, there had been numerous deliberate and accidental imports during the years of the British occupation. As the islanders felt the warmth of that most delicate and delightful season of the year creep over their fields and streets, invading even the cavernous mouths of their underground shelters, they were encouraged not only by the Easter Festival — always celebrated in southern lands more than Christmas — but by the comparative absence of daylight bombing. They were not to know that this was due to the withdrawal of planes for the campaign in Greece and the offensive in the western desert, but it was part of an Easter bonus all the same. But the night raids continued and on the 29 April the dockyard area of Cospicua was hit as well as the outlying townships of Zabbar, Zurrieq and Zebbug. On the following night Cospicua was again bombed, and the village of Kalkara on Grand Harbour, as well as Valletta and Sliema. Casualties fortunately were few, and those mostly in the farming township of Zebbug which was unprepared for such attacks (Zebbug means 'olives' in Maltese), but many houses were damaged or demolished, thus adding to the never-ending problem of refugees.

A member of the 1st Battalion Hampshire Regiment which had come to reinforce the island in February 1941, straight from service in the desert, recorded some years later his remembered images of Malta at that season of the year.

'To us Poor Bloody Infantry from the desert, with its undulating expanses of sand from horizon to horizon, Malta appeared as it must have looked to those early Arabs and Moors, especially in the spring of the year with the grass in the low-lying Marsa area and bright yellow chrysanthemums all the way from Porte des Bombes to Pieta Creek.

The solid limestone houses of the villagers with pumpkins ripening in the sun on the flat roofs, colourful washing there, too, gave promise of companionship after the bleak months in North Africa where even the nomads ceased to roam. There were crops in the tiny fields surrounded by the never-ending lines of stone walls, and fig trees and olives as well as orange and lemon orchards. . . .[3]

Under the spring sun the island was as always at its most gracious — a far cry from the dusty aridity of summer when it shows its North African face and is almost as barren as the desert which that soldier

68

remembered. On the high garigue, among the bare rocks, stony ground and sandy patches were scattered low bushes of thyme, rosemary, sage and many other herbs — as well as grape hyacinth, garlic, Star of Bethlehem and narcissus, to name but a few flowers whose brief spring would soon be extinguished, leaving their dusty seed-heads in the parched land of summer. Everywhere, alongside the white roads, and growing thick in the lanes that were too narrow for even the smallest army trucks, waved the yellow Cape Sorrel. Legend had it that this had been introduced by some English woman from South Africa in the early nineteenth century, since when it had spread all over the island and was known in Maltese as *Haxixa Inglesa*, the English Weed. The fields were still green and the island garlanded in flowers.

Meanwhile the German armies were advancing in Greece and the British forces (too little and too late) confronted by overwhelming air power were falling back, finally to be evacuated. On 27 April 1941 German troops entered Athens.

CHAPTER ELEVEN

War and Weather

The fast mechanized columns of the Afrika Korps were sweeping everything before them in the desert to the south. In the east the German 12th Army was overrunning Greece. Agonizingly conscious of German tank and air superiority on both flanks of their besieged island, the people of Malta looked out over a sea where the enemy's grip was tightening around them and where as April drew to a close the prospects of the summer looked bleak indeed. One of the only sources of hope, though unperceived as yet in the island, was that the port of Tobruk in Cyrenaica was being held even as the enemy was moving up to the borders of Egypt. Tobruk in due course was to become, like Malta itself, a thorn in the side of the triumphant Axis powers, another besieged garrison, but this time able to strike back from the land.

The withdrawal of part of Fliegerkorps X seemed a bonus at the time. Although the news of defeat came to them over cable radio, it was natural enough that its long term effect on Malta was not at first perceived. The relief from the Luftwaffe attacks seemed enough in itself on those fine days when, curiously, official announcements and news broadcasts could still be heard issuing from houses that had been deserted or too badly damaged to be occupied. Out of dusty bakelite radios which had been left switched on the crackled voices sounded strange on the still, blue air amid white rubble or glassless window frames.

But the news of the final withdrawal from Greece and the occupation of Crete when it came by word of mouth — and rumour in an island where almost every family knows one another runs faster than any bush fire — was fully understood. Not only was the British army having to be evacuated from Greece but the Mediterranean fleet was also taking such punishment from the air that its victories at sea would be rendered meaningless. By 24 April over fifty thousand troops had reached their evacuation beaches in Greece, some near Athens, and others at selected points in the Morea. That the losses from warships engaged in escorting the troopships in this evacuation were not greater was due to the fact that the Luftwaffe had not been able to move their bases forward fast enough to catch up with the disciplined retreat (described by Rear-Admiral Baillie Grohman as 'magnificent — especially considering that they had been fighting a rearguard action for some weeks, from Salonika almost to Cape Matapan'). Evacuation could only be carried out during the hours of darkness for fear of the Luftwaffe, and on any occasion when this was disregarded the result was disastrous. One troopship late in leaving Nauplia was sunk as soon as daylight discovered her. Two destroyers sent to pick up the survivors, having collected some seven-hundred men from the scene of the sinking, were themselves sunk by dive bombers as they headed for Suda Bay in Crete. Only forty-one sailors and eight soldiers survived out of the hundreds involved. The writing that had been on the wall since the attack on *Illustrious* by Fliegerkorps X was now plain for all to see: ships could not operate safely or efficiently in the face of massive air superiority. Crete was to prove the final scene where this fundamental of modern warfare was to be made explicit.

Another fundamental rule in warfare later to be pronounced by General Montgomery — 'never march on Moscow' — was about to be broken by the German dictator during that year. Incomprehensible though it seems with hindsight, Hitler in his fanatical absorption with the conquest of Russia and the destruction of the 'subhumans' who lived in that giant land, was to close his eyes to the potentials of the desert campaign. In this area, the only one where the British and Germans could get to grips, there lay at that moment the key to the whole struggle. A concentration of German forces behind the spearhead of Rommel's Afrika Korps would undoubtedly have swept the British back and out of Egypt and the Middle East. The Suez Canal would have come under Axis control, the oil of the Persian Gulf would have been at the disposal of the Axis and the British would have been deprived of this essential of modern warfare as well as being ignominiously expelled from the African continent. The rankling wound of the war in the west with Britain would have been removed at a stroke. At his leisure, and without any further worries about sources of oil for his military machine, Hitler could have turned his attention to the invasion of Russia. But he never saw the desert war as anything other than an unfortunate sideshow into which he had been dragged in his desire to bail out his incompetent partner. In Greece and the Balkans he had had to intervene to save Mussolini's face and so as not to leave his right flank unguarded, or in a state of confusion, when he made his major move east later in the year. The arrival of the British in Greece, honour bound to come to the aid of an ally even though at grave disadvantage to their main interests, caused Hitler to take the Greek campaign seriously. He recalled what the British had tried to do via the Dardanelles in the First World War, and a threat to his flank and to the Rumanian oilfields could not be tolerated when he was about to march on Russia. Yet Hitler, who prided himself on a mastery of grand strategy and military geopolitics, by failing to see what success in the desert could have meant to him and how it could have ensured a successful invasion of Russia by two giant prongs striking into the heart of that country (one from Europe and the west and the other from the east), deprived himself of ultimate victory. His eyes were European eyes; he could see the east only in terms of Russia.

Even at this moment when the evacuation of the troops from Greece had not yet been completed, an event was taking place in the Mediterranean in which Malta figured conspicuously. This was an elaborate dual convoy operation code-named 'Tiger', in which the great risk was taken of passing right through to Egypt a convoy from the western end made up of transports full of tank reinforcements for the Army of the Nile at the same time as two convoys from the east for Malta. Churchill, unlike his adversary, was fully aware of what the loss of Egypt and the Suez Canal would mean and was determined, when the German Panzers had shown their hand in the desert, to reinforce General Wavell as far as possible. The risk was considerable, for convoys passing from Gibraltar all the way through to Egypt had not been considered acceptable since the arrival of the Luftwaffe in the central Mediterranean. However, in the hope that the German air force would be fully stretched with the Greek and desert operations, the gamble was taken and justified. The convoy from the western end was escorted by Force H from Gibraltar, the only loss occurring when one of the transports was mined and sank in the narrows of the Skerki Channel. This area, which was later to be the setting for many desperate actions involving convoys to Malta, was shallow and mine infested, ideal attack ground for torpedo boats, submarines, and torpedo aircraft, but on this occasion it was completely neglected by the Italians. Except for the loss of this one transport the convoy made a successful passage, Force H withdrawing to Gibraltar as Cunningham's Mediterranean fleet took over as escort to Egypt.

On its way to the rendezvous Cunningham's fleet had also successfully covered the two highly important convoys to Malta. This was one of the most creditable moments of the Mediterranean sea campaign to date for the fleet from Alexandria — battleships, cruisers and destroyers alike — at a time when it had been working at full stretch since the campaign had started in Greece. Although in need of a respite — which they were not to get — the safe escort of these two convoys into the beleaguered island was to sustain Malta and ensure the island's efficiency throughout the long summer that lay ahead. One of them was a slow convoy consisting of two tankers carrying 24,000 tons of oil fuel, and the other a fast one of four supply ships with troops, food, ammunition and the thousand and one other requisites needed by the garrison and the people.

The successful passage of these two convoys through to Malta must largely be ascribed to the state of the weather at the time, for without it there can be little doubt that, although the Mediterranean fleet had the carrier *Formidable* with them for fighter cover, the convoys would certainly have been spotted and heavily attacked. Indeed, a great many enemy aircraft were reported on the fleet's radar, clearly searching for them and their precious cargo ships but, as Admiral Cunningham reported, the weather was 'thick with low cloud down almost to our mast-heads'. The admiral comments in his autobiography that 'for the time of the year the weather was most unusual', a curious remark coming from one who had served in the Mediterranean in the First World War and often during the inter-war years and who might well have called himself, in the words of Nelson, 'an old Mediterranean man'. It was very typical sirocco weather, which is more common in the month of May than any other. Starting in the desert as a dry, dusty, southerly wind, varying in direction from south-east to south-west and known as the 'Khamsin', it picks up moisture as it crosses the sea. The hot desert air cools from contact with the sea's surface, the relative humidity rises sharply and the resultant sirocco wind is warm and hazy and full of moisture-laden cloud. Known as the 'Xlokk' in Maltese it is this which causes the buildings and gutters in the island to stream with water, the enervating air exacerbating tempers and causing even the mildest to swear while they sweat.[1] But since the war and the bombing the besieged islanders had learned to bless this normally cursed wind for the respite that it gave from air attack. It was during just such a period that these two all important convoys were approaching the island. Traditionally known as Calypso's isle from the secret 'hidden' island of the goddess in Homer's *Odyssey*, Malta, low lying on the face of the sea, was now completely obscured by cloud.[2]

Admiral Cunningham learned while at sea that the island was encircled by more than the sirocco cloud, it was completely mined in. During their night raids the Regia Aeronautica had been sowing mines in all the approaches, and the Vice-Admiral, Malta,[3] reported to the commander-in-chief that the destroyer flotilla stationed in the island could not sail to escort in the convoys because it could not get out of harbour, and that the channel normally used could not be swept because all the minesweepers capable of dealing with magnetic mines had been lost or put out of action.

Fortunately Cunningham had among the escorts for the convoys one corvette which was equipped for magnetic minesweeping, but one ship alone would clearly not be capable of dealing with the situation around Malta. A method was quickly devised by the fleet torpedo officer,[4] and a signal was sent to Malta instructing the authorities to blast a channel out through the approaches to the island with depth charges. Fortunately there were plenty of depth charges available and to the thunder of underwater explosions a channel was gradually cleared outwards from Grand Harbour, the pattern of exploding charges having the effect of countermining or otherwise disturbing the firing mechanism of the magnetic mines which closed the approach channel. Even so, when the *Gloxinia*, Cunningham's lone corvette equipped for magnetic sweeping, preceded the convoys into the harbour at least a dozen mines that had survived the previous rough treatment went up in thunders of spray. Under the steamy cotton wool clouds of the south wind the convoys safely reached Grand Harbour and were unloaded, unseen by any aerial reconnaissance. The special supply ship, HMS *Breconshire*, whose name was to become famous and synonymous with the siege of Malta during the months to come, also entered Marsaxlokk, the southern harbour, with fuel and ammunition. As the most critical period of the war for the Mediterranean fleet developed to the east around the island of Crete, Malta stood replenished, refuelled and rearmed. The limestone fortress was all set to confirm the German opinion that 'a gross error had been committed [by the Italians] in not starting the war with the conquest of Malta.'

CHAPTER TWELVE

In Another Island

Following the success of the German army in Greece it was almost inevitable that the next scene of action should be the great fish-shaped island of Crete, lying across the foot of the Aegean Sea and dominating all the eastern Mediterranean to the south. The capture of Crete would mean that from its airfields the Luftwaffe could have Alexandria and Suez and the Canal within their reach and could make the passage of allied merchant and naval ships in support of the ground forces along the North African coast so hazardous as almost to cut this lifeline. As yet the German navy, with its U-boats and light craft, had hardly been committed to the Mediterranean, the area by tacit agreement being considered the prerogative of the Italians and their fleet. The dominant pressure on the Mediterranean theatre was then to be exerted by the Luftwaffe and here again, as in the Battle of Britain, Marshal Goering was not only supremely confident but determined to obtain the laurels of victory for his own service. Units of Fliegerkorps X, as has been seen, had been detached from Sicily to join Fliegerkorps VIII in Greece. The latter could deploy over seven-hundred aircraft for the operations in Greece and the subsequent attack on Crete, several hundreds of them being dive bombers. These would have been sufficient in themselves to devastate the airfields available to the British who, in any case, after fighting a rearguard action in the air all the way down Greece were reduced to a few Hurricanes and some old Gladiators.

It might have seemed reasonable for the bulk of the German troops to have been transported for the invasion of Crete under the escort of the Italian navy, protected all the way by German fighter aircraft. After all, the British after their withdrawal from Greece had transported sixteen-thousand men to hold the island of Crete, the bulk of the troops being taken to Egypt to reinforce the desert army. Under constant air attack and faced by large-scale landings which the Royal Navy it might have been thought (quite wrongly) would have been unable to prevent — because they would be required to work in narrow waters without fighter cover and under dive-bomber attack — the occupation of Crete could have been planned in a conventional manner. But the Germans, partly mistrustful of the Italians' ability to provide adequate protection at sea for troop convoys and partly because Goering wished the whole operation to come under the aegis of the Luftwaffe, had decided to take Crete by airborne assault. General Kurt Student, who commanded Flieger-korps XI, consisting of the Parachute and Airborne troops, was the author of the scheme. He was naturally eager to try out his élite corps and was confident that its use would lead to a far swifter operation than conventional landings. Such a large-scale airborne assault had not been previously tried during the war, and it was hoped that the very surprise of its nature would swiftly overwhelm the British defence.

But even if nothing could be done to prevent the attack, the projected airborne invasion of the island had been known to the British since the end of April. Ultra had given warning from the moment that gliders and transport aircraft had begun to assemble in Bulgaria, and the build up of Luftwaffe bombers, dive bombers and fighters had also been known. The sheer weight of the preparations determined the urgency of the German High Command to complete the occupation of Crete as quickly as possible. Hitler had himself given his approval to the scheme, for he was anxious to see the whole campaign in Greece and the Aegean concluded before turning to what really concerned him — the invasion of Russia. That this too was known about due to Ultra is now common knowledge — even the fact that Stalin was warned in advance by Churchill of the German plans. In the case of Crete, not only was Churchill informed some time prior to the invasion, but General Freyberg in command of the allied forces in the island was furnished with the German plans in elaborate detail. General Kurt Student was a German of the almost obsessively meticulous order and was determined to ensure that every unit involved in the forthcoming operation was kept fully briefed. The result was a stream of signals read by Ultra, giving full warning several weeks in advance — from the date that the invasion would take place to landing grounds and the strength of airborne formations.

This being so, the inevitable question must be asked — why then was Crete lost? Ultra information could only forewarn a general or an admiral of some intended enemy move, but there was little that he could do about it unless he had the necessary weapons at his disposal. In the case of Crete there was nothing that could be done to bring the strength of the RAF up to anything approaching practical standards. The Hurricane squadrons which had fought their way down through Greece were reduced to under a dozen aircraft and the few Gladiators of the Fleet Air Arm were too old to cope with the waves of Messerschmitt fighters that escorted the bombers and transport planes. In the first stage of the action, when the Luftwaffe had begun softening up the island prior to the main assault, these few survivors of the many weeks of fighting were reduced to four Hurricanes and three Gladiators. Hard pressed in North Africa, with few enough planes even to defend Malta, there were no reserves left for transference to Crete before the blow fell on 20 May. Only the day before, the seven remaining aircraft (rightly judged incapable of withstanding the wave poised over the island) were sent back to Egypt. There was no fighter defence at all. What surprised subsequent commentators on the campaign — and more than surprised General Student — was that it almost seemed as if the airborne assault had been anticipated. But it was true that General Freyberg might well have learned from sources in Greece of the build up of gliders and transport planes and of the presence of paratroops on the mainland — and certainly in that case he would have prepared his defence around the most likely airfields. This seemed good enough cover for Ultra.[1]

The attack began with heavy bombing around Canea and Maleme airfields, and was followed by waves of gliders coming in to land. But this landing, which should have driven away the handful of troops that were all that might have been expected to be left to guard the airfields, did not seem to have the desired effect. In fact, General Student's airborne troops ran into stiffer resistance than had been anticipated. Losses were heavy on both sides, but Maleme airfield, which had been expected to fall within the day, still remained a battlefield at nightfall. Similarly at Canea the invaders were firmly held and the ground remained disputed.

With his crack paratroopers in trouble at both these landing places General Student may have hoped for better things on the airfield of Heraklion and Retimo, but here too they met with unexpectedly fierce resistance. The key to the battle for Crete was the landing ground at Maleme where it was hoped to bring in the Junkers 52 transport planes carrying the 5th Mountain Division as reinforcements. The airborne assault on Crete might indeed have been completely defeated if General Freyberg had thrown into Maleme two New Zealand infantry battalions which were held in reserve at Canea. Aware, however, that the bulk of German reinforcements must come by sea General Freyberg held back the New Zealanders to deal with the expected landing. Had he but known that during the night of 21 May Royal Naval ships sweeping north of the island had encountered these seaborne reinforcements and that all of them had either been sunk or turned back, Maleme airfield might have been held. As it was, the German transport planes landed, Maleme was taken, and the way was clear for massive reinforcements by air. Crete was lost.

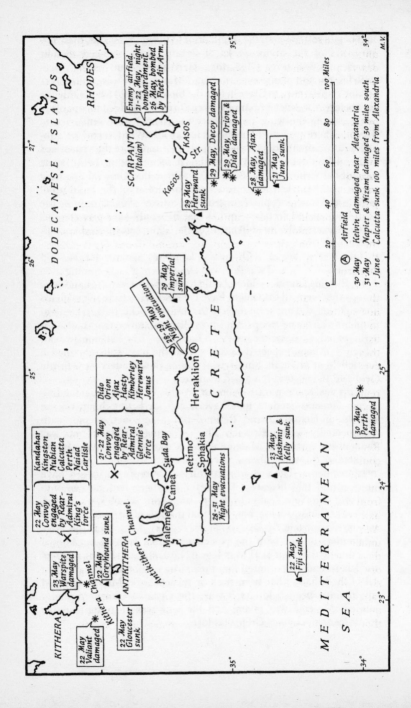

KITHERA

22 May Valiant damaged

22 May Gloucester sunk

22 May Greyhound sunk

23 May Warspite damaged

Kithera Channel

ANTIKITHERA Channel

Antikithera Channel

DODECANESE ISLANDS

RHODES

SCARPANTO (Italian)

Enemy airfield. 21–22 May, night bombardment. 26 May, bombed by Fleet Air Arm.

KASOS

Kasos Str.

29 May Hereward sunk

29 May, Decoy damaged

29 May, Orion & Dido damaged

28 May Ajax damaged

31 May Juno sunk

29 May Imperial sunk

28–29 May Night evacuation

Dido
Orion
Ajax
Hasty
Kimberley
Hereward
Janus

21–22 May Convoy engaged by Rear-Admiral Glennie's force

Suda Bay

Kandahar
Kingston
Nubian
Calcutta
Perth
Naiad
Carlisle

22 May Convoy engaged by Rear-Admiral King's force

Heraklion Ⓐ

C R E T E

Maleme Ⓐ Canea

Retimo

Sphakia

28–31 May Night evacuations

23 May Kashmir & Kelly sunk

22 May Fiji sunk

30 May Perth damaged

M E D I T E R R A N E A N   S E A

27°   26°   25°   24°   23°

35°

34°

Ⓐ Airfield

Kelvin damaged near Alexandria
Napier & Nizam damaged 30 miles south
Calcutta sunk 100 miles from Alexandria

30 May
31 May
1 June

0   20   40   60   80   100 Miles

M.V.

The fact remains that Heraklion and Retimo airfields were held until the general evacuation of Crete by the allied forces had been ordered; the former not being abandoned until 28 May and the latter not until the 30th. This was proof, if such was needed, that the landings by General Student's airborne forces, which had been expected to clear all the airfields within a few hours ready for reinforcements by the transport planes, had failed. At every point where these crack troops had been thrown in they had been held and had suffered such heavy casualties that the German command was in a state of despair. What seemed so inexplicable to the Germans at the time as well as to subsequent writers on the Battle of Crete — the failure of the paratroopers to secure the airfields within a matter of hours — is clearly explained by the prior knowledge obtained from Ultra. Once Maleme airfield had been captured, however, and the way cleared for massive reinforcements, the loss of the island was inevitable since the allies had no fighter cover and their ground troops were ceaselessly harassed by the overwhelming numbers of Luftwaffe fighters and divebombers.[2]

The political decision to hold Crete, taken with the full knowledge that the Luftwaffe would overwhelm the skies and that there could be no response from the RAF or the Fleet Air Arm, was an act that was to have the gravest consequences for the Mediterranean fleet. The list of warships sunk, severely damaged or so badly damaged that they had to be sunk to prevent them falling into enemy hands, covers every type of vessel afloat from destroyers to cruisers and battleships. Operating in confined waters with two objectives — to prevent reinforcements reaching the island by sea, and to withdraw the allied troops when the order came — meant that ships without air cover had to be constantly active in waters where from the Greek mainland, Aegean islands and in due course Crete itself, the Luftwaffe and the Regia Aeronautica could enjoy a field day such as only political folly could ever have offered them.

The ships were operating under such conditions of almost continuous attack that it was not uncommon for them to have to retire from the scene of action because all their anti-aircraft ammunition had been used up. At one point, in response to a message from the Admiralty which Admiral Cunningham said he'd found 'singularly unhelpful', he was prompted to respond: 'The experience of three days in which two cruisers and four destroyers have been sunk, and one battleship, two cruisers and four destroyers severely damaged shows what losses are likely to be. Sea control in the Eastern Mediterranean could not be retained after another such experience.' He went on to say that 'the effect of the recent operations was cumulative, and that the officers, men and machinery were nearing exhaustion.'[3]

Yet still no major German reinforcements had been able to reach Crete by sea, such transports and escorts as had attempted it having been sunk by the fleet units patrolling to the north of the island or forced to turn back under cover of darkness. Radar also played a part in one of these major actions, a convoy attempting to reach Crete at night being badly shot up, despite the gallantry of its Italian escort which, without this modern advantage, endeavoured to protect its charges against attackers who could see through the dark. The last British reinforcements were sent into Crete as late as the night of 26-27th — the order finally coming through from London to evacuate the island on 27 May. Yet even as late as the 26th Winston Churchill was cabling General Wavell — 'Victory in Crete essential at this turning point of the war. Keep hurling in all you can.'

An example of the total impracticability of the prime minister's command was the story of the landing ship HMS *Glenroy* which was sent up from Alexandria at the last moment to try and land more troops on the island at a time when the British, Australian and New Zealand forces were everywhere in retreat.

The *Glenroy* escorted by the *Coventry* [anti-aircraft cruiser], *Stuart* and *Jaguar* [destroyers] was also on her way to try landing troops at Tymbaki [on the south coast of Crete]. They were bombed during the morning of 26 May and at 6.20 p.m. were heavily attacked by dive bombers and then by low-flying torpedo bombers. The *Glenroy* avoided the torpedoes, but was slightly damaged and had some casualties from near misses and machine-gun fire. Three of her landing craft were holed, and a large dump of cased petrol on the upper deck was set ablaze. To cope with the fire the *Glenroy* had to turn south to bring the wind aft, and one of the landing-craft at the davits had to be jettisoned. With eight hundred troops on board and a large cargo of petrol the situation was most unpleasant; but when the flames were mastered the convoy again resumed its course for Crete.[4]

Finally, owing to the loss of time incurred the *Glenroy* was turned back because her late arrival would have meant landing troops in daylight — an impossibility with the Luftwaffe everywhere dominant. The blood bath that was the sea around Crete would not be cleared until the last of the allied forces who could reach any of the embarkation points had been taken off.

As the evacuation proceeded, day after day the harbour of Alexandria presented a panorama of increasingly disastrous proportions: ships of all classes with gaping holes in their decks or sides, cruisers with gun turrets blasted apart and gun barrels pointing askew at the sky, a destroyer with so much of her stern blown off that it was amazing her propeller shafts and screws had remained to drive her back to port, and other vessels that looked as if only the breakers' yard awaited them. By 1 June all those who could be taken off the island had been returned to Egypt — over sixteen-thousand men, leaving some five-thousand or more still in Crete to surrender; some took to the mountains. The admiral's covering despatch summed up what had been achieved and at what cost.

> Apart from the cumulative effect of prolonged seagoing over extended periods it has to be remembered that in this last instance ships' companies had none of the inspiration of battle with the enemy to bear them up.... They had started the evacuation already over-tired and they had to carry it through under conditions of savage air attacks such as had only recently caused grievous losses to the fleet.

The fatigue of the constant bombing attacks and long periods at sea under those conditions was such that both men and ships were at breaking point. The surviving destroyers, those maids of all work, were worn to pieces, even when they had not been badly damaged. It was not unusual for a man to be rescued from one sinking ship only to board another destined to be sunk and survive to join a third which, if not sunk, was hit. During those two months before, during and after the Battle of Crete, one of the cruisers had spent fewer than ten nights in harbour — and then only to refuel and reammunition. The days at sea were not days on patrol but of constant action stations. But, as Admiral Cunningham wrote, 'it was impossible to abandon the troops in Crete. Our naval tradition would never survive such an action.' The cost, however, was greater than anything that might ever have been expected: two battleships, the *Warspite* and the *Barham* and the aircraft carrier *Formidable* so badly damaged as to be beyond local repair and to be out of action for some months, three cruisers and six destroyers sunk, two cruisers and two destroyers damaged beyond local repair, and three cruisers and six destroyers damaged sufficiently as to be out of action for some weeks.

The navy had fulfilled its prime function: throughout the whole of the battle no warship or transport of the Axis powers had succeeded in reaching the island. Apart from this and the evacuation of so many fighting men, it was difficult to discern anything else on the credit side. What could not be foreseen was that the Cretans in company with some of the allied survivors in the mountains, later to be

81

reinforced by other special agents landed at night from submarines, were to make the island a permanent running sore in the side of their occupiers. The Cretans had a long tradition of guerrilla warfare, dating back to the centuries of their occupation by the Turks. From the same almost inaccessible caves in the high, remote mountains they would defy the German occupiers just as their ancestors had defied the Ottoman Empire. But the most important outcome of the battle (which can now be attributed to Ultra information) was the fact that in the course of the airborne attack Fliegerkorps XI, the only paratroop and airborne division in the German army, had been practically annihilated. No further airborne operations were ever carried out by Goering's Luftwaffe, and when at a later date further proposals were made for a similar attack on Malta the events of Crete were well remembered.

The whole of Malta was a giant fortress, whereas Crete had been a large island with many landing places available and held by an insufficient number of men. Hitler's own comments about the nature of Malta's terrain and the thousands of stone walls which turned it into a death trap for gliders and paratroopers, making any form of airborne assault almost impossible, combined with the memory of Crete, were to preclude any invasion. Of course none of this was apparent to the people of Malta at the time. The news of the attack on Crete by paratroopers naturally caused great concern among the islanders, suggesting that a similar attack might soon be launched against them. Many — servicemen and civilians alike — anticipated a return of the Luftwaffe to Sicily now that Crete had fallen. What they could not know was that Fliegerkorps VIII was about to be withdrawn to the north for Hitler's Russian campaign starting on 22 June, and that Fliegerkorps X had abandoned the airfields in Sicily and was now responsible for the whole of the Mediterranean theatre. Since the war in the desert was the main Axis preoccupation those units of Fliegerkorps X which were not stationed in North Africa were concentrated in Greece and Crete, giving them operational access to Egypt and the Suez Canal.

The Mediterranean fleet would find that the eastern waters of the sea were now heavily threatened and convoys to beleaguered Tobruk were increasingly at hazard. So too would be all future convoys to Malta. But for the moment Malta was threatened by no more than the Regia Aeronautica, the scale of whose attacks had long since become of relatively little importance, at any rate from a military point of view.

The summer of 1941, which many in Malta had anticipated would be even more fearsome than the previous winter, would prove to be a time of relative tranquillity during which the island would begin to hit hard at the lifeline between Italy and North Africa. Once German attention was concentrated on the Russian front the importance of Malta would be somewhat lost to sight. With Operation 'Barbarossa' engrossing Hitler's attention, the small island to the south of Sicily was temporarily overlooked.

CHAPTER THIRTEEN

The Besieged Strike Back

Living on tight rations is difficult to get used to, but after a time the body becomes adjusted and it is then that the steady monotony of the diet begins to wear down the morale. During the autumn of 1940 and the winter and spring that followed, garrison and civilians alike were kept vibrant by the air attacks and by the constant feeling of vice-like pressure that firmed the spirit without breaking it. The summer without the attentions of the Luftwaffe, with fewer night raids, and with the daytime raids made by the Regia Aeronautica — high up, ready to turn back at the sight of bursting flak against the summer sky, or the silver glint of fighters' wings rising to meet them — induced something like a melancholy resignation among the islanders.

The war now seemed interminable. The reports from the desert — except for the stubborn resistance of the defenders of Tobruk — were indeed melancholy, and the fall of Crete had engendered a deep fear. The obvious countermeasures could not escape notice: the airfields were being mined and the few other possible landing places were being obstructed. But the inhabitants could now at least escape out of the railway tunnel, the bomb shelters, the caves and modern catacombs, from the damp walls that had housed them, knowing well that only a week or two would see all of these refuges as dry as bone again. But the dryness itself would soon become oppressive; the summer sun is the enemy in southern lands. Spring and autumn are the happy times, the winter is dull and damp and windy, but the summer — the season of *la grande chaleur* — is the time when the ennui that seems to rise like a steam from the hard blue sea engulfs peasant and priest alike. Both had survived the first twelve months of this second great siege equally well — the peasant because centuries of unremitting toil on that difficult earth and stone-hedged land had bred men and women accustomed to hard lives and simple joys, and the priest because the disciplines of the faith had trained him under the same austere sky. The townspeople, shopkeepers and civil servants, small businessmen and others, were less well equipped. The dockyard workers, skilled and unskilled, were as tough as their country cousins, but many of their small houses lay in ruins and their slightly more sophisticated forms of entertainment had come to a standstill.

The cheap entertainment for all classes in Malta during the summer months had always been the sea: the Maltese were as native to the water as fish. Fishing itself with rod and line as well as swimming in the luke-warm water were pastimes that never cost a penny. Fresh water itself was never too great a problem during the siege (whatever else had been forgotten during those years that the locust had eaten, the water supply for a growing population and a large fleet had been borne in mind) but its supply had often become disrupted through mains being burst under bombing. Very few among working people as yet had baths with running water and where they existed, even if the mains were intact, it was more than likely that home supply pipes had been broken. All beaches that were anything like beaches were out of bounds because they were potential landing areas and most of the coastline, except in very rocky or otherwise unapproachable parts, was similarly forbidden. Hazards were everywhere and it was difficult to find a place in which to enjoy the simple pleasure of bathing. The soldiers and the gunners in their remote concrete pillboxes, scattered all round that mostly inhospitable coast, might spend much of their free time living in the water, but the dockyard and townsfolk, unless they were lucky, were condemned to sweat and swelter as the sun grew steadily higher at noon. *Le cafard*, that old familiar of the French Foreign Legion, was not unknown in Malta — the island lies further south than the latitude of Tunis — and its cockroach mumblings were insistent in the summer.

As yet the shadow of real hunger had not visited the island thanks to recent convoys, and reserve stocks of essential commodities had been built up. The system of kerosene distribution which had been maladministered and had become a source of black marketeering was radically altered, and policemen accompanied the kerosene carts through townships and villages to ensure a fair supply. There were still large stocks of butter (little in demand among a Mediterranean people) but other unrationed goods were beyond the reach of all but those with private money or large incomes, and although stone cutters and miners earned a good wage the average for Maltese servicemen and Government employees was about five shillings a day. Bread, that staple diet of the Maltese family, had not yet been rationed, but bread supplies tended to sell over the odds and it was not unusual for working men's wives with families to feed to have to spend several hours a day walking from one place to another to find bread at a reasonable price.

Far from Malta, at the eastern end of the sea, further attempts had been made by the Axis powers to seal off the British from the vital oil supplies and thus bring the Mediterranean struggle to a close. These hinged on an attempt through a pro-German administration in Iraq to drive out the British forces which were stationed in that country by agreement. The operation depended upon the Vichy French administration in Syria (which had been far from neutral in its conduct) supporting an Iraqi rebellion, and allowing German aircraft to make use of Syrian airfields. Seeing that the German aim was ultimately to occupy northern Syria, thus threatening Egypt through Palestine, the British were forced to launch an expedition into Syria — all this shortly after the disasters of Crete and the withdrawal in the desert. Had these eastern manoeuvres by the Axis been successful Malta's part in the history of the war would have soon been over. The British, however, succeeded in compelling the pro-German Vichy French general in Syria to capitulate in July. During the naval operations in support of the army, working off the Syrian coast in the face of shore-based French aircraft, several destroyers were damaged — a further blow to the Mediterranean fleet at a time when it could ill afford it. The fact that Syria from now on was controlled by British troops relieved the pressure at the eastern end of the sea, but the weakness in the fleet resulting from all these campaigns meant that the task of supplying Malta from Alexandria — in view of the Luftwaffe's presence in Crete — would be increasingly difficult.

In the meantime, as if it were some earlier siege (as had in fact happened in 1565), those within the walls began to sally out by secret ways to attack the enemy's supply lines. Again, they could only do this when the latter were distracted by more important events and, of course, the cover of darkness was essential for such sallies to be made at all. (When those besieged in a fortress begin to break out and attack their investors in broad daylight it is a clear sign that their morale is so high and the surrounding forces so weak that the siege appears to be drawing to a close.) In June the Axis forces were concerned by a counterattack launched by General Wavell in the Western Desert, the main aim of which was to relieve the garrison of Tobruk. The distraction existed — and the very fact that this was the moment when the supply line to the Axis forces in North Africa was most important provided added incentive for the besieged to strike out.

The sortie by night was still the tactic adopted by the bombers operating from Malta. During the worst period of the spring, before the Luftwaffe had been withdrawn for the Greece and Crete operations, the last of these Wellington bomber squadrons had been withdrawn to Egypt, but by May they were back and by June there were sometimes two squadrons of bombers available, as well as at least one squadron of Blenheims and two of Fleet Air Arm Swordfish. The strength of the island as an air base, which had been reduced to almost nothing over the winter, began to increase. The old Swordfish, lumbering but accurate with their torpedoes, achieved the major successes on the sea routes between Italy and North Africa. The Wellingtons' bombing of the North African ports, while not so successful in sinking ships, caused considerable disruption in the loading and unloading of the transports upon which the Axis desert armies relied. In the villages and scattered farmsteads of Malta the country people heard the thudding of the engines overhead at night and knew — as their ancestors had once known from the hoofbeats of their cavalry raiding the Turkish encampments — that their defenders were active. The importance of this to the morale of a beleaguered people is scarcely measurable. One hundred and twenty-two bomber sorties were made out of Malta between the fourteen days from 30 June to 13 July — a record for the island since the beginning of the war. The submarines used the dark tunnel of the sea to make their forays against the enemy's supply lines. In the early days of the large 'P' and 'R' class these patrols had been heavy with suspense (as indeed they always were), for in the pellucid Mediterranean waters submarines were often spotted by aircraft and losses were heavy. The smaller and far more manoeuvrable 'U' class, six of which were for a time based on the island, were soon able to achieve success on the convoy routes in the restricted confines between Sicily and North Africa.

The submarine headquarters were on Manoel island which lay north of Valletta in Marsamuscetto Creek, the island itself being connected by a causeway to the land and distinguished by a large eighteenth century fort designed to protect the capital from this quarter in the days of the Knights. Originally garrisoned by five-hundred men it now housed the submarine command, workmen, artificers and spare crews, crews resting from patrol and, lying alongside, the submarines themselves. Where eighteenth century cannon had once glowered seaward, anti-aircraft batteries now pointed skyward. 'Fort Manoel is the classic example of a Baroque fortress — bold yet precise, elegant yet a hard functional machine.'[1]; it was to become a cornerstone of Malta's function during these years. Both the fort and its surroundings were to be heavily attacked during a later stage in the siege and, so dangerous did the whole area become, submarines 'resting' from patrol often had to lie submerged on the bottom to escape the rain of bombs.

Apart from attacking Axis shipping the submarines had other functions during these years, some of which were to become vital to

87

the later landings in Sicily and southern Italy. As a by-product of their patrols submarines would surface after dark and, particularly in Calabria where the railway lines ran close to the coast, shell bridges and railway lines, or land raiding parties to disrupt these and other communications. Months later, as the planning for the allied attack on Sicily got under way, Malta submarines would embark parties with folding canoes to make detailed studies of potential landing areas, take inshore soundings, investigate beaches, and check on the strength of enemy defences. The information that could not be gained through aerial reconnaissance or through the radio waves reaching Malta would have to be hardly won by individuals operating under cover of night, and slipping back into the shelter of their submarines before the eastern sky lightened and the bright day set in. If so much of the espionage success achieved during the war has rightly been attributed in recent years to the code and cypher breaking of Bletchley Park, it must not be forgotten that the old method of reports brought back by 'spies', who had crept into enemy lines during the night, remained as important as they had been in earlier centuries. Many of these brave men disappeared without trace.[2]

Acting in conjunction with aircraft — those invaluable Swordfish equipped with torpedoes — the submarines began to wreak havoc on the convoy route to Tripoli. The area off the Kerkenah Bank, which was marked by a number of navigation buoys, was one of the great hunting grounds and it was here that commanders whose names and whose submarines were to become part of wartime legend found their *raison d'être*. In March 1940 three of the Malta submarines — *Unique*, *Utmost* and *Upright* — all scored successes in this navigationally hazardous and much-mined area.

When a heavy concentration [of shipping] on the Tripoli route was reported on the 8 March, every available boat was sent to sea. The *Utmost* (Lieutenant Commander R. D. Caylet), recently returned from patrol, was off again after only 24 hours in harbour, and on the 9th torpedoed and sank the Italian transport *Capo Vita*. The next day Lieutenant A. F. Collett in the *Unique*, whose patrol had been extended for the same reason, sank the *Fenicia*. The *Utmost* was off the Tunisian coast again on the 19th and, falling in with a convoy of five German ships with supplies for the Afrika Korps on the 28th, torpedoed two of them, the *Heraklia* and the *Ruhr*. The former sank but the *Ruhr* was towed to port. The same convoy was further depleted on leaving Tripoli on its return journey when the *Galilea* straggling astern of it, was torpedoed and severely damaged by the *Upright*.[3]

88

Only a month earlier *Upright* under her captain, Lieutenant E.D. Norman, had sunk an Italian cruiser, the *Armando Diaz*, off the Kerkenah Bank. This cruiser in company with another of the same class had been quite unnecessarily hazarded by the Italian command as escort to a large convoy of German transports — unnecessarily because the British had no surface forces at this time in the central Mediterranean. This was well enough known from air reconnaissance over Malta and a cruiser, which was no threat to a submarine, was at the same time an ideal target.

Lieutenant Commander Malcolm D. Wanklyn, VC, DSO, in *Upholder* was himself a one-man scourge of the convoy routes. Between the period April 1941 and March 1942 *Upholder* sank ten merchant ships (three of which were troop-carrying liners of over 18,000 tons), one destroyer, two U-boats, and damaged a further cruiser and three merchant ships. He and *Upholder* were finally lost off Tripoli in April 1942. While Malta was sending out submarines like these it was hardly surprising that the time would come when, unable to contain losses so great, the Italians would begin to demand large-scale action against Malta while Rommel, bitterly aware of the men, munitions, petrol, tanks, guns and transports that were failing to reach him, would begin to call for an antidote to the poison of 'that scorpion in the sea'. In fairness to the Italian convoy system it has to be remembered that in these early days their ships were without anything approaching the British Asdic (Sonar) or RDF (Radar). Blind on the surface at night and with only hydrophones for listening to the darkness below, they struggled bravely to maintain the supply line to their desert armies, while being increasingly harassed by the aircraft and submarines operating out of that island which their Regia Aeronautica had earlier claimed had been 'rendered completely inoperative'.

Large minelaying submarines from Alexandria also played an important part that summer in bringing to Malta such limited quantities of essential stores as they could carry in their mine bays. After unloading they then took aboard their outfit of mines from the underground stores and proceeded north to lay them, for instance, around much-used ports like Palermo. One of them having discharged these two main functions of her patrol went on to use her torpedoes on an Italian submarine and a merchantman and, when the latter refused to sink, surfaced and sank her by gunfire. The 'Magic Carpet' as this supply system by submarines become known to the islanders could only be of limited and temporary service and Malta had not received a real convoy since May.

The *Rorqual* and the *Cachalot* were two of these visitors from Alexandria which, their identity signalled on a dark night off the island, would come lifting their whalebacks down the swept channel to Grand Harbour. The watchers on the shore — and there were many who now slept out in the warm summer on quaysides and paths and paving slabs — would see the water streaming phosphorescent from their casings, a light fume drifting over the surface, and hear the muffled thump of their diesel engines. As the 'boat' passed they would catch the oily hot-metal smell lifting from the conning-tower. Sometimes on those nights the air-raid sirens would wail to announce what had become almost routine hit-and-run raids. Sometimes the all clear would go without any raid having taken place. The radar plot had signalled a formation approaching the island which had suddenly faded and disappeared. Extra close attention was paid at first to see whether this was merely a diversion, and if the plot would suddenly thicken from another quarter. But after this had happened once or twice it was realized that some of the pilots, familiar from the past or by report with the Medusa-like terror that the island inspired, preferred to drop their bombs in the safety net of the sea and return to their comfortable quarters in Sicily.

CHAPTER FOURTEEN

The Hot Summer

On 22 June 1941 German forces invaded Soviet Russia. Hitler reckoned that Britain could make no move, his right flank in the Balkans and Greece was secured, and the Mediterranean theatre was dominated by the Luftwaffe and the Afrika Korps. He had chosen this moment to risk that strategic nightmare which the Germans had tried to avoid throughout their military history — a war on two fronts. Stalin, forewarned but strangely unbelieving that his late partner could have so duped him, or that the hostile British under Churchill (of all people) would have informed him correctly, could do little as the mechanized grey waves rolled forward. The British could only hope that the two *hostes humani generis* would exhaust one another — and make such excursions as they could on the one front where they were active, while their enemy's main attention was engaged elsewhere. In view of the failure of General Wavell's counter attack in the Western Desert the revictualling and reinforcing of Malta was more than ever important.

Sweltering under the summer sun the naval fuel carrier HMS *Breconshire* and six large merchant ships waited empty beneath the protection of the island's barrage. They had long ago discharged their contents, but had been forced to remain immobilized because they could not be brought out for fear of air attack. Concern was also growing about the need in Malta for mines and torpedoes for the submarines, torpedoes too for aircraft, ammunition for guns, petrol for aircraft, oil fuel for ships and shore installations — and, as well as all these, food for the garrison and the people. In June 1941 planning had started for a large convoy to replenish the island and at the same time to take away these empty ships that were urgently needed elsewhere. Operation 'Substance' was designed to forward a convoy from Gibraltar under the escort of Force H as far as the Skerki Channel, the fleet from Alexandria at the same time creating a diversion with the intention of deceiving the enemy into thinking that this convoy was designed to pass right through the Mediterranean to the east.

On the night of 21 July the convoy entered the Straits of Gibraltar (it was always necessary to pass convoys through at night because of the many agents in the area). As so often where the cold ocean meets the warm sea, there was thick fog in the straits and the troopship *Leinster* ran aground. Unfortunately she was carrying among much else RAF personnel to maintain the aircraft in Malta, but even this was of less concern than any of the other heavily-laden merchant-ment would have been. As the convoy moved on to the east with fighter cover provided by the *Ark Royal*, Force H with the addition of the battleship *Nelson* moved north of it to provide protection as far as the Skerki Channel. Meanwhile Cunningham's fleet made their sortie from Alexandria, having sent two submarines to the west of Crete to make wireless manoeuvring signals that would suggest to the listeners that the fleet was operating in that area. This stratagem had the desired effect, drawing out the Luftwaffe and Regia Aeronautica over the area, while the battle fleet turned back over night to Alexandria. In the western Mediterranean, although the Italians had at this time three divisions of cruisers and four battleships, no surface move was made against the convoy as it advanced towards Malta. The Regia Aeronautica, however, had some success in an attack by torpedo aircraft and high level bombers on the convoy as it neared Sicily. One cruiser was crippled and forced to turn back to Gibraltar and one destroyer was sunk. The Italians were skilled in such a combination of high level bombers and low level torpedo attacks. In the last dangerous night through the narrow Skerki Channel motor torpedo boats registered a hit on *Sydney Star*, which finally reached Malta alone and apart from the rest of the convoy, having survived further bombing and torpedo attacks in the kind of saga that was to become only too familiar on what was already euphemistically known as 'The Malta Run'.[1]

Despite the losses Operation 'Substance' was a great success, with six large merchantmen laden with essential supplies reaching the security of Grand Harbour. Now that the Luftwaffe was away from Sicily, it was reckoned that the island's barrage and its fighters could keep the Regia Aeronautica away while the valuable stores were unloaded. At the same time *Breconshire* and the six empty merchant-ment were escorted back through the Sicilian Channel on their way to Gibraltar. At either of the two main points of the operation — the passage of the convoy to Malta through the Sicilian Channel or the return of the empty ships — the judicious use of a cruiser squadron by the Italians could have led to a disaster, but they remained inactive in harbour. Previous encounters with British surface ships and the recent loss of *Armando Diaz* to the submarine *Upright* had not helped morale.

The convoy reached Malta on 24 July to be followed, once reconnaissance planes had established the presence of the ships in harbour, by a high-level raid. As had become increasingly familiar, the raiders dispersed before the barrage. The many Maltese who had thronged the roads and walls around Grand Harbour, to look with affection and some comfort on the merchantment berthed below, stayed to cheer as the barrage lifted and the Hurricanes came in among the disorganized attackers. How often during those years, at times when they were not entirely deserted because of the weight of an attack, did the old ramparts and curtain walls erected in the days of the Knights echo with the cheers of the people as the fighter pilots rode the sky above! These were only to be exceeded by the roars of applause, hand-clapping and tears that were to greet the arrival of torn and bloody ships from savaged convoys in the months that lay ahead. . . .

On the night of the 25th an incredibly brave, but in the final analysis foolhardy, attempt was made by the Italians to destroy the ships of this convoy whose presence unloading in Grand Harbour so mocked their Regia Aeronautica. The history behind this venture goes some way back in time. The Italians had always been adept at actions involving individual gallantry and cavalryman dash. In the First World War they had sunk the Austrian battleship *Viribus Unitis* as it lay in harbour by attaching mines to it from a small submarine (the father of Count Ciano, Mussolini's foreign minister and son-in-law, had been among the crew on that occasion). The Italians had begun work on such specialized attack craft as midget submarines, high speed motor torpedo boats, and what amounted to manned torpedoes, at the time of the Abyssinian war. The *Decima Flottiglia Mas* (The Tenth Light Flotilla) was responsible throughout the Second World War for everything connected with this type of operation, ranging from explosive motor boats (EMBs) piloted by one man seated in an ejector seat so that he could blow himself clear before the moment of impact with his target, two-men chariots known as '*maiale*' or 'pigs', and skin-diving frogmen. The 'pigs' were slow-speed torpedoes on which a two-man crew sat astride wearing breathing apparatus, manoeuvring themselves until they were below their target. The detachable warhead was then removed, clamped to the keel and a time-fuse set, the 'pig' meanwhile withdrawing to safety. (Later in 1941 three of these were to change the whole balance of power at sea when they entered Alexandria harbour and crippled the battleship *Valiant*, the fleet flagship *Queen Elizabeth* and blew the stern off a large tanker.) The Tenth Flotilla had already conducted successful operations in Gibraltar harbour, while six EMBs during the Crete campaign had penetrated the defences at Suda Bay, sunk the cruiser *York* and damaged a tanker. The naval authorities in Malta had long been alert to the possibility of some attack being made by one or other of the specialist craft

93

assembled by the Tenth Light Flotilla, and the gunners had been trained to expect them.

An attack on Malta had indeed been planned for a long time, but an awareness that the island and its harbour were defended to an extent to be found nowhere else in the Mediterranean, and that the garrison under siege were on the *qui vive* far more than at Gibraltar or at Suda Bay (which was an open anchorage with temporary defences), had been enough to cause some hesitation. A parent craft and escorting motor torpedo boats had to cross the Malta Channel from Sicily, launch their small attacking craft at that fearsome harbour, pick up survivors — if any — and get away again before daylight. It was a daunting task from the start and one which, if the Italians had had a full appreciation of Malta's radar system, would never have been attempted. Indeed on several occasions in the past coastal batteries had opened up at night on unseen targets at sea, firing under radar control, it being assumed by the gunners at the time that these were probably mine-laying motor boats. But, since it is known that members of the Tenth Flotilla had come over on one or two occasions to examine the lie of the land and test out defences, it may have been they who provoked this 'blind' firing.[2] If so, it is even more incomprehensible that the Italian command could have envisaged that an assault such as the one they prepared could have any chance of success. Mariano Gabriele the official historian of *Operazione C3: Malta* refers to it as 'the unfortunate action'.

Starting from the great harbour of Augusta in Sicily on the night of 25 July the attacking forces consisted of a parent ship, the naval auxiliary *Diana*, carrying eight of the small EMBs which were intended to attack the convoy in Grand Harbour once the defences had been breached, and two motor torpedo boats each towing a two-man 'pig'. One of the latter was to enter Marsamuscetto and hopefully find a target among submarines at Fort Manoel. The other was to blast a way through the outer defences of Grand Harbour, thus creating a breach which would enable the EMBs to tear in and make their headlong attack on the merchantmen. Even if the defences had been so simple that the piercing of one would have given access to the inner harbour where the ships lay (and they were not — they were defences in depth) it was almost unthinkable that any boat, however small and however fast, would have got down the length of Grand Harbour without being blown to pieces. The approach of the EMBs and the two-man submarine was to be covered by an air raid, the noise of the bombs, and the thunder of the barrage in theory covering the whole attack sequence from the sea.

The parent ship *Diana* was picked up early on radar: this was the first thing to go wrong for the Italians. The second was that the air raid when it came was too short and over too early; the 'cover' for the attack by sea was lifted long before it was needed. The harbour defences were always alert, but especially so when there was a convoy in. The radar report of a vessel to the north of the island brought everyone to one hundred plus degree of readiness.

Diana stopped about twenty miles from the island and put her EMBs overboard, they and the motor boats carrying on towards Grand Harbour. The plan was for Major Teseo Tesei, who had been actively engaged in experiments with manned torpedoes since the 1930s and had been one of the principal promoters of the operation, together with his crewman, Chief Diver Pedretti, to make for the viaduct that ran out to the breakwater from the shore by Fort St Elmo. Having reached it, he and his diver would attach their warhead to the defences and blow them up, this in theory giving access to Grand Harbour. The EMBs, taking the explosion as the cue, would then charge through the gap.

The exact pattern of events will never be known since neither Tesei nor Pedretti were ever seen again, but the first explosion at the foot of St Elmo (which should have been masked by the air raid) brought all the alert gunners into action. They were mostly Maltese of the RMA, and the guns were mostly six-pounder pom-poms, Bofors, and small arms. They opened fire as all the searchlights illuminating the entrance to Grand Harbour were snapped on. One of the EMB pilots seems to have reached the entrance under the viaduct, for it was either his boat exploding against the defences, or Tesei's warhead before him, that brought down the whole span in a tangled heap of metal. This 'entrance', such as it was, to Grand Harbour was now irretrievably blocked. Meanwhile, caught in the full glare of the searchlights, the EMBs as they raced towards harbour were blown to pieces. The Maltese gunners had waited many months for attack from the sea, and when it came they let their feelings of frustrated vengeance come to the boil in the waters outside. Within two minutes most of the attackers were dead and every boat was sunk. All the bravery in the world could not avail against such a savage curtain of metal.

The people of Valletta were on their roofs and in the streets. The families sleeping outside and on the vantage points of the Upper and Lower Barracca were witnesses to that astonishing display; fire and light, parabolas of tracer, and a sea exploding in flames. With the dawn the Hurricanes were overhead and a battle took place with the escort of Macchi fighters that had been promised the attacking team for first light. There was in any case nothing for them to escort back to Sicily. *Diana* had long ago turned away after bringing her charges to the dropping point, the EMBs were destroyed, and the motor boats which had covered them and the two-man torpedoes to the harbour periphery were caught by the Hurricanes before they could make good their escape. In the dogfight above the scene three of the Macchis were shot down and one of the Hurricanes. The pilot of the latter baled out and got into his dinghy. As the sea lightened he sighted a stationary torpedo boat and paddled over to it, only to find that all the crew had been killed. He took possession and hoisted a white flag. Later in the morning a Fleet Air Arm Swordfish equipped with floats landed alongside and took him off; the Italian torpedo boat was towed back intact. Miss Ella Warren, MBE, who at that time was among the many British women engaged in plotting duties with the navy, later wrote: 'Among things salved from the boat was a little mascot white furry dog, with a red bow; what girl gave it to what boy? We named him "Bruno-Bianco" and he swung on a cord above my typewriter and his little black eyes gave nothing away'.[3] The crew of the two-man torpedo who had intended to make for Manoel Island and the submarines experienced some difficulties with their craft and were forced to abandon it. They were later captured swimming ashore in St George's Bay, which is a good two miles to the north of Marsamuscetto, suggesting that they had been confused by the bays and inlets of the coastline and had never been on the right track for their target area. Never was Italy's Medaglia d'Oro, albeit posthumously, more fittingly awarded than to Major Teseo Tesei and Chief Diver Pedretti. They and their companions had tackled the most formidable fortress harbour in the world and had died beneath the guns of Fort St Elmo, where once the flower of the army of the Grand Turk had similarly perished.[4]

CHAPTER FIFTEEN

Aspects of War

Four days before the seaborne attack on Grand Harbour the island had once again shown its striking power. Malta-based Blenheim bombers, alerted to the passage of a convoy of three Italian and one German transport, closely followed by a tanker, on their way to North Africa, struck in a mast-high attack; an ammunition ship blew up and the tanker, set on fire, finally drifted immobilized to become a total loss on Kerkenah Bank. The Blenheims specialized in low-level attacks and, although there were no more than two squadrons at a time based on the island, they achieved a success against shipping that was hardly equalled even by the submarines.

Acting in close cooperation with the torpedo-carrying Swordfish of the Fleet Air Arm, they combined to spread havoc on the Libyan supply route, sometimes the one finishing off a ship that the other had torpedoed and sometimes the torpedo carrier finishing off a ship that had been bombed but not sunk. By October 1941 over sixty per cent of the supplies designed for North Africa were failing to reach their destination. Rommel who had seemed poised over Egypt, even though the port of Tobruk still remained untaken, constantly complained in that routine nightly communiqué (read by Ultra) of almost every kind of shortage. Shortage of fuel came first on the list, then demands for equipment, and then criticism of the Italians for stretching his land supply line by unloading at Tripoli instead of Benghazi five-hundred miles further east. Undoubtedly Rommel was a general who believed in the old principle of always asking headquarters for more than you need in the hope of getting something like what you want, but the shipping figures bear out his complaints. By November 1941 over seventy percent of supplies were failing to reach North Africa. The bravery of the Italian merchant marine and their escorts who daily and nightly faced these attacks by air and sea was remarkable. As for Rommel's complaints about the failure to use the port of Benghazi sufficiently, the coastal sea route from Tripoli to Benghazi was constantly patrolled by submarines out of Alexandria, while the port itself was raided almost every night by RAF bombers from Egypt. His problem was that narrow lifeline between Italy and North Africa against which Malta pressed like a knife.

At the height of the siege the people in the island were dominated almost entirely by the raids, the deaths and the woundings, the shattering sound of so many guns numbing the mind, the roar of aircraft, the rumble of collapsing buildings, and — worst of all — the scream of falling bombs which seemed to menace each and every listener with personal dismemberment and death. At such times all ordinary considerations of life; making money, making love, making a meal, making something connected with one's trade or craft, were subordinate to the simple demands of survival. But in the summer and autumn of 1941 the shelter life could largely be abandoned, and many photographs witness the gipsy-encampment atmosphere that grew up around the mouths to the tunnels and cavern-like entrances of public and private shelters: mothers and children, bare-foot as often as not, sometimes round an improvized cooking stove (kerosene was short, but fortunately the staple diet of bread and oil with a little tomato paste was all that most wanted in the hot weather), Maltese soldiers in uniform, priests as much a part of the people as they always were in Malta, and the revered old, sitting on wooden chairs or boxes that had once held foodstuffs.

As everywhere else at that time the war itself was the enemy and in the blank face of the monstrous evil and disruption of life the survivors on this raft of a crowded island were drawn together in the warmth of friendship. Apart from the many British servicemen (hardly foreigners since generations of close companionship and intermarriage had made them part of the island scene), there were members of the old British empire, New Zealanders, Australians, and Canadians, some in ships, some in aircraft passing through to the Middle East, and some in the RAF stationed in Malta. There were many parties for, although spirits were scarce, beer at that time still held out, and local wine (mostly of doubtful parentage and brewed under conditions ranging from the ingenious to the absurd) was drunk by soldiers, sailors and airmen more for effect than for palatable pleasure. Known to some as 'jungle juice' and to others, familiar with the results if taken in excess, as 'screech', it enlivened many licit or illicit gatherings. Men who served during the siege remembered apart from the hardships and the horrors not just the inevitable tedium of war but such things as 'the mournful echo from an uncovered well' and 'the sweet-scented stephanotis around the kitchen door and the colourful oranges and lemons catching the sunlight. . . .'[1]

Much of the atmosphere of those days is best perhaps expressed in the words of a Chinese sage: 'A man getting drunk at a farewell party should strike a musical tone, in order to strengthen his spirit

... and a drunk military man should order gallons and put out more flags in order to increase his military splendour.'[2]

A travelling concert party had been marooned on the island when the siege began and continued throughout to carry on as if on an extended tour. The Malta Amateur Dramatic Association, a staunch growth from the inter-war years of light comedy and drawing-room drama, still thrived, though its ranks were now largely filled by men and women most of whose time was spent either on the guns or underground in plotting or cyphering operations. Individual units put up their own teams of entertainers, and the RAF, true to their reputation of being more raffish than the other services, had a band called the 'Raffians'. Small bars still opened throughout the island from Gzira and Sliema to such as remained in Strait Street, Valletta; this was the street where once by tradition the Knights had fought their duels, but which had long ago been taken over as the sailors' bar and brothel and cheap café quarter. Known to generations of servicemen as 'The Gut' it had achieved a world-wide reputation among seagoers but, bombed in places, deserted in others, it was already but a shadow of its former rorty self.

More and more as the weeks and months passed the people of the island and their many uniformed visitors went back to almost medieval village patterns of life. With roads both bad and bombed, with travel discouraged and petrol strictly rationed, with civilians unwilling to be far away from their homes and servicemen unable to be far from their place of duty, there was a return to life within small circumscribed areas. The country people had always lived like this, and now the refugees from dockyard areas and towns learned to share similar restricted patterns of living. Like miniature Japanese gardens these expanded into an infinite variety as the eye became used to a microscopic view. There was a bar or two, a store (however little in it) — the one a meeting place for the men, the other for the women; usually a square however small; a particular street corner under (almost certainly) the statue of some saint, known to be shady when the sun stood high; and some natural feature — knoll, ridge, or declivity — where towards sundown a breeze or faint, moist air could be felt drawing off the sea. Life was circumscribed, but all the more fresh and memorable for that.

'It was evening coming on to dark. To the west, the sky was a vivid orange streaked with purple.... A few stars had begun to shine. The sound of generators on three British destroyers in the harbour seemed a natural part of the evening. The city was behind us, past the old, enormous hospital of the Knights and the narrower streets of downtown. We could hear very little of it. Just Ester and I at the great door of her house with the brass-dolphin knockers, the ornate

99

shoe-scrapers on both sides of the upper step.' Or: 'The room I was living in was small but comfortable. Through the window, I could see part of a headland towering high above the sea. The rest of the cliff was invisible. Sometimes at night, when all was silent and no air raid was on, I would lie still on my bed and listen to the distant sound of the sea far below breaking against the bottom of the cliffs.'[3]

Writing in the 19th century in his *History of the Knights of Malta* General Whitworth Porter had concluded his account of the Great Siege with what might have seemed imperialistic rodomontade, but which proved prophetic: 'English hearts and English swords now protect those ramparts which formerly glistened with the ensigns of the Order of St John; and should occasion ever demand the sacrifice, the world will find that British blood can be poured forth like water in defence of that rock which the common consent of Europe has entrusted to her hands. On such a day the memory of this great siege will have its due effect, and those ramparts already bedewed with so much noble blood, will again witness deeds of heroism, such as shall rival, if they cannot excel, the great struggle of 1565.'[4]

British blood was indeed 'poured forth like water' not only on the land as the general had envisaged, but in the air, on the sea and under it, 'in defence of that rock'. The great distinction between the story of this second great siege and that earlier one is that the accounts of 1940–3 give full credit to the Maltese people themselves. In the histories of the siege of 1565 it was inevitable that in the light of those times it was the Knights, the 'noble blood', who occupied almost every corner of the canvas. Nameless peasantry, their wives and children, merited little except commendations for their general bravery and stoic endurance. The Abbé Vertot, Count Zabarella, General Porter and many others tended to ignore the people of the island, forgetting that with a cowardly or even indifferent population the siege could neither have been won, nor endured at all. The Maltese over all the years — and to this day — have held a Thanksgiving Mass on 8 September to commemorate the raising of the siege of 1565, while the boatmen of the principal villages and townships around Grand Harbour maintain the traditional *dghaisa* races in those oared boats which equal the gondolas of Venice in their elegant lines while surpassing them in the extravagance of their colour and decoration.

But these, and the firework display that followed, will not have been in evidence during the years of war, and it is doubtful if many of the men in the British services will have known much, if anything, of the siege that had preceded the one in which they were engaged by nearly four centuries — nor anything at all of the later siege of the French in Valletta by the Maltese themselves. Yet the roots of the islanders' resilience were as old as the leathery-leaved carob tree and if, as some claim, the ancestry of their small nation could be traced back to the Carthaginians then it is worth remembering that the siege of Carthage was one of the most fiercely contested in the whole of ancient history. Islanders always tend to be fiercely patriotic, every island being superior to its neighbour,[5] but usually they are adjacent to large countries to whom their language, religion and patriotism are subordinate. The Maltese were different: they were set alone in the sea and they had given their allegiance to the British at a time when their survival was threatened. But they had retained their own language, customs, basic laws, and their own patriotism. Britain, though a protecting power, was far away. Had they become a colony or dependency of Italy their Catholic faith would have blended with that of the Italians, there would have been more intermarriage, and their own language and customs might well have been submerged. As it was, the islanders had a great affection for remote Britain, but had now developed a curiously deep hatred of their neighbours, the Italians. People with whom for centuries their fishermen and merchantmen had shared the same sea had violently attacked them. Many were intermarried, many bore Sicilian (if not Italian) names, they shared the same faith, and the Maltese upper classes and many of their middle classes spoke Italian in preference to Maltese ('a kitchen language'), if they did not speak English. The feeling of revulsion, when the first bombs fell, was very deep indeed. It was deep where it really mattered — in the hearts of the dockyard people and the country farmers and their wives. They often shared more in common with the red-faced British soldiers than they did with their employers and the upper strata of their own people.

Admiral Cunningham in his memoirs tells the following illuminating story: 'During the early Italian bombing a petty officer steward, one Talliana, had been left behind at Admiralty House. One morning he brought news to my wife that an Italian bomber had been shot down, adding fiercely that if the Maltese laid hands on the crew they would be lynched there and then. My wife remonstrated, pointing out that the Italians might retaliate against our airmen, and that in any case lynching was against International Law. Talliana regarded her with a pitying sort of expression. 'International Law not in Malta, Signora," he said, shaking his head ... ' There are many similar stories.

In almost identical words had the Maltese, after the fall of Fort St Elmo in 1565 (when the Turks had mutilated the dead bodies of the defenders), refused to take any more prisoners. 'St Elmo's Pay,' they had shouted as they cut their throats. The expression is used to this day in Malta for any action in which no quarter is given.

CHAPTER SIXTEEN

The Fall of the Year

September, before the rains come, is the harshest time. The lion sun of summer burns just as fiercely and the whole island is baked out, not a green thing to be seen save the prickly pear (those 'figs of India' which feed both man and beast) and, ageless as the bony land from which they climb, the carob trees opaque with dust. Even the sea looks hot; it is certainly warm, cleansing but not refreshing to the swimmer. At such times, as throughout much of summer, the observer turning his eyes from the still, very dark blue water towards the sky will encounter a curious phenomenon. The great dome above, while free of cloud, is not the picture-postcard blue that might be expected but white — sometimes curiously dazzling like the white-washed walls in Greek islands, and at other times milky and soft. Whereas in the Aegean the summer sky, broomed by the northerlies, is crisp and sharply blue, and over much of Italy it is the misty azure of a hundred Renaissance paintings, this Maltese sky — reflecting back perhaps the harsh, rocky landscape — is in distinct contrast to the sea. Against the white skies of September 1941 few aircraft rose — in defence of the island at least. With Fliegerkorps X engaged in the eastern Mediterranean and over the desert, the Italians concentrated almost entirely on night bombing. Even this was on a lesser scale than before, but was carefully designed to cause the maximum irritation to the besieged while encouraging them to waste priceless ammunition brought in by convoys at such cost. The technique was to send over from Sicily an almost continuous stream of single bombers, coming in high and straight, and usually on a course to unload over Grand Harbour.

To combat night bombing the defenders had earlier set up a Malta Night Fighter Unit composed of some flight of Hurricanes. The problems involving such a unit were, as the Commander Royal Artillery, Malta put it at the time, that the conditions were quite unlike those to be found in England or anywhere else. 'Not only were the airfields within the gun-defended area, but it was usual for aircraft to arrive either from Egypt or Gibraltar nightly, for bomber flights to take place almost nightly, or for the Fleet Air Arm to carry out strikes or reconnaissance. Night fighters were usually up, and the enemy was almost invariably present.' All this activity in the night sky over an island only seventeen miles long by nine miles at its greatest width presented a kind of almost continuous three-dimensional chess game. 'The problem of dealing with all these factors (of which the most difficult were the arrival of strangers from Gibraltar inadequately briefed as to our plans, and the return of damaged bombers from Sicily, who were not always able or willing to comply with the rules) necessitated very clear cut instructions to the guns and searchlights, as well as to the air defences.... Simplicity was essential, since personnel changed very rapidly, and any extended period of inactivity almost always meant beginning the work all over again, educating the pilots and the fighter controllers in the details of control.'[1] The islanders who slept fitfully in their shelters during these 'nuisance raids' (they did relatively little damage) could hardly have imagined the technicalities of the radar and communications war that was being conducted over their heads.

The night fighter unit was a fascinating example of the interlocking of the searchlights, the gun operations unit, and the Hurricanes themselves. In Britain, with factory sources of supply quite close at hand, it might by now be possible to be wasteful with ammunition for the purpose of maintaining civilian morale, but in Malta the primary consideration was always the tenuous sea or air links that had to provide replacements of everything. In the scheme evolved for the destruction of bombers at night one of the main requirements was the conservation of anti-aircraft ammunition. The radar of the artillery together with the searchlights were used in combination to direct the fighters onto the target. The island was divided into two sections, Valletta being on the dividing line, each of which was patrolled by a Hurricane kept informed by radio of the course, speed and height of the approaching raid. (No orders were given to them as they would have been in daylight interception.) When the raid was some fifteen miles off the island the Hurricanes, each within its patrol zone, would position themselves on either side and on converging courses towards the target. The result was that as soon as it was caught in the searchlights there was a Hurricane to port and starboard on closing courses.

The resulting analysis showed that, on average, out of every seven raiders that crossed Malta's coastline five were picked up by the searchlights, three out of every five were attacked, and two out of these three were shot down. The figures were good, but not quite good enough. Too many were getting through to Grand Harbour, and the sinking of the destroyer *Maori* by a direct hit was but one of a number of incidents that led to an improvement in the night fighter arrangements. To make the most efficient use of anti-aircraft fire together with the night fighters the sky, as well as being divided in two sectors, was now layered — the Hurricanes operating above a fixed height and the guns below them. While this somewhat increased the expenditure of ammunition it led to much greater efficiency, and this system with but minor modifications continued to be used throughout the siege. It was good also for the morale of all those islanders who, unable to be spectators (and thus occasionally to see a bomber caught in the searchlights being shot down), were only listeners to a raid. They could hear from their shelters the sound of the guns which, fearsome in the early days, had now become reassuring. It gave them all that satisfactory feeling of 'hitting back'; they, from below the earth and rock, identified with the gunners who in the night above, crisscrossed with searchlights' beams and lazy tracer and fiery explosions, kept them protected.

During the later summer and early autumn the aircraft strength of the island was gradually built up. More Hurricanes arrived, brought by aircraft carriers from Gibraltar to flying-off range, until the island could muster about seventy of these invaluable all purpose fighters. Not only had they now taken over night fighter duties but, equipped with bomb racks, had been turned into fighter bombers. (Later when the important September convoy was entering Grand Harbour they operated in this capacity against Comiso airfield in Sicily, serving to ground the Italian fighters at this crucial moment.) The island now had for attack, apart from its Fleet Air Arm Swordfish, a number of Marylands, two squadrons of Blenheims, seventeen Wellington bombers, and a few radar-equipped Wellingtons which proved invaluable in guiding the torpedo-carrying Swordfish on to their targets at night. The latter, also used as mine layers, sank or damaged between the May and November of 1941 about a quarter of a million tons of shipping. The Blenheims striking by day at masthead height (and incurring the inevitable losses) accounted for about 50,000 tons over the same period. Even the German High Command, with their eyes firmly fixed on the progress of the great advances on the Russian front, could not entirely ignore Rommel's almost nightly cries of anguish at the failure of supplies to reach him.

With the winter approaching, and the Mediterranean fleet from Alexandria fully engaged with their coastal operations in support of the desert army and the supply of the all important garrison at Tobruk, it was clearly a good moment to run a convoy through to Malta from the west. This was a large one, consisting of nine merchant ships carrying 85,000 tons of supplies and 2600 troops, and had as escort three battleships, one aircraft carrier, five cruisers and eighteen destroyers. The escort normally provided by Force H from Gibraltar was one battleship, one aircraft carrier, and two cruisers as well as destroyers. The reason for the considerable increase was the hope that, expecting the usual force, the Italian fleet might be tempted out to give battle. Elaborate deception methods were employed to disguise the size of the convoy and the fleet, the convoy being passed through the Straits of Gibraltar in two groups on the night of 24 September, the heavy ships hauling well to the northward shortly afterwards while the body of the convoy kept along the Algerian coast where they were certain to be sighted and reported. The deception that there was no more than one battleship in the escort succeeded with Italian intelligence, and Admiral Iachino assembled a fleet of two Littorio-Class battleships, five heavy cruisers and attendant destroyers and set out from Naples.

Throughout the night of 26 September Admiral Iachino maintained a south-westerly course. The weather came down with patches of haze over the sea and low cloud. The Italians hoped that during the following day bombers from Cagliari in Sardinia as well as from Sicily would successfully soften up the convoy and its escorts, leaving them scattered and ripe for an attack by the fleet in the afternoon. But Wellington bombers out of Malta laid on a heavy raid of Cagliari that night, parked aircraft being set on fire and bomb dumps blown up, and hangars wrecked. The result was that although the fleet and the convoy had to accept a number of torpedo-bomber attacks the whole scale of air activity was diminished, and the only damage was to the flagship HMS *Nelson*. She was hit on the stem by a torpedo and had her speed accordingly reduced. At 2.30 that afternoon a Malta-based reconnaissance plane reported two Littorio-class battleships, four cruisers, and sixteen destroyers less than eighty miles from the convoy on a converging course. Admiral Somerville aboard the damaged *Nelson* ordered his other two battleships and the rest of his force to steer to engage, and the *Ark Royal* to launch a torpedo strike. It seemed that for the first time a fleet action in protection of a Malta convoy might indeed take place.

The visibility had been gradually worsening all day, the thunderclouds of autumn lofting over the Mediterranean and haze lying over the sea. The poor visibility and some confusion in radio communications, combined with a change of course by the Italian fleet, resulted in the Swordfish aircraft failing to find them. Meanwhile, Admiral Iachino had become suspicious. He knew that there was an aircraft carrier in the force opposed to him but W/T traffic combined with reports that the Regia Aeronautica had sighted more than one battleship led him to the correct conclusion that he was in danger of falling into a trap. Since he had strict orders not to risk an action unless he enjoyed assured superiority of strength, and since he might equally expect an attack at any moment by carrier-borne planes emerging suddenly out of the clouds and haze, he wisely turned his whole force back for Naples. Swordfish aircraft continued to look for him on his last reported line of advance until compelled to return to the *Ark Royal* through lack of fuel. So ended another battle that never was — Admiral Somerville and the heavy ships returning as usual to Gibraltar, leaving the cruisers and destroyers to take the merchantment through the narrows to Malta. He could be confident that the Italians would not risk a night action involving capital ships, and that the convoy's escort could cope with any other surface vessels that might challenge them in the Skerki Channel.

At sunset the cloud and haze cleared away and a fine moonlit night exposed the ships advancing towards Malta to a number of attacks by torpedo bombers coming both in pairs and singly, and having the convoy silhouetted by the moon. They pressed home their attacks with resolution and it was more by luck than anything else that only one of the ships, a large merchantman, was hit. *Imperial Star* had a very typical mixed cargo for Malta — several hundred crates of bombs, five-hundred tons of kerosene, five-hundred tons of refrigerated meat, grain, flour and small arms ammunition, as well as three-hundred passengers. Fortunately she did not explode or go down at once, being a well-built modern ship of 12,000 tons, and they were taken off safely. Despite all the hazards through which the convoy had passed she was the only ship to be sunk, and the battleship *Nelson* was the only other to be damaged.

The following morning the first of the escort entered Grand Harbour in advance of the merchantmen upon whose stores and supplies, troops and technicians, the whole besieged island depended. The news had of course been passed round in advance, those words which everyone was poised to hear: 'There's a convoy coming in!' Having now lived constantly — every day, week after week, month after month, for over a year — with the pustulous face of war ever present, there was no one who did not understand (feel within their own frame as it were) what had been endured to bring in those heavily laden merchantmen. And when the advance guard swept in with such panache — how else could they respond?

> ... the whole population of Malta appeared to be lined up in serried cheering masses along the shore, as the cruisers, with guards paraded and bands playing as though returning from a peace-time cruise, passed through the breakwater and up the stretch of sheltered water with which the Mediterranean Fleet had been so long and so intimately acquainted.'[2]

The golden moment hangs suspended like a fly in the amber of time — still recalled by old men on drowsy harbour evenings, and by many others who will never write their memoirs. Despite the loss of *Imperial Star*, at least 60,000 tons of stores had reached Malta in the convoy. This meant that, quite apart from military supplies, the seven months reserve of essential commodities for the island was once more brought up to scale. Kerosene and coal were to remain in short supply, but in all other respects the island could face the winter with confidence. This was just as well because, although no one could have known at the time, it would be nearly ten months before another convoy of any size would reach the island again.

CHAPTER SEVENTEEN

Individuals

Obsessed with the campaign in Russian, Hitler could hardly pay attention to the cries for help that were proceeding from the Mediterranean theatre. Mussolini's war was not his and the Mediterranean was a side-show. He would not be distracted from the great German crusade — reflecting, as it did, that earlier one carried on centuries before by the Teutonic Knights in Prussia and the Eastern Territories. (He conveniently forgot that it was this same *Drang nach Osten* which had led to the knights' terrible defeat at Tannenberg and the complete eclipse of their Order.) The German Supreme Command, however, could not ignore their commitment in the south and Rommel's persistent calls for some action to be taken to ensure that supplies got through to his desert army. These were reinforced in September by Vice-Admiral Weichold, the German liaison officer with the Italian Naval Staff, who informed the High Command that the current situation was untenable and that the Italians were unable to provide adequate protection for the convoys. He asked for 'radical changes and immediate measures to remedy the situation, otherwise not only our offensive but the entire Italo-German position in North Africa will be lost.'

In effect he was asking for some Luftwaffe squadrons to be redeployed to Sicily. It had been clear enough when Malta had been heavily under attack that the convoys had proceeded without overmuch interruption. But Hitler refused to withdraw any squadrons from the east, although he did agree to the diversion of Fliegerkorps X from its concentration in Egypt, the Canal Zone and the desert war, to the protection of convoys bound for North Africa. No units, however, were moved to Sicily, and all that happened was that convoys from Greece down to Benghazi were brought under the protection of Fliegerkorps X operating from Greece and Crete, while those units which were engaged in the desert were given the additional duty of protecting coastal convoys. Far from having any effect on Malta the result of these orders was merely to ensure that the Luftwaffe in the Mediterranean was spread more thinly over a wider area, leaving the island unmolested except by the Regia Aeronautica.

After their disastrous losses on the short route to Tripoli, west of

Malta, it was natural that the Italians would change to the easterly route — through the Messina Straits and then out into the Ionian Sea, making a great curve to keep outside the range of Malta's aircraft before heading south for Benghazi or Tripoli. This was the route normally taken by the fast passenger liners (now converted to troop ships), but it was being increasingly used by merchantmen carrying stores and supplies. West of Sicily and then along the Tunisian coast had too often proved disastrous for convoys, for the eyes of reconnaissance planes out of Malta (and often the ears of Ultra information) were quick to alert the British to their passage. The longest route was the safest, but it had the great disadvantage that the ships had to pass through the narrow funnel of the Messina Straits, which was naturally under close observation by submarines and aircraft out of Malta.

In the first week of September two transports were hit by torpedoes from Swordfish in this area, one sinking and the other being towed back to Messina out of commission for many months. A week later a reversion to the western route proved no more helpful and a convoy, attacked first by Swordfish at night and escaping under smoke, was located again next day by Blenheim bombers coming in at masthead height. One ammunition ship was hit and blew up, for the high price of three Blenheims. In the dark hours of the following morning, however, the same convoy — its route plotted and its destination known — was again attacked by Swordfish and another ship carrying ammunition exploded. Rommel's planned offensive to capture Tobruk in September looked further and further away.

For some time, in view of the absence of the Luftwaffe from Sicily and the relative safety of Malta as a base for surface units once more, Admiral Cunningham had been in communication with the Admiralty as to the desirability of reviving Force K. This had been a striking force of four destroyers and a cruiser, which had been stationed in the island in April to increase the weight of attacks on the Axis convoys to North Africa. This was a task in which for a time it had succeeded admirably, on one occasion catching a convoy off the Tunisian coast and sinking all five heavily laden transports as well as the escort of three Italian destroyers. This was the kind of conclusive action 'in the Nelson style' which only a surface force could execute. Submarines and aircraft might sink one or two ships in a convoy, but only warships could sink them all.

The operations around Crete had effectively put an end to any further ships being available for Force K and intensive minelaying had rendered operations out of Grand Harbour increasingly hazardous. On one of its last expeditions the ships then forming Force K had returned safely to the island, only for one of their number to be mined alongside the breakwater, completely blocking the entrance channel for several days. Circumstances were different now, however, and a surface force operating from Malta along with the submarines, the RAF bombers, and the Fleet Air Arm torpedo-carrying planes (a squadron of Albacores had also joined the Swordfish at Hal Far), might be expected to reduce Rommel's chances of mounting an offensive even further. Owing to his numerous commitments, which now included the Red Sea, Admiral Cunningham found himself unable to provide any ships for a new Force K, but the Admiralty had agreed with his conclusions and were preparing to send out from Britain a striking force of two six-inch gun cruisers and two of the best armed fleet (heavy) destroyers. They would arrive in October, but meanwhile the submarines out of the island were to make another decisive strike.

The preparations for assembling a convoy of almost any size in Italy were almost impossible to disguise and so long as Malta could dispose of an efficient air-reconnaissance unit (which she continued to do throughout nearly all the siege) the chances of a convoy getting far without being observed were very slight. In many respects, even though their convoys had to traverse thousands of miles from Britain round the Cape of Good Hope, always at risk in the Atlantic to the deadly efficiency of the German U-boats, they had a better chance of bringing men and material unobserved to their forces in the desert than had the Axis powers. It was true that, since the Luftwaffe had been operating in the east, Port Said, Alexandria, the Suez Canal, and the assembly point at the head of the Red Sea had all come within their range and the hazards had increased, but they were still relatively small compared with those of the convoys run from Italy or Greece. These had to assemble at a few known points and their destination by sea was always known because of the very limited number of ports in North Africa. The British, once they had got their men and supplies into Egypt, were at liberty to deploy them as and when they wanted. The Axis powers had to take theirs into two ports that were constantly bombed and through waters that were always menaced — by Malta. The conclusion was obvious, but it was not fully acted upon for a few months.

In the meantime the known destination of a particular convoy, as well as its port of departure, played a large part in an ambush that was carefully set up by four of the Malta submarines. It was true that sometimes this information was supplied by Ultra, but on this occasion, as on very many others, it was the work of reconnaissance planes out of Malta. They operated with immense skill and almost unbelievable disregard for the earlier established rules of such work and covered ports and harbours almost daily, bringing back from heights of no more than 5,000 feet large-scale photographs that rendered any attempts at secrecy about naval units and ships assembling for convoys completely futile.

Since the disclosure of the Ultra Secret there has been a tendency to overcompensate for the inevitable omissions of earlier war histories by ascribing almost everything to the brilliant intellects and technical abilities of the hitherto unknown 'backroom boys'. This is an error, and particularly so in the case of Malta where, despite the island's prime position in the field of intelligence, so large a part of intelligence gathering was done by individuals flying aircraft, operating submarines or, at a later stage, paddling ashore on to enemy held territory in canvas canoes.[1] The war as fought from Malta was in itself a particularly individual one, and the very nature of the besieged island gave full vent to the extremely individualistic nature of the British. This was shown in such characters as the quiet, brilliant Scottish Wanklyn as well as in other submarine commanders of wildly flamboyant natures. Every gun battery, every army unit, every ship, and every squadron had at least one or more whose private talents and whose oddities would hardly have fitted them for any kind of promotion in peacetime, but which flowered under the peculiar exigencies of the siege. Since it would be invidious to make an arbitrary selection from such a wide gallery at this remove in time, let one man stand duty for them all — particularly since it was the practice of low-level reconnaissance which he introduced to Malta that led to so much coveted information.

'Wing Commander A. Warburton,' says an official history of *The Air Battle of Malta*, 'first came to the island at the end of 1940, and specialized in reconnaissance flying, with only short interruption, throughout the period covered in these pages [the whole of the siege].' His friend, A.J. Spooner, the captain of a Wellington operating from Malta who knew him from early days, describes how

... in Egypt [he] borrowed a Beaufighter, stripped it of all armour plate, guns, ammunition etc, installed vertical cameras and flew it to Malta. He dismissed the Baltimore [the official reconnaissance plane] with a wrinkle of his disdainful nose. 'No bloody good. But this Beau,' he said, 'is the fastest aircraft in the Mediterranean....
With this I can reconnoitre any place at any time at any height.'
He photographed the Italian fleet in their naval base of Taranto in appalling weather from less than a hundred feet. He navigated himself all over the Mediterranean — without adequate meteorological services or navigational equipment. He went when they expected him and when they did not. He always came home undamaged, often followed by an armada of enemy fighters. He

carried no guns or armour. He refused to fly with regular aircrew. He chose to fly with AC2 Haddon and L.A.C. Shirley, their role on board being to change the camera spools and to count aloud the enemy fighters following him. He liked to take his coat off and to assist in servicing his own engines — a task for which he was not qualified. He would fly in almost any clothes provided they were *not* the official ones. A thigh-length pair of sheepskin leggings which he had acquired in Crete were characteristic. Above this he would wear army battledress with air-force stripes (he was now acting flight-lieutenant). He preferred an Ascot cravat to a tie. He was proud of his ash-blonde hair, so let it grow to near shoulder length. He had a notoriously grease-stained cap which he used to wear at times — on top of his flying helmet even. Against orders he smoked as he flew. He would take little part in mess life at Luqa, but instead could be found on occasions playing cards with the airmen at the dispersal site in one of the homemade huts there. Yet on one occasion, at a time when most of us had run out of buttons, polish and smart uniforms, he turned up in the mess immaculately dressed in order to meet the new group-captain. He was like that — utterly unpredictable. He lived in Valletta with a charming cabaret artiste, and he drove himself to work in an old car.... Although not by nature a normally contented person, I believe that he found himself — and happiness — in Malta. And later, when posted to other Mediterranean bases, he found unofficial ways of returning to the island that welcomed him and appreciated him.'[2]

It was air reconnaissance that revealed three ocean liners gathered in the harbour of Taranto. Clearly a troop convoy was assembling and since their destination could only be Tripoli, Benghazi not being able to handle them and being even more subject to bombing attacks, it was decided in Malta to lay a trap for them at the 'toe of the sock', the approaches to Tripoli itself. Four of the U-class submarines from the island, *Unbeaten, Upholder, Upright* and *Ursula* were accordingly stationed along the coast towards Tripoli, starting at a point one-hundred miles to the east where it was known that such convoys usually made their landfall. *Ursula* was last in the line at the entrance to the swept channel which began thirty miles east of Tripoli, the others were spaced some ten miles apart eastwards of her. Coming from Taranto the convoy naturally took the expected route, and, escorted by five destroyers, steered at high speed through the night of 16 September, being first sighted in the early hours of the following morning by *Unbeaten* which was at the end of the line and too far away to get into an attacking position. Her immediate radio

A *karozza* among the ruins.

The most heavily bombed place on earth.

Land freshly turned by ancient ploughs.

The welcome sun outside the sheltering darkness.

A convoy enters Grand Harbour in 1942.

H.M.S. *Ark Royal* torpedoed and sinking.

Changing a worn out four-inch gun on a destroyer.

Albacores with torpedoes fly off on a mission.

Farmers and servicemen get in the harvest.

Stores transferred from a lighter to waiting lorry.

Interior of a family air raid shelter.

Quarrying new tunnels to enlarge Headquarters.

Clearing blast debris off and around a bus.

report was received by Wanklyn in *Upholder* who steered on the surface to intercept. When he came to fire his spread of four torpedoes his usual skill came into play, but it was reinforced by luck for him and *mala fortuna* for the Italians in that two of the liners, as they zig-zagged, happened to coincide across the path of the torpedoes — making in effect, though at different ranges, one target. One was hit aft and brought to a standstill, and the other received her death blow. There were in fact comparatively few casualties, most of the troops getting away in the boats and life rafts. Wanklyn finished off the stricken liner the following morning. The third, which happened also to be the fastest of the trio, was missed astern by *Ursula* at the mouth of the swept channel and reached Tripoli safely, the sole survivor apart from the escorts. But at such a moment, when Rommel was waiting for men as well as machines, this was a further insulting blow to his hopes of a desert offensive. As Count Ciano, the Italian foreign secretary, wrote in his diary for 6 October: 'The supplies for North Africa are becoming more and more difficult. Only twenty per cent of the material set aside for September has been shipped and delivered.'

The authorities in Malta were well enough aware that the constant run of successes against Axis shipping which was crippling the Italo-German armies in North Africa would one day invoke the Furies. The Maltese people — artisans, businessmen and peasants alike — were extremely shrewd and recognized that unpalatable fact. They would not have survived as a separate race in the Mediterranean through all the centuries if they had not been as shrewd as they were tough. While they rejoiced in the damage that the island was causing their enemies they had felt the weight of that enemy before and, while the winter came on with its first downpours of rain, reviving the damp, unhealthy life of the shelters as a prospect (though not as yet a necessity), they felt uneasy as well as hungry.

'Fears of starvation began again as early as six weeks after the previous eight ship convoy had sustained Malta. There were many who expected some relieving measures in the situation, and no doubt there were some in the way of replenishment of ammunition, petrol, spares and foodstuffs, but any effects there must have been in this respect were certainly not visible.'[3] The government, looking ahead, was certainly not going to increase rations with the winter approaching, and in fact had already engaged a group of experts to report on how to eke out their existing stocks. No one knew when another convoy could be expected and, though minelaying submarines still brought in their limited and specialised cargoes, and a few merchantmen still ran the blockade alone and unescorted from the western end,[4] no one could predict when the next large convoy would arrive. The memorandum on 'Rationing in Malta' when completed for the government told them little that they did not know about stocks in the island or what possibilities there were for further cuts in the rations. After mentioning that 'the rations of coffee, tinned meat and tinned fish are very tight and could not be reduced without further hardship', it went on to stress: 'Bread is much the most important article of consumption with the people of Malta.... It is undesirable that any rationing of bread should be attempted.'

As has been said before, it was indeed the staff of life to the people and the excellent crusty Maltese bread, baked in wood-fired ovens, had long been about the best bread in the whole Mediterranean basin. (No wood had been imported for a long time, of course, but the great beams and fittings from wrecked houses, store houses and other buildings as well as wrecked ships and boats were gleaned in these days as if they were gold — to bake the wheat.) Adulteration had inevitably set in and since there was as yet no overall control of the bakers (that was to come) many people complained that, apart from the difficulty of getting it, the bread was often heavy and strange-looking through having been mixed with potatoes. These too were a problem since Malta had always had to import seed potatoes on account of the climate, and if they failed there was no substitute.

After the first winter rains when the island streamed, the sea around turned muddy, and every crack or fissure in every building was searched out by the weight of the downpour, all the land began to be feathered with green. Troops familiar with the desert, who knew how the passage of a single rain cloud could revivify seeds that no one would have suspected to lie hidden beneath the sand, would have recognized the phenomenon. Every year in Malta October began a second spring — perhaps the best months of the year, coming as they did after the barren summer when the eyes had ached with the glare of bare earth and rock. Now once again for two months or more wild flowers would rise everywhere and the scent of narcissi efface the dusty smell of summer. The harsh burning temperatures had dropped to about seventy degrees Farenheit throughout the day and the sky was a rinsed pale blue.

People had not come to terms with the endless oppression of war but they had adapted their lives to accord with it — in a curious way as if peace had never existed. Reality was in the gun barrels against the sky, the ululant sound of the sirens, the torn buildings and the yellow scars where old walls had had their skin ripped off to reveal the fresh stone beneath. Washed tattered clothing blew in the breeze on improvized lines stretching out from shelter mouths, and iron pots with little in them sat over makeshift fires made between limestone blocks. People felt hungry, but not as yet starved.

News passed by word of mouth quicker than by the savaged telephone system or the slow and carefully-deliberated information released over the radio. There had been a stir at the harbour mouth, crunch of the sea under the moving forefoot of a warship arriving. . . . The two six-inch gun cruisers, *Aurora* and *Penelope*, new to their light grey Mediterranean paint, accompanied by the two heavy destroyers *Lance* and *Lively* were entering Grand Harbour.

CHAPTER EIGHTEEN

Striking Force

Approached from seaward there was no more imposing harbour in the Mediterranean than that which is justifiably called 'Grand'. On the right, Fort St Elmo, its guns pointing skyward in those days, a star-shaped fortress built over the site of the one that had defied the Turks in 1565, hunched heavy shoulders in protection of the grid-plan city of Valletta behind it. Undulating over the hill of limestone on which it was built, the light shining clear down the mathematical lines of the streets, Valletta's sides were protected by great curtain walls. On the Marsamuscetto side the nineteenth-century spire of the Anglican cathedral made its sharp statement against the flat-roofed palaces and houses of the City of the Knights, the masterpiece of the sixteenth century architect Laparelli.[1] Called after its Grand Master *Humillima Civitas Valettae* — the Most Humble City of Valletta — there were those from the seventeenth century onwards who had maintained that it should have been called 'The Most Proud'. Certainly during this siege, fulfilling its function of a fortress city, it was indeed most proud and the scars and shattered buildings — showing here and there like the gap teeth of an old fighter — did not diminish its grandeur. From Fort St Elmo the broken iron girders of the viaduct to the breakwater, destroyed in the Italian attack, hung down or pierced the surface of the water where they effectively closed the gap. Behind them the boom defences of the harbour sealed it yet again. Spreading back as far as the Upper Baracca and the Great Ditch beyond (which protected the city from the landward side) rose the walls of the city that had caused a Turkish spy, visiting Valletta just after it had been built, to report to the Sultan: 'We shall never take this place!'[2]

Opposite Fort St Elmo and on the left of the breakwater — completed by the British in 1906 to protect their battlefleet from the Gregale (the fierce north-easterly wind of winter) as well as from potential attack by the new weapon, torpedoes — lay Fort Ricasoli. This late seventeenth century fortress had been built to seal the harbour mouth, providing a complement to Valletta's Fort St Elmo. Running out on a narrow strip of land, this was a longitudinal fort whose curtain and bastions rose sheer from the water's edge to seaward. On the harbour side, looking over Rinella Bay towards the

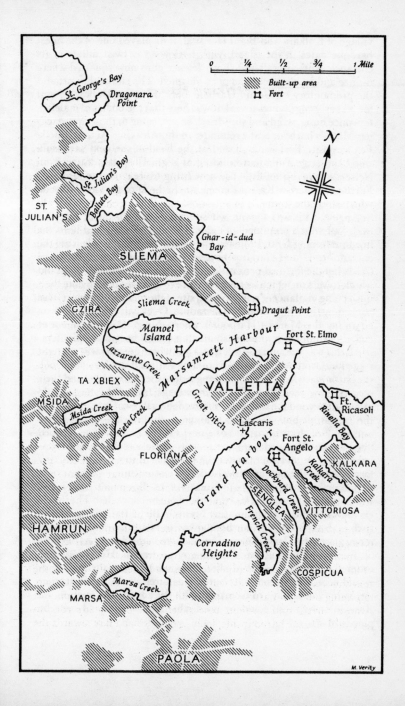

village of Kalkara and Bighi Hospital, it displayed one of the finest baroque gates in the island, with barley-sugar twist pillars at its entrance. Anti-aircraft and shore defence guns now squatted where bronze and iron cannon had once gleamed. The end of this fort and the promontory on Grand Harbour bore the name Gallow's Point for, as early engravings reveal, it was here that the bodies of malefactors once hung, wind and sun-dried, as a warning to those approaching Malta's harbour and a reminder to those leaving. Across Rinella Bay opposite Fort Ricasoli and at the head of the next peninsula stood the large Palladian building of Bighi Hospital, dating from Nelson's days, but of little use now being overexposed to air raids. Further on, across Kalkara creek, at the head of the peninsula on which stood the township of Vittoriosa was the largest fortress of all, St Angelo. This was a giant, whose scars bore evidence of many air raids but which remained as indomitable as when it had been the headquarters of Grand Master La Valette in 1565. A mile from the entrance to Grand Harbour beyond Fort St Angelo and Dockyard Creek lay the fortified peninsula of Senglea, distinguished by its old watch towers on which were carved an eye and an ear to denote their unsleeping vigilance. French Creek, site of the modern drydocks, was backed by the whale hump of Carradino. Over half a mile further on again lay the Marsa ('Harbour') where this great sleeve of water ended in tumbled buildings, small ships, tugs, barges and lighters.

All this was the arena — but it was one where not only was the fight staged but from which issued from time to time the ships which took the battle elsewhere. It was not long before the two cruisers and their escorts, now refuelling after their passage from Gibraltar, would move out beyond the breakwater, guarded by its two forts, and — like the impossible bull which gets in amongst the crowd — create havoc outside. Not that the arrival of a new Force K could have escaped observation. Coupled with the recent severe losses due to Malta-based aircraft and submarines the presence of this surface striking force caused the Italian Naval Staff to discontinue — even if only temporarily — all convoys to North Africa. Rommel's complaints were now reinforced by a fact that could not be concealed. The listeners in Malta and the coordinating brains in Bletchley Park knew that such a situation would not be allowed to continue, since it would mean a complete Italo-German breakdown in the desert. At the time of diverting Fliegerkorps X to convoy protection, Hitler had also ordered six U-boats to the Mediterranean theatre and their presence would soon make itself felt, but it was already clear that further measures would have to be taken. With the advent of winter on the Russian front there could be no doubt that there would soon be planes to spare.

The absence of any convoys meant a long wait for Captain Agnew of the *Aurora* and the ships under his command but at last, as was inevitable, the Italian Naval Staff had to bow to the pressure exerted on them from the High Command; a convoy must be run through to the Axis armies to ensure that they could at the very least stave off an attack which the British were clearly preparing. So on 8 November a convoy of eight freighters escorted by six destroyers issued out from the Messina Straits, eastward bound towards the coast of Greece where they would be joined by a further smaller convoy, the whole then turning south for Tripoli. Despite the fact that the convoy was given an air escort throughout that day it was still sighted by a patrolling Maryland out of Malta, whose report caused Captain Agnew's Force K to get under way at dusk. In anticipation of any such move the Italians had already stationed a submarine watch on the approaches to Grand Harbour, but it must have been inefficiently maintained or the submarines 'put down' by destroyers dropping depth charges prior to the emergence of the cruisers and their escort, for Force K steamed out at high speed through the breakwater and headed east without being attacked or reported. In the words of a marine who was aboard HMS *Aurora* at the time: 'We sailed in a hurry, in fact some men were still ashore, and the captain of *Penelope* went aboard in a launch just as his ship was going through the boom.'[3]

To avoid confusion in night actions the two destroyers *Lance* and *Lively* and the cruisers *Aurora* and *Penelope* fought as one ship. Steaming at twenty-eight knots at close stations, each keeping in the other's wake, they were at liberty to open fire on anything that was not either dead ahead or dead astern of them. As has been seen from earlier engagements, the British were highly trained in night fighting whereas the Italians were not and they also had the immense benefit of radar, which again the Italians did not. The convoy which had been located as it left the Messina Straits had, apart from its destroyer escort, a close support force commanded by Vice-Admiral Brivonesi, consisting of two heavy cruisers *Trieste* and *Trento* and four destroyers. In theory this should have been quite sufficient to cope with anything that the British could bring out, but in view of the deficiencies mentioned above it was to prove useless. It was a brilliant moonlit night and the second convoy, consisting of two merchant ships and two destroyers, was just joining the main body when Captain Agnew picked them up. Reducing speed to twenty knots he led his ships round to the north of the convoy, silhouetting them up-moon, and turned on a parallel course. There had been a report of other ships astern of him but he had ignored this to concentrate on his target.

119

The other ships were Admiral Brivonesi's cruisers and destroyers which he had positioned astern of the convoy, maintaining a patrol on a north – south line to ward off any threat that might develop from the direction of Malta. Without radar he was dependent on visual sighting, and his lookouts had failed to observe the British slipping between his force and the convoy. Indeed, the first that Admiral Brivonesi knew of the enemy's presence was when there were flashes and explosions from the direction of the convoy some three miles to the east of him. Force K steaming parallel with the convoy and its escorts came up first with the destroyer at the rear and left it damaged and out of action. Two further destroyers were sunk in the action which followed, the situation being to some extent made easier for the British by Admiral Brivonesi coming to the conclusion that the convoy was under air attack and giving the order for all ships to make smoke. The destroyers on the far side of the convoy from Force K were confused by the smoke blowing over them and to all intents and purposes were put out of the action. Brivonesi discovered his mistake too late when the mast supporting his radio aerial was shot down, leaving him unable to communicate with his squadron. Meanwhile Captain Agnew in *Aurora* led his ships almost at leisure in the destruction of the convoy, nine ships being sunk and a tanker left ablaze. About one hour and a half after the first sighting Force K turned south-west for Malta. Such was the course that might automatically have been expected and it was athwart such a course that Admiral Brivonesi should have laid his ships. Inexplicably (unless subsequently revealed in the Italian courts martial) he turned to the north to intercept the British squadron. (He and Captain Bisciani in command of the close destroyer escort of the convoy were subsequently deprived of their commands.) The ultimate humiliation was yet to come, when the submarine *Upholder* put in an appearance at dawn and sank one of the remaining destroyers.

The sudden urgency with which Force K had steamed out from Grand Harbour the previous night had made it quite plain to any Maltese in the vicinity of the waterfront that a convoy must have been sighted. Next morning the people were waiting at every vantage point — guns' crews in the old forts, men, women and children thick on the roofs and in the windows of the houses in Valletta, and dense along the shoreline. Their cheers rebounded off the limestone battlements as they welcomed the great ships back. As the marine aboard HMS *Aurora* put it in his letter: 'Arrival back in Malta was pretty exciting because the Maltese knew just about before anyone that we had been in a successful action, and they used to line the front and all viewpoints waving and cheering. . . .' This action, the first of several, was but the shining tip of the iceberg that

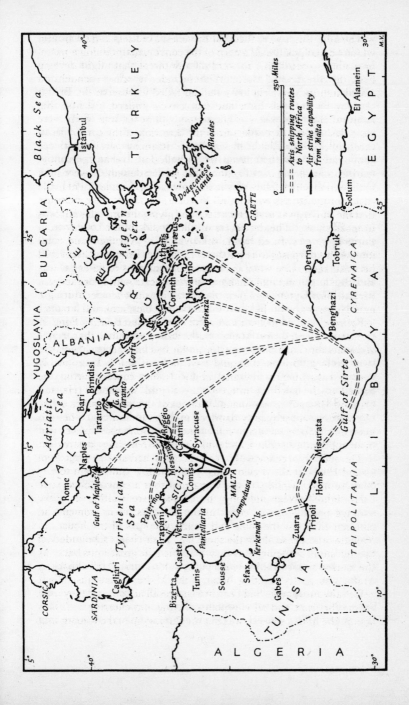

was sinking the Axis in the Mediterranean. In the previous month, on the night of the 16-17 October, sixteen Wellington bombers out of Malta had carried out a heavy raid on Naples, hitting docks, factory buildings, the Arsenal and a torpedo factory. As well as their normal 1000lb bombs, they dropped a number of 4000 pounders — the first time bombs of this calibre had been used anywhere in the Middle Eastern theatre of war. In the same month airfields in Sicily were attacked, as well as roads and other targets on the North African coast, by Malta's Blenheim bombers. Meanwhile the submarines continued to take their usual steady toll. The Italian mercantile marine was being destroyed. With understandable alarm the German Vice-Admiral Weichold noted: 'In October 1941 the African tonnage dropped to 50,000 tons — a third of the monthly average of the past seven months. Of this, almost 63 per cent was either sunk or damaged; in the whole month only 18,500 tons of shipping space arrived safely in Libya.... In November the total tonnage used fell to 37,000; of these 26,000 tons were sunk and 2,100 tons damaged. This was 77 per cent – the highest percentage of lost and also the remaining 8400 tons was the lowest monthly delivery... the battle for Cyrenaica (Western Desert) was not decided during a month of actual land fighting, but rather by these external factors.'

Radar-equipped Wellingtons were used by the RAF working in close liaison with the surface forces, the former preceding the aircraft at dusk in the direction in which a convoy had been reported and the latter picking up the convoy and then guiding the attacking force in its direction, as well as illuminating it with flares on moonless nights. Sometimes, as has been seen, the convoy would have been reported by one of the reconnaissance planes out of the island but at other times the reasons why Force K would make a sudden departure were unknown to those taking part. Commenting on his liaison work one of these Wellington pilots observed: 'A typical sortie worked out like this. It would start when the Navy received an intelligence report from one of their "men on the pier" that a supply convoy was due to pass through the Straits of Messina or was to leave Naples or Palermo on a certain tide. Naval navigators would then work out where the enemy was most likely to be at various times during their passage to North Africa....'[4] The mysterious figure 'on the pier', of course, carried a signal for Captain Agnew containing information that had been decyphered and construed by those anonymous men and women working in the hidden fungivorous tunnels below Lascaris Bastion.

Without radar and without efficient sonar the Italian navy made a brave effort to get convoys through to the Axis forces in North Africa. If besieged Malta was always deeply concerned about oil fuel for its ships (doubly so when a surface force was based there) and petrol for its aircraft, the Italians throughout the war were also hard pressed, being dependent almost entirely on the good will of their German partner to see that supplies from eastern Europe were adequately available. Often they were not, and the restricted movements of Italian battleships were not always due to the grand policy of keeping a fleet in being. Now, what one writer has termed 'Massacre on the Libyan Supply Route'[5] was regularly taking place; a battle-ship was even brought out to cover one convoy and heavy cruisers for others, while light cruisers were used to run petrol supplies through for the Axis air forces and mechanized armies. Even this did not always succeed, and late in November that year one convoy escorted by three heavy cruisers, two light cruisers and attendant destroyers, was attacked after leaving the Messina Straits by RAF bombers, Fleet Air Arm Swordfish and Albacores. One of the cruisers was torpedoed during the day and had to return to Messina, while a second cruiser was torpedoed that night by a submarine and also forced back. At this point the Italians, expecting the arrival of Force K or further air and submarine attacks, recalled the whole convoy. A few days later Force K did indeed strike and two German ships laden with ammunition, bombs, petrol and transport for the Afrika Korps were blown up and sunk as they tried to slip by on the eastern route to Benghazi.

The combination of the onslaught at sea and a fresh British offensive in North Africa proved almost fatal to the Axis in the Mediterranean theatre and if it had not been for the outstanding military talents of Rommel it probably would have been. The British advance starting on 18 November had caught him by surprise, but he struck east into Egypt to threaten his enemy's supplies. Then, on the news that Tobruk was on the point of being relieved, he turned west again and after heavy fighting in the desert succeeded in preventing the junction between the Tobruk garrison and the New Zealand Division — thus at one stroke depriving the British and imperial forces of the main object of their offensive. Had he had his supplies, armour and reinforcements, he might have continued his advance into Egypt, cut the British off from their base and broken through the 'soft' defences of Alexandria and Cairo to reach the Canal.

Such had been his intention, but it was defeated at sea by the air, submarine and surface naval forces operating out of Malta. Even as it was, Rommel could no longer maintain the land blockade of Tobruk and, reporting that he would have to abandon Cyrenaica, he began to withdraw towards Tripolitania on 11 December. Known to Ultra his moves could in any case have been anticipated, but little could have been done to prevent a general of his calibre from extricating his hard-fighting forces. By the end of that December Tobruk was finally relieved, after a siege that had lasted two-hundred and forty-two days. The closing months of the year had shown the other besieged fortress, Malta, at the peak of its capacity for disrupting the enemy's supply lines, and able to view the success of the British forces in the desert to some extent as the by-product of its own efforts. This warm feeling, which was shared by the islanders, seemed like a cheerful prelude to Christmas which, austere though it was bound to be, was a longed for break in the overall harshness of war. But before then, unknown to most, whether servicemen or civilians, things had already started to go wrong with the balance of power in the Mediterranean. Hitler had ordered more U-boats into the sea, and Fliegerkorps II had been ordered to transfer from the Russian front to Sicily and North Africa.

CHAPTER NINETEEN

A Hard Winter

Inside a fortress there is a special kind of claustrophobia, an insularity quite beyond that normally associated with islands. The news from the greater war beyond their immediate embattled walls is heard only as a distant rumour, comforting in so far as it shows that the besieged are not quite alone, and doubly comforting when it is about supplies or some damage inflicted upon the enemy that must ultimately weaken his hold upon their position. The news of 7 December 1941 that the Japanese had attacked Pearl Harbour, thus bringing America into the war, was heard first with astonishment and then with a warmth of fellow feeling. Japan was far too remote to come within the ordinary Maltese's sphere of thinking, but many had relatives in America as they had in other parts of the English-speaking world. No one on the island could possibly understand what the fact might mean in terms of the overall picture but everyone could understand that it meant there was now a massive ally on their side, thousands of miles distant indeed, but construed as a menace to the enemy that besieged them.

About a week beforehand there had been an ominous sign in the sky over the island — high up, a distinctive twin-engined shape known to all, a Junkers 88 on a reconnaissance flight, something not seen for many months. A few had already been warned that 'information' suggested that there might soon be a return of the Luftwaffe to the airfields of Sicily. What the many had long suspected (without access to any secret sources) was about to be revealed.

Something similar had happened nearly four hundred years earlier when the great corsair and tactician, Dragut Rais, had arrived on the scene in Malta a few weeks after the attack had begun. The siege, previously somewhat indifferently handled, suddenly acquired a new direction and force: guns were sited on Tigné Point facing Fort St Elmo to the north, and on Gallows' Point (where Fort Ricasoli now stood) to bombard St Elmo from the south.[1] The overall strategy of the attack on the island was also drastically reshaped. So it was from the moment that Field Marshal Kesselring took over the command of Fliegerkorps X in the eastern Mediterranean, of all the German forces in Sicily, and of Fliegerkorps II, under General Lörzer, now transferred from Russia to Sicily and North Africa.

The blitz on *Illustrious* had been a kind of 'one off' performance. This had then been followed by heavy raids using massed bombers, in the belief that this would be sufficient to break the island's defenders and above all its civilian people, as such attacks had done when applied to cities in Europe. But the German and Italian experience in the air had subsequently shown that Malta was every bit as indomitable as London and, because of its nature, presented quite a new problem to Luftwaffe thinking. Geographically speaking the island was, as its defenders boasted, 'unsinkable'. The civilian population in their air raid tunnels had developed a way of living that no one had been able to do in the bombed cities of Europe, and the islanders seemed to be completely wedded to the British cause.[2] Luftflotte II, as Kesselring's whole command was known, was governed by an overall directive issued by Hitler himself, now back in Germany from his advance headquarters on the eastern front and able to see the whole scale of the war again from a European viewpoint. First of all, the order went, Kesselring's forces were to concentrate on achieving mastery over the area between southern Italy and North Africa, thus ensuring the passage of convoys between the two. Secondly, they were to prevent the passage of enemy convoys through the Mediterranean. Both parts of this order meant that Malta had to be suppressed.

Luftwaffe losses had been extremely heavy in the first assault on the island, and they were again to be used like a bludgeon — but this time with a difference. Instead of staking everything on a few large saturation raids, the bludgeon was to be applied intelligently as well as incessantly. (Something had been learned from the Italian tactics of keeping the defenders permanently without rest or sleep.) The campaign was to fall into three phases: firstly, the air defences were to be neutralized by forcing the defenders to expend their personnel and their ammunition; secondly, the airfields were to be rendered inoperable and any aircraft caught on the ground destroyed; thirdly, the dockyards, shipping, harbour installations, and lines of communication were to be destroyed. (Ammunition soon had to be rationed, as well as food, to a degree never known in any other place during the whole course of the war.) It would be fair to say that, but for the quite exceptional nature of the garrison (which included everyone on the island at the time) and of the men who managed to fight the shattered remnants of convoys through to sustain it, Hitler's aims would have had a good chance of success. Until the nuclear scientists succeeded in their morally dubious achievement, no area on earth ever endured such an explosive power as the one that was now to fall on Malta.

The lone Junkers 88 had been the portent of things to come. A few days afterwards, like an old gage of battle flung down before an opponent, something strange occurred in Grand Harbour.

... Nick Harrison and I were talking in the Castile Square when suddenly we heard a familiar whine. I queried Nick saying: 'Surely that is an ME?' We both turned round in time to see a single ME 109 with a yellow nose, flying down the length of the harbour with its guns blazing, and at enormous speed. Nick, who was an expert at these things, said at once that he thought it was a ME 109F, which was the very latest German fighter. If this were true, it boded ill for the RAF in Malta, as not only was Malta's airfields space largely given up to bombers, but the fighters we had would be outclassed by this type of Messerschmitt.[3]

Things had begun to go wrong for the British long before the appearance of the Luftwaffe over Malta. Despite the objections raised by the German Naval Staff, Hitler had ordered six U-boats to the Mediterranean in September and he now ordered a further four. The result of these new dispositions was soon seen when, on 12 November, the *Ark Royal* was torpedoed by U.81 and sank some thirty miles east of Gibraltar. This famous ship, so often previously 'sunk' by the German radio, was a grievous loss, coming at a time when two of Britain's carriers were away being repaired, a third was being docked after a grounding, and the number of such ships was sadly few. It was the *Ark Royal* which had consistently managed to 'feed' Hurricanes into Malta over the previous months, and she was returning from just such an expedition at the time. This meant that Force H no longer had a carrier, the supply of aircraft into Malta dried up, and Force H could no longer escort convoys to the island. Less than a fortnight later, Cunningham's Mediterranean fleet from Alexandria also suffered a disaster. Operating in conjunction with surface forces out of Malta, Cunningham with his three battleships — *Queen Elizabeth*, *Barham* and *Valiant* — had been 'trawling' along the North African coast when U.331 penetrated their destroyer screen and put three torpedoes into *Barham*. The old warship rolled over to port, blew up and sank, taking 56 officers and 812 ratings with her. This was but the beginning of a series of heavy blows to Britain's naval forces that was to change the balance of power in the Mediterranean to an extent not even rivalled by the Fleet Air Arm attack on Taranto in 1940.

But before this turn of the tide became apparent in the island and the Luftwaffe had had time to get settled into Sicily, all the signs seemed to point to the continuance of a successfully aggressive future. The harbour watchers (of whom there were many hundreds) argued from the presence of Force K that the battle was being won, a feeling that was reinforced by the arrival of two more cruisers, *Ajax* and *Neptune*, and the fleet destroyers *Kingston* and *Kimberley*. The presence of this addition to the surface forces on the island meant that, while the Axis convoys were even more threatened, the expenditure of oil fuel doubled. While maintaining some essential reserve, there was at that time only enough fuel for all four cruisers and fleet destroyers to make three sweeps of normal range from their base. The *Breconshire*, the only fast fuel-carrier available, was a converted merchantman which could carry 5000 tons of oil fuel and a certain amount of petrol: without her many runs between Eygpt and Malta no surface force could have operated, shore installations would have failed, and even the submarines would have been confined to harbour. To some extent Malta existed and maintained its fighting capability for some time on the slim thread of one ship.

Lack of radar and inadequate training in night fighting techniques led to another disaster for the Italians on the North African run. Two light cruisers, the *Da Barbiano* and *Di Giussano*, had been loaded with case petrol at Palermo (urgently required by the Axis forces in the desert) and sent out with a torpedo boat to make a fast run from the west of Sicily down to Cape Bon and thence along the coast to Tripoli. Their departure was observed by Malta reconnaissance and an obvious target for Force K was presented — but owing to the oil-fuel shortage at that moment the ships could not be despatched. A strike by torpedo aircraft was accordingly arranged, although the chances of finding two fast ships at night were not promising. Outside of Admiral Ford and his staff in Malta no one knew that by sheer chance four fleet destroyers, the *Sikh*, *Maori*, *Legion* and the Dutch *Isaac Sweers*, were at that moment on their way from Gibraltar to Malta bound as replacements for Cunningham's fleet. They would be nearing Cape Bon at about the time that the two Italian cruisers were anticipated in the area. This was the night of 13-14 December.

'The Maltese knew just about before anyone. . . .' Bad news could almost always be contained within a tight group, but good news was allowed to find its own mysterious source of leakage — from a signalman to a friend, to a Maltese sailor, to a civilian, and so to all the waterfront. When Commander Stokes in *Sikh* and the three other fleet destroyers steamed in line ahead through the breakwater in daylight on 14 December ships' sirens were sounding on the bright air and the whole population, as it seemed, was out to welcome them. On the following day *The Times of Malta*, that unique newspaper which never missed a day's publication despite conditions that at times few newspapermen could even have imagined in a nightmare,

128

maintained the regularity of its imperial prose style: 'The spectacle as the victorious destroyers entered Grand Harbour, amid the cheers of the populace, which were returned by the bluejackets lining their ships, was one that will not easily be effaced from memory. The ships were welcomed by cheering crowds lining the Lower and Upper Barraccas, St Angelo and every vantage point. The cheering conveyed a simple message of pride and gratitude, of sympathy and shared resolve, and of appreciation for the heavy blows they are dealing the enemy in the waters around Malta.'

Having received the message about the Italian cruisers from Admiral Ford in Malta, the four destroyers had been dashing for Cape Bon to try and come up with them. By chance only (the cruisers had temporarily reversed course to throw torpedo planes from Malta off their track) the destroyers — at action stations, guns' crews and torpedo tubes at the ready — encountered them off the dark loom of the Cape. Hit by shell and torpedoes both of the cruisers were sunk, the Italian torpedo boat being left behind to pick up the survivors. This was the news that had brought out the crowds along that ancient waterfront. It would be a long time before they would hear anything that gave them again such a sensation of riding the flashing crest of a victorious wave.

Quite often, after sliding out of the dark harbour on one of their convoy hunts, Force K had drawn a blank and been back before dawn with nothing to show for their efforts except expenditure of oil fuel. On another occasion they would make a successful attack in the night — nothing but flames on the sea to show that the predator had struck before returning to its lair. But there had always been the danger of the gamekeeper — those battleships used as escorts — or the sharp spring of a mined trap closing. It was the danger of the heavily mined waters off the North African coast, some of the areas known to the British but others uncharted by them, that had earlier caused Admiral Cunningham to dissuade the Admiralty from asking for any further ventures by the battlefleet in bombardments of the enemy held ports. He was well aware how quickly one or more capital ships could be lost and how irreplaceable they were. After the loss of *Ark Royal* and *Barham*, the cruiser *Galatea*, torpedoed and sunk off the entrance to the swept channel into Alexandria by a German U-boat, was a further blow to a dwindling Mediterranean fleet. With the war now breaking over the Far East, the Australians and New Zealanders were wanting back their destroyers and frigates, which had played an invaluable part with Cunningham's forces, while the South Africans were asking for their anti-submarine group for the Indian Ocean; these small ships which had proved their efficiency many times in the escort of troops and stores along the desert coast were now more than ever needed in the face of the new submarine threat.

A severe blow was about to befall the British fleet in an operation which had involved passing the *Breconshire* through to Malta on one of those invaluable runs that enabled the surface forces to stay operational. Admiral Iachino, who had been covering a convoy to Tripoli with his battlefleet (three battleships, two heavy cruisers and ten destroyers) wisely refused to engage a British force from Alexandria in a night action, even though the latter had no more than four light cruisers and attendant destroyers. He had turned for home after seeing his convoy near enough to the harbour. That night, however, Wellington bombers and torpedo planes out of Malta attacked Tripoli heavily and the convoy was forced to anchor outside the port. On receiving this news, Force K, consisting of *Aurora*, *Neptune* and *Penelope*, with the destroyers *Lance*, *Lively*, *Havelock* and *Kandahar*, dashed south from Malta to try and catch them outside. Some twenty miles east of Tripoli they ran into an unknown moored minefield. In the struggle to help one another and at the same time get clear of the minefield *Neptune* was lost with all hands save one, *Aurora* badly damaged, *Penelope* slightly less so, and the destroyer *Kandahar* so severely damaged that she had to be sunk. Something that Cunningham had feared might happen to his battlefleet off that dangerous coast had now almost wiped out Force K.

The spectacle of stricken ships limping into the harbour was not new to the island and the dockyard was always in the business of repairing ships. They already had the cruiser *Ajax* in hand, out of action because of mechanical defects, and they now had two more cruisers with serious damage that needed dry-docking to repair. All this went along with the permanent normal maintenance jobs of submarines, minesweepers, harbour craft and any other odd fish that swam within their reach out of the sea around. It was now that the underground workshops — fuel lines and other facilities, many of which owed themselves to the unending labours of Admiral Ford to ensure that the island could repair its damaged ships as well as the hospitals did its wounded men — proved themselves invaluable.[4] They were to continue doing so during the black turmoil of the ensuing months.

If Malta had been an island under almost continuous siege since 1940 it was not until the end of December 1941 that the people learned what 'siege' really meant when a voice had spoken from the 'High Diwan'. Hitler's personal Directive No. 38 to Field Marshal Kesselring on the subject of Malta had been not unlike that of the Sultan Suleiman the Magnificent at his Diwan in October 1564. The latter had told his assembled ministers, admirals and generals that he envisaged the day when 'The Grand Seignior, or his deputies, masters of the whole Mediterranean, may dictate laws, as universal lord, from that not unpleasant rock, and look down upon his shipping at anchor in its excellent harbour.' For the immediate future, however, he had issued the ultimate directive: 'Those sons of dogs! I say now that, for their continual raids and insults, they shall be destroyed!'

On 4 December 1941 the Luftwaffe appeared again over the island, timing their first raid for the hours of darkness. They brought from Russia a deadly seriousness to the annihilation of this arrogant island and a contemptuous fury. During the first five weeks of campaign there were ninety-three daylight air raid alerts, and one-hundred and twenty night alerts. There were only two nights completely free from attack.

CHAPTER TWENTY

New Year 1942

Christmas 1941 was probably the most depressing in recorded history. Everywhere throughout the world it seemed that might was proven right, and that naked aggression would always triumph. There had been terrible winter seasons in other wars, most notably World War I, but never a time when at every point of the compass there seemed no hope — except for men who had deliberately rejected the cardinal virtues, including hope itself. In the Far East the triumph of the forces that had treacherously attacked America seemed to be borne on such a victorious tide that their onrush looked irreversible. The Mediterranean was poised like a fulcrum between Hitler's war against Russia and this new war instigated by Japan. On 10 December the news that the old battle cruiser *Repulse* and the new battleship *Prince of Wales* had both been sunk by Japanese dive bombers brought no comfort to people in an island which suffered every day and night from the high scream and the thunderous roars of bombs.

The worst news was the crippling of Cunningham's remaining two battleships in Alexandria harbour on the morning of 19 December. Although everyone had been forewarned by events in Gibraltar and Malta, and it was well known that the Italian 10th Flotilla would certainly try to exercise their skills on the main British fleet, the precautions taken against them were quite insufficient. This time, and fully compensating for their failure at Malta, the Decima Flottiglia Mas achieved a triumph with their two-man 'torpedoes'. The flagship *Queen Elizabeth* and the *Valiant* were both so severely damaged as to be unseaworthy and the tanker *Sagona* and the destroyer *Jervis*, lying alongside her, were both severely damaged. This meant that, with the Italian battlefleet increasingly active in the central Mediterranean, Cunningham could no longer oppose it with his own battleships. With the Luftwaffe striking daily and nightly the island of Malta was imperilled as never before.

It was at times like this that a native insularity coupled with the siege mentality served people in good stead. What mattered was here and now — in the immediate vicinity. Other things could look after themselves, and indeed would have to; here was the current raid, here was the tunnel, the air raid shelter, the immediate family and neighbours. Outside, the dark of the world. It is significant that everyone who has written about those times, Maltese or foreigner, civilian or serviceman, has always commented on the strength that the islanders derived from their faith. In every air raid shelter of any size there was always a priest, an altar, a lamp burning, and the rites of the Church available. Even in small private shelters there would almost invariably be part of a corner where a statuette, a coloured reproduction of a favourite saint or the Madonna, would stand in a small aureole of light — an oil or candle-lit glow that quivered and twisted against the rough-hewn walls when the bombs were dropping. Holy Malta, as the old people had always called it (paying no attention to the scepticism of some of the young, let alone the cynicism of foreigners) was in itself a very real presence, helped and preserved by very many saints as well as the Holy Family. Apart from the prescribed prayers there were prayers for many occasions — and special ones had been approved by the archbishop for the terrible circumstances of this new war.[1]

Mussolini's fascists, in their endeavour to reclaim their 'Catholic brothers from the yoke of the Protestant British', had also maintained that the language of the Maltese was only a dialect of Italian. How many of them would have recognized the following words, said often in those days in the shelters by thousands of young and old?

> 'Missierna li inti fis-smewwiet,
> Jitqaddes ismek,
> Tigi saltnatek,
> Ikun li trid Int, kif fis-sema hekda fl-art.'

They are the opening lines of The Lord's Prayer in Maltese. Except for a number of Italian loan words, which then suffered a sea change and were declined like Arabic, there was as much resemblance in the languages as there was in the temperaments of the people.

Indeed, the temperaments of the races involved in this struggle present an interesting study and, even allowing for the many different gradations between the individuals, it is still possible to make out a composite picture of attackers and defenders, bombers and bombed. As far as the Maltese were concerned the instigators of the war were the Italians. This had seemed somewhat unbelievable to many in 1940, although no one in pre-war Malta could have been ignorant of the fascist attempts to arouse anti-British feeling and to popularize the new regime in Italy. There had been the inevitable disagreements during the inter-war period between the British and Maltese at governmental level and the British had revoked the constitution in 1933. These were things on which anti-British elements could well play, but at a private level, so many were the friendly everyday contacts between the two peoples that, despite the inevitable flare ups which happen in garrisons and naval ports, what prevailed was a feeling of rough friendship. Much was forgiven on both sides for the sake of a long relationship — more like a marriage than that to be found in any other colony. Against this had to be set the Italian culture adopted by many of the middle class and more prosperous Maltese, although in the relatively sparse ranks of the old upper class Mussolini tended to be regarded as a vulgar buffoon (but dangerous). For the working classes, whether from the dockyard and harbour areas or from the country, Italian fascism had little appeal — except the inevitable one to poor men of any organization or party that promises better things. Comparatively few working-class Maltese spoke anything but somewhat 'basic' English, and fewer still any Italian at all. Theirs was a typically Mediterranean culture, but with North African undertones, deeply impressed over centuries by the influence of the Catholic Church and somewhat less so by the simple pragmatism of British servicemen. Those Maltese who had travelled at all — as ratings in the Royal Navy, aboard merchantmen, or even in fishing boats no further than Sicily — were well aware that the living standards of the Italian working men were far lower than their own and that the 'new' Italians of fascist persuasion appeared to dislike and attempt to patronize them.

In the battle for their island the Maltese were literally fighting for their country: this stony land of blinding light; their churches, the glories of their towns and villages now daily desecrated by bombs which, they remembered, had first been dropped by the Italians; their homes and familiar streets and loved places threatened as never before in a hard history. They indeed had a real stake in the war, since they could not believe that people who had killed and injured so many of them and ravaged their country would ever treat them humanely if they were to conquer. They had long ago cast in their lot with the British and they did not see (as some post-war Maltese politicians would maintain)[2] that if it had not been for the British presence they would not be involved in the war at all. Their position was completely unshakeable.

The official Italian position was quite clear. It had been stated over and over again by Mussolini and others, and formed the subject of many books. One of these, *Il Mediterraneo*, may do duty for them all: 'By the will of the Mediterranean people, by the affirmation of their national independence, the "British episode" in this sea is finished — that period, during which, for some length of time, they included the basin of this sea in the security system of their imperial communication routes.'[3]

134

The young Italians who formed the officer class of the Regia Aeronautica, as well as in their army and navy, were very largely of the fascist persuasion. How could they not be? The regime had promised them an African empire (though the last of that was now imperilled) and in *Mare Nostrum* (words which, along with *Imperium Romanum*, were unspoken after a short time at war) had seemed at first, with its fine new ships, to promise what it could fulfil. Disillusion rankled at the heart of young flying officers and certainly, as far as Malta was concerned, they had lost too many of their number to feel much enthusiasm for that target — though they continued to show themselves excellent in torpedo-bombers against convoys. Yet still, like the naval officers of the 10th Light Flotilla in their explosive high-speed boats and manned torpedoes, they were capable of exploits of dashing bravery. The real trouble was that the aircraft with which Italy had entered the war were already obsolescent. Their fighters were not the equivalent even of the old Mk I Hurricane, and their bombers were slow and lacked armour. Worst of all was the fact that the aircraft production of Italy was not geared for the rate of wastage incurred in a war like this, with the result that aircraft had to be husbanded almost as jealously as warships. They wished to swagger with the great, and yet they knew in their hearts that the role was beyond them. They had seen the performance of the Luftwaffe and knew they could not emulate it.

As for Malta itself, it was a constant affront. They knew how many planes it had claimed and how many navy and merchant navy men that Scylla of a rock had seized.[4] The fact that the Chief of the SMG (*Stato Maggior Generale*) was apt to repeat, like Cato the Elder some two-thousand years before, '*Delenda est Carthago*' — 'Carthage must be destroyed' — was not likely to impress them. They were well aware that before Operation C3 could even be seriously considered the combined Italo-German airforces would have to bomb the island into the silence of death. It was not likely to be easy. So far as they had any personal feelings, they hated 'the English' who had seemed to mock them on the sea and in the air, and they felt an inordinate dislike of the 'Arabic peasants' whose obduracy seemed like an affront to their culture and their pride.

The attitude of their allies the Germans is more difficult to define because the records of those who took part are inevitably few and the consenting silence of post-war years in Europe has been allowed to erase the memory of what was at the time, after all, much publicized as the 'Kampf um Malta'.[5] German newspapers and magazines featured many articles, as well as pictures of the Stukas diving like hawks over that strange, shining island, with its streets like dark chessboard patterns, of bomb bays opening to release their tumbling cargo, and of storage and ammunition dumps boiling up in great white clouds — strangely prophetic of those mushroom clouds that were later to terrify the world.

The first wave of Luftwaffe pilots who had attacked *Illustrious* and then the island had been borne forward in the complete confidence of past successes. The masters of Europe thought they had nothing to fear, and felt disdain for such a humble target as a Mediterranean island defended by a few British and inhabited by peasants. Their losses taught them a salutary respect for the word 'fortress' and an understanding of its meaning. Fliegerkorps II, under General Lörzer and directed from above by Field Marshal Kesselring, came to Sicily with a different outlook on war and, although at that time they still represented a triumphant Luftwaffe, they had no illusions about their current target. Some of them had been in the Battle of Britain and most, apart from new intake, had recently been in Russia. One of them, later shot down and hospitalized at Mtarfa said: 'It was great fun fighting the Russians, one being able to destroy usually four or five aircraft in a day.... My CO has forty victories, and my No. 1 on this last flight is a man with twenty-eight victories.'[6] If Malta was an objective which Fliegerkorps X had been unable to take, then their successors were determined to prove it was within their capability. Like most fighting men they lived almost entirely within their own world. They thought little of Sicily, and the winter there this year was as cold as anywhere in Europe — though not as cold as it would be in Russia. On 4 January Blenheims out of Malta had attacked Castel Vetrano airfield and destroyed a number of German planes, the raid being followed up the same night by Wellingtons which left many more burning and had blown up a petrol dump. Malta was an airfield and a navy base. It was disrupting the German campaign in North Africa and as such had to be neutralized prior to invasion. Invasion was still considered the real objective and Operation Hercules was very much talked about, even though there was a tacit feeling among the Germans that their allies would be unable to cope with their side of the bargain. If the latter felt an almost feline distaste for the island, the Germans as the year wore on were to acquire an implacable resentment of it.

The fourth party in this siege, the British, had by now become so much part of the island — from, among many other units, the 2nd battalion of the Devonshire Regiment (who had been there since 1939) to the men of the Hampshire and Cheshire Regiments who had landed from Alexandria in February 1941 — that they were as native to the scene as the King's Own Malta Regiment or the Royal Malta Artillery. The one thing they had to endure that the Maltese did not, was absence of mail from home. When mail did get through (sometimes in submarines) it was invariably many weeks late, and many of these men came from industrial cities, ports, or London itself; places under constant attack. Anxiety about their families fuelled their resentment of the war itself. For in all those years it was the condition of war, and therefore of those who had instigated it, which provoked the deepest hatred. No one could actually grasp the loathsome Cerberus head of that monster, but it was represented by every attacking plane. The man who was defending from this small, strange island his own very different and distant one was not in fact weakened in morale by absence from home, but lent an additional vehemence that even his Maltese neighbours at the guns, who saw their own homes being smashed, could hardly feel. More often than not — and this was especially true of those living in pill-boxes on the coast or out in country districts — they had already been adopted by local families. They had in their own phrase 'their feet under the table somewhere' — not that there was likely to be any more to eat at a cottage table than there was on an empty packing case at the back of a gun emplacement.

Christmas 1941 — the day itself, but only the one day — was again observed by both sides. It in no way resembled the previous year's. Everything was much harder, townscapes had changed, and damage and deaths had accumulated. Children's parties were given wherever possible, rations had been saved, and there was still drink for the adults (rum which mysteriously disappeared from naval stores seemed to turn up in strange bottles all over the island). Toys for the children had seemed an insuperable difficulty, except for repainting old ones and passing them from one family to another. This was one of the more easily solved problems of the time.

Now the hours of leisure of the soldier in the garrison were very difficult to fill. Transport was out of the question owing to the petrol rationing, and the vast majority found themselves stuck in the middle of the country with only five or six companions, living in what are known as Elephant Shelters. The CRA [Commanding Officer Royal Artillery] seized upon this and said: 'The Gunners will make toys.' The result was the day before Christmas a most magnificent collection of toys (over two thousand were on view) all made by the soldiers out of their own local resources. They ranged from accurate scale models of MTBs down to the inevitable Spitfire and motor cars, and included two magnificent forts, complete with model soldiers, made from bully beef tins, and one working model of the interior of a theatre.... The ingenuity that the soldiers had displayed was something to marvel at, and there were very few of the toys that Hamleys would

137

not have been proud to sell in the days of extravagance before the war.'[7]

The previous Christmas season had witnessed that rarest of all sights in Malta, a sprinkle of snow over the high ground, but this year was marked by something almost equally unusual, steady rain. After the dark shut down — crisply as it does in that latitude — the black-out, the shelter life, the absence of entertainment, and all-night raids, the hunger and the cold were almost insupportable. And now, as if the elements themselves conspired, the damp permeated house and shelter and worn winter clothes. In the records of the island those months of 1941-1942 are known as 'The Black Winter'.

CHAPTER TWENTY-ONE

Raids and Rain

In the old days when they brought up the great siege guns, man-handling them into position and laying them carefully to concentrate on one weak part of the wall, the besieged knew exactly what to expect. Day after day the bombardment would go on, frightening at first, then monotonous, then frightening again as it became clear that the wall was collapsing. Then the besieged would look beyond the smoke and the guns and see what they expected to see — the massing lines of the enemy waiting for the bombardment to lift as a breach opened in the wall and the ravaged city beyond shone through against the sky. That was the sight that made the waiting soldiers suddenly spill forward at the shining prospect of plunder. But more often, and especially if the besieged were well ordered as at Rhodes in 1530 and Malta in 1565, the investing troops would be met by the sight of yet another wall — constructed by the defenders out of torn houses and the remnants of the perimeter. All was to do again.

The chronicles of such sieges tend to make monotonous reading for, except for brilliant and savage incidents — like fireworks against a summer night — they are little more than the sound of the metronome of war steadily beating.

Monday 18 June: The bombardment of St Elmo continued, two further cannon having been added to the battery firing on the Spur. Ceaselessly by day and night, these guns kept up their fire. *Tuesday 19 June*. The new Turkish battery was almost ready. Their trenches had gone so far that our men, drawing water to throw on the breastworks, were now in great danger. So many of them were killed that there was little hope of getting any more water. During the night a small powder mill in St Angelo caught fire. It blew up and killed eight men who were working or sleeping there....[1]

These extracts from the diary of Francisco Balbi di Correggio, a Spanish arquebusier who fought in the siege of 1565, tell us as much, or as little, as do accounts written in 1942.

The sirens sounded and we manned our gun. We did not have long to wait before the heavy AA guns gave us the direction of the first wave of twenty-five planes and as soon as they commenced their dive another twenty-five came in from the opposite direction. Now dust clouds were blowing over from the centre of the city, which had taken the brunt of the attack. We could not see or hear anything above the noise of the world's most formidable barrage; stones were falling, shrapnel coming down like rain and planes dropping from the sky. It was terrifying, and more planes were coming in. We saw very little of this wave because of the clouds of dust which now enveloped us.

The latter was written by Bernard Gray, a journalist from the *Daily Mirror*, who had smuggled himself into the island aboard a bomber from England and who was greeted by an icy Governor Dobbie with the words: 'We would rather have had a sack of potatoes than you.' Later, in an equally determined endeavour to get himself to Alexandria to join the army in the desert, Gray inveigled a berth aboard a submarine bound for Egypt, but this time he was unlucky — the submarine never arrived.[2]

The main difference between the records of the earlier siege and those of the Second World War was that the attack now came from the air and that, instead of curtain-walls and bastions protecting the enceinte of a fortress or a fortified township, fighter planes provided the outer defence, and artillery the inner wall. The whole island was now the fortress although, even as in 1565, the heaviest blows still fell on certain selected points. The account of air raid after air raid can have little meaning to those who have not experienced them, and every raid was as individual as a fingerprint — even though it was directed at the same specific target area. A bad raid, to be remembered and talked about by one man or one group of people, was clearly one where the action was in his or their vicinity. The overwhelming impression conveyed by all was the hurricane of noise — the barrage itself, as it were, providing the main scream of the great wind; and the diving roar, falling bombs and collapsing buildings being the heart of the storm where the hurricane walks through a city, smearing houses over streets and wiping out landmarks with a casual hand.

'The towns and villages lay much in ruins. The heavy limestone blocks of which the houses were constructed were vast heaps of rubble. Whole streets were blocked and areas cut off.'[3] And again, 'The once beautiful harbour had become a foul lake of wrecks and more than ever a dangerous gauntlet to run. . . . Docks, wharves and store houses were now rubble of cordite grey stone, the once white stone buildings were scarred, looking like eyeless sockets where bombs had struck.'[4]

The simple record in itself tells everything — and nothing: 'On January 14 1942, there were 14 alerts in the space of 19 hours, lasting in all 9 hours; and on February 7 the Island had 17 alerts within 24 hours.' On 25 February the *Times of Malta* (which sometimes appeared with its edges damaged by fire) wrote: 'For some eighty days now there has been a period of almost continuous alerts. With few respites, days and nights have been enlivened with the sound of tense air battles, anti-aircraft guns in action, and the whistling and crash of falling bombs.' On 15 February the Regent Cinema in Kingsway, the main street of Valletta, received a direct hit and an unknown number of civilians and servicemen were killed.

The world is not contained by facts and figures; they do not contain emotion. Blake drank damnation to Newton for explaining the rainbow, but the great mathematician never for a moment explained or conveyed what the sight of that tenuous peacock arc has meant to myriads of human generations on the face of the earth. Perhaps a few fragments from an unrelated source convey better something of what was felt by people who were present in the great siege of Malta 1942.

It was something formidable and swift, like the sudden smashing of a vial of wrath. It seemed to explode all round ... with an overpowering concussion and a rush of great waters, as if an immense dam had blown up to windward. In an instant the men lost touch with each other. This is the disintegrating power of a great wind; it isolates one from one's kind. An earthquake, a landslip, an avalanche, overtake a man incidentally, as it were — without passion. A furious gale attacks him like a personal enemy, tries to grasp his limbs, fastens upon his mind, seeks to rout his very spirit out of him. ... He had struck his head twice; he was dazed a little. He seemed to hear yet so plainly the clatter and bangs of the iron slice flying about his ears that he tightened his grip to prove to himself that he had it there safely in his hand. He was vaguely amazed at the plainness with which down there he could hear the gale raging. Its howls and shrieks seemed to take on, in the emptiness of the bunker, something of the human character, of human rage and pain — being not vast but infinitely poignant. ... The heavy iron plate turned on its hinges; and it was as though he had opened the door to the sounds of the tempest. A gust of hoarse yelling met him: the air was still; and the rushing of water overhead was covered by a tumult of strangled throaty shrieks that produced an effect of desperate confusion. ... Pieces of wood whizzed past. Planks, he thought, inexpressibly startled, and flinging back his head. At his feet a man went sliding over, open-eyed, on his back, straining with uplifted arms for nothing: and another came bounding in like a detached stone with his head between his legs and his hands clenched.[5]

Perhaps Joseph Conrad, writing about a typhoon in another century and another sea, conveys something like the actuality of being caught in a bad air raid better than any contemporary, let alone columns of statistics. Yet the *fact* of two-hundred and sixty-two air raids in January and two-hundred and thirty-six in February is something that one must attempt to understand to obtain any idea — or to grasp however remotely — what that siege was like. Aboard ships under heavy air attack men sometimes jumped overboard — a fruitless exercise since either the ship would survive and sail on, leaving the man to drown, or the bursting bombs would kill him with their metal and the compression of the exploding sea. Off an island there was nowhere to jump, any more than there was aboard a ship. True, Malta could not sink — although there were some in those days who recalled an old story that Malta was like the head of a mushroom, supported on a slender stalk of rock which would one day become eroded by the constant surging of the sea and the head would fall back into the depths from which it had once sprung.

Worse in some ways than the bombing was the wet. Mediterranean buildings, especially in Malta where they were all of stone, are damp, draughty, and cold in the winter. Built to an open-plan design to accommodate six months of sunshine, four of which are like the torrid zone, with marbled, tiled or stone floors, they are not built for warmth. Windows and doors dry out and warp over the long summer, the carpenters working often with indifferent woods are not highly skilled like the stone masons, and icy draughts abound. Many a traveller shivering in Seville, Algiers, Malta, Athens or Istanbul during the winter months has cursed the roseate enthusiasm of travel agents. Malta, exposed to every wind that blows over the central Mediterranean, mops up the rain and breathes out damp — especially in a winter as wet as that of 1941-2.

A temperature of forty-five degrees Fahrenheit which, as a thermometer reading would occasion no concern in a northern country, can produce aguelike shakes unless one is warmly clad as for wintry Scotland. Yet the Mediterranean peoples never seem to be prepared for the winter months, never have adequate winter clothes, nor proper heating for their houses. They endure the winter as the inhabitants of Britain endure the summer, on the six or seven yearly occasions when the latter get anything approaching the Mediterranean norm. In besieged Malta, where most of the residential areas had by now suffered bomb damage, and those houses fit to be occupied had often lost windows, doors or other fittings, living conditions were horrendous. Except for some of the grand houses, the Mediterranean *palazzi* to be found in Mdina, Sliema and other select parts of the island like Lija and Balzan, fireplaces were almost unknown — the shortage of wood and high cost of coal having always made them almost exclusive to the well-to-do. As has been seen, it was difficult to find wood even for firing the bread ovens, and in 1942 an organization was set up to collect wood officially from the débris of ruined buildings. (Over twenty tons a day was being collected all over the island by the midsummer of 1942.) Coal gas for lighting and fires, only found in Valletta and other central areas, soon became unavailable. Electric heaters were practically unknown and in any case the electricity itself was uncertain, even when it was not completely cut off. Kerosene was the only reliable form of heating and lighting, and kerosene was strictly rationed. In the shelters families slept huddled together to try and escape the all-pervading cold and damp.

The weather, so maleficent to the health and spirits of underfed people, was almost equally damaging to the island's striking role. It was true that the submarines had not suffered badly from the air attacks as yet, and such surface forces as remained (including two cruisers) were still operational, but the airfields had never been designed to carry their current load. They were without efficient bays or pens, and were constantly under bombardment. In the third and fourth weeks of January, when Rommel was making a reconnaissance in force in the desert — and a convoy vital to him was being escorted to Tripoli — one-hundred and fifty sorties were made against the island. Quite apart from this, the weather again — although on occasions it limited the enemy's attacks — markedly reduced Malta's air striking power. Gales, torrential rain and much low cloud persisted throughout January, and the fighter airfields of Hal Far and Ta Qali became waterlogged, necessitating the transfer of fighters to the constantly attacked and overcrowded main bomber airfield at Luqa. All this meant that during the British army's final advance in January the amount of supporting sorties out of Malta was reduced by at least thirty per cent.

A problem peculiar to Malta because of the smallness of the island was that if the weather suddenly closed down over the air bases — as it did so often at that time — there were no other landing grounds to which aircraft could be diverted. A big island like Sicily had airfields in various places, where completely different local climate and visibility might obtain, but Malta, 'unsinkable' though it might be, suffered from the same deficiency as any aircraft carrier alone in the sea. Meteorological information was unobtainable from any source outside the island, which meant that the maximum weather forecast could cover no more than six hours. The result was that aircraft away on missions often had to be recalled at the threat of any change. Weather records from that winter show bad weather, lashing winds and cold rain very often and, at the turn of the year, violent electrical storms. The same weather that often grounded aircraft in Malta might let through bombers from Sicily which, having completed their mission, were able to use the cloud cover to make good their escape.

With no battleships to give cover to convoys for Malta from the eastern end of the sea and with no aircraft carrier for the Gibraltar end, it might have seemed that Malta was cut off. But, so long as the British army held Cyrenaica and the airfields on that coast, cover could still be provided by planes from North Africa and Malta combined. This was shown in the mid-January convoy when three merchant ships out of four managed to reach Grand Harbour; the fourth which had developed engine defects and had been diverted to Benghazi was hit in a dive-bombing attack and had to be sunk as she was carrying large quantities of ammunition. A destroyer was also torpedoed and sunk by a U boat, but all in all the ability to get ships through when the island was under such heavy attack was some encouragement to the authorities, as well as the people on the bastions and waterfront, and was a tribute to the cooperation between the island and the desert air force.

Admiral Cunningham was writing to the Admiralty at the time stressing that 'the employment of airforces in maritime operations should provide sufficient aircraft to give us control of the Central Mediterranean where at present we have no battleship. It is vital that the number of aircraft should be apparent to the enemy immediately to hide our weaknesses from him, which, if known, would permit him to establish himself in his objective in such a way that it would be impossible for us to regain our present position.' He was concerned at the drain on his forces imposed by the new requirements in the Far East and was well aware that the invasion of Malta was still a possibility, especially now that he had no capital ships to oppose the Italians. 'If we fail to deter the enemy's heavy ships during the next months from establishing control of the Mediterranean, he will achieve reinforcements of his forces in North Africa, be in a position to secure Malta and endanger our Middle East forces.' Looking ahead in an accurate prophecy he wrote: 'Our return to Europe can be obtained from North Africa and it is in Europe that we must defeat Germany. For this reason we must consider the retention of control of this theatre as our main objective.'[6] Retention of control meant retention of

144

Malta, for without the island the whole sea and probably the war was lost.

With Force K reduced to the *Penelope* and three destroyers, and with the island airfields largely out of action through constant bombing and the heavy weather, the inevitable had been happening on the Libyan convoy route. Escorted on one occasion by the whole Italian battle fleet, and regularly by heavy cruisers and one battleship, the convoys had been getting through and the Axis forces were regaining their strength in fuel, fresh armour and reinforcements. The British on the other hand were now at the full stretch of their supply line in the desert, and the most westerly port, Benghazi, had been so badly damaged by earlier British bombing that it was taking a long time to get it serviceable again. As happened more than once in the desert war, one side built up supplies and threw the enemy back; then in its turn it became over-extended, and the enemy with shortened lines of communication built up his supplies and the seesaw shifted once again.

Malta was the pivotal point of this movement and when, as now, its striking power was almost exhausted, the inevitable could be expected. With adequate fuel and fresh armour Rommel struck in the desert on 21 January, and eight days later Benghazi was retaken. By 6 February the British had fallen back to a line a few miles to the west of Tobruk, and most of Cyrenaica was lost. This meant that any convoys from Alexandria to Malta must now pass through the corridor dominated by Crete in the north and Axis airfields on the Benghazi hump in the south. Malta was to outward appearances suppressed and, in the face of overwhelming airpower and threatened by the only battlefleet in the Mediterranean, might expect an invasion.

CHAPTER TWENTY-TWO

Awaiting Invasion

In a New Year broadcast to the people of Malta the Governor had anticipated likely events by giving detailed instructions of what was to be done in the event of invasion. Church bells, which had previously been rung to indicate the local all clear after air raids, would now only be rung when invasion was imminent. This would be a clear enough signal to everyone wherever they were, since Malta has hundreds of churches, and none but the stone deaf could have escaped the clamour of them all sounding together. Everyone should preferably stay at home, but at any rate within their own villages or towns, and the streets were to be immediately cleared. The protection officers in each area would be kept informed by the central government and would be in local control. This protection office organization had been set up in 1940, quite separate from the special constables and air raid wardens, and was composed of responsible citizens — very often members of the judiciary or the medical service, and invariably assisted by the parish priests. They already had powers to requisition buildings for housing refugees, to order the construction of air raid shelters, and some control over the issue of essential commodities through their local shops. They were now to be provided with stores of provisions to cope with any immediate emergencies in their districts. As in Britain, signposts and milestones had long since been removed or defaced, and in any case an invader trapped within the Daedalus-type maze of most Maltese towns and villages would have been as lost — and probably as dead — as an unwelcome visitor from the Barbary Coast three-hundred years before.

Operation Hercules was indeed being discussed at Axis headquarters, and before the spring was out would have been the subject of talks between Hitler and Mussolini in person at the Berghof on 30 April. A curious thing about this meeting of the two dictators and their staffs (and one which shows how badly coordinated was the Axis High Command) was the fact that, although there were generals and field marshals present, there were no admirals from either side. Since Operation Hercules was high on the agenda, this seems surprising to say the least, but may be no more than an indication that Hitler never regarded the assault and capture of

Malta as feasible. The Italians pressed for an early invasion, and indeed this was the best moment that could possibly have been chosen. However, despite the reduction of the British Mediterranean fleet, Malta's RAF bombers, Fleet Air Arm torpedo planes, and submarines had given the Italian naval authorities sufficient respect for the island's capabilities against surface ships without any naval threat being necessary to deter them. Despite all the arguments put forward in its favour, Hitler still regarded the operation with scarcely concealed mistrust. He could see from the many aerial photographs that the island was quite unsuitable for glider landings, and its massive fortifications — few of them, in fact, later than the eighteenth century except the Victoria Lines — were hardly designed to inspire confidence in a would be aggressor.

Hitler probably felt that by diverting Luftwaffe forces and U boats to the Mediterranean theatre he had done as much as he could at the moment afford. Let Rommel get his major offensive, code-named 'Theseus', under way in the desert and then, presuming on its success, there would be time to consider 'Hercules' again. By the end of April, however, relying on Kesselring's confidence that 'Malta was completely neutralized', he was prepared to come to an agreement with Mussolini that an assault on Malta should indeed take place, but after Rommel's offensive in the desert which was designed to begin on 26 May. Rommel was eager to advance right into Egypt, but the Italians were more cautious (knowing the difficulties of the supply routes) and a compromise was reached. If all went well, the desert offensive should halt on the Egyptian border before the end of June, after which everything was to be turned against Malta. The preliminary date for the island's invasion was fixed for 10 July.

What Hitler principally mistrusted about the operation against Malta was that it must be largely an Italian affair — troops, ships, embarkation points — and thus he had good reason to anticipate failure. The war must be won in Russia. Let the German and Italian air forces continue softening up Malta to such an extent that it was completely suppressed which, Kesselring notwithstanding, he still somewhat doubted. He was indeed eager to see Rommel in Egypt and to establish that other pincer to the east of his great adversary, but not at the expense of some costly air and seaborne expedition which the Italians might mismanage. On the surface, however, Italian pride must not be ruffled and their natural concern about the serious losses to their navy and merchant fleet, occasioned by the British presence in the island, must be soothed by the promise of future action *after* success in the desert.

Essential fuel supplies were still reaching Malta, though a bare minimum, by fast single ships like the *Breconshire* and *Glengyle*, but they could only enter or leave during the dark hours. Daylight was dominated by dive bombers and fighters from Sicily, the latter having so much confidence now through the lack of fighter opposition that even small villages were terrorized by lone fighters swooping down their dusty streets and spraying anything that moved with machine-gun fire. A fleet destroyer, *Maori*, one of the few remaining to escort the *Penelope* if this survivor of Force K was to provide protection for an incoming convoy, was hit and sunk in Grand Harbour. The submarine base on Manoel Island was under very heavy attack, land mines having destroyed much of the shore facilities and living quarters. The sole fleet minesweeper left in operational order was riddled with machine-gun bullets and could only be used at night. The first part of the Luftwaffe's task — putting the airfields and the aircraft out of action — seemed well on the way. A minimum of four ships a month had been calculated as necessary to keep Malta functional, a target which had been fulfilled in January but which looked increasingly difficult with almost every day that passed in the following month. In an endeavour to get away the *Breconshire* and three empty merchantmen from Malta during the dark of the moon, and at the same time run in a convoy, Cunningham despatched the anti-aircraft cruiser *Carlisle* and eight destroyers as close escort to three fast freighters on 12 February. Not one merchant ship reached Malta. The Axis airfields now commanding the whole of the Benghazi bulge meant that any convoy was almost a whole day west of Crete without any fighter protection, and the amount of fighter cover that might be expected from Malta in the last, closing phase of the convoy operation grew thinner day by day. Air attack after air attack on a scale that had never been known at sea before (even during the Battle of Crete) ensured that despite the heavy fire put up by the cruiser and the destroyers, first one freighter and then another was sunk by the bombers. The last to go, her engines disabled by the explosion of a near miss, had to be sunk as there was no chance of towing her to Malta before daylight. The only good thing to emerge from this operation was the transfer of the empty ships, including the invaluable *Breconshire*, to the Alexandria force and their safe arrival at that end.

It was hardly surprising that before the end of February new regulations were issued governing the sale of bread and flour. The reason that nothing similar had been attempted before was perhaps the report issued the previous autumn on the whole subject of rationing which had stressed the undesirability of attempting to ration bread, since it was 'the basic diet of the Maltese'. The new regulation meant little more than that families might only buy from the one breadseller with whom they were registered, that no other 'farinaceous foods' (pastries, cakes and biscuits) might be made and that pasta (never so popular with the Maltese as with the Italians) was rationed. This move was, of course, no more than the thin end of the wedge and it was inevitable that bread rationing would have to be introduced before very long. The current black market and the fighting queues at bread shops or bread carts were worse for morale than any rationing could be. Before the end of April the Governor, Sir William Dobbie, would be compelled to announce this unwelcome, but over-delayed legislation.

Some wheat was of course grown on the island, but it could never be enough to feed the population which had mutliplied first of all under the rule of the Knights and then exploded under the improved sanitation, health service, and (not to be forgotten) availability of work made possible by the British. Grain to feed the inhabitants had always been a major problem and the islands had not produced enough to satisfy local needs even before the arrival of the Knights in the sixteenth century. In the past, by a special arrangement (Malta being considered as part of the kingdom of Sicily), the Order of St John had been able to import grain duty free from that island granary of the Roman Empire. Often, though, if there had been bad harvests in the north the galleys of Malta had raided the Moslem North African routes for grain cargoes — and at times had even seized Sicilian ships which were trying to avoid their Malta quota and sell the grain at better prices elsewhere. Famines had not been unknown in those centuries, and the word still held a hereditary menace for the Maltese. Under the British, with their ready supply of cheap grain from the Empire, it had been almost forgotten, but it was to be remembered again in this second siege.

Wheat was now being milled 'to the highest practicable extraction rate' (ninety-five percent) and was then mixed with maize or barley. We have seen how adulteration with potato flour had already become part of the millers' practice, but the bread as now issued came hard to a people whose main item of diet it was, and who were used under normal conditions to hot crusty loaves of white bread. (The bread van's arrival in a Maltese village, scenting the air with its loaves straight from the baker's oven, is still one of the great daily occasions in village life.) Now it was becoming dark and tough — and early in May it would be rationed to under half a rotolo (less than 14 ounces) per person.

Food was already beginning to occupy people's thoughts to the exclusion of almost everything, except self-preservation. Potatoes, after their introduction by the first British commissioner Alexander Bell (one of Nelson's captains) early in the nineteenth century, had become one of the island's principal crops and in the 1930s had even

149

become a major export. But in 1942 the entire potato crop had to be bought over by the Government and then reissued at a low, subsidized price on a ration. Because potatoes would not germinate in Malta's soil the seed had always to be imported and the loss of a ship carrying the whole seed crop for 1942 led to an acute shortage.[1] Unlike the inhabitants of northern cities during the war the Maltese were not short of vitamin C, but even here, on an island which is normally a market garden for fruit and vegetables, there was very little to be had.

Whole areas had been taken over by the military, farms destroyed by bombing, labour was short because of the call up of so many young men, and in the spring of 1942 hardly any part of the island was safe for men out in the open during daylight hours. The roaming fighters from Sicily would even come down to sea level and turn and fly up the *wieds* or rocky gulleys to machine gun the cement pill boxes often placed to command their approaches — and peasant shooting was all part of the day's excursion over Malta.

As the siege grew steadily worse through that terrible spring and summer even the simplest foods grew as scarce as luxuries once had been. *Soppa ta l'Armla*, Widow's Soup (so called because even the poorest peasant's widow had been able to make it with the aid of the small plot at the back of her house) became a gourmet's dream. It consisted of whatever vegetables were available, one egg (dropped in at the last moment just before eating) and a small ricotta cheese made from sheep or goat's milk. But eggs were almost priceless, one bean could cost a penny, and the familiar herds of goats that were part of the Maltese landscape had sadly dwindled, or vanished into the hills and remote hamlets. No longer did they come every morning in their dozens right into built-up areas like Sliema and Valletta, their full bags swaying, up and down the man made steps and alleys to be milked into cans at the doorsteps. (In Valletta, where some of the houses were many storeys high, they had even been taken up hundreds of stairs to the doors of the sick or bedridden.) Pigs and rabbits had vanished — or were guarded with a shotgun — and cats, which can look very like rabbits (once skinned, with head and tail removed) turned up in many a pot. Later in the year the fruit of the prickly pear as well as the carob bean, usually animal fodder, were as sought after as the normally abundant fruit of the island. The weather that year was bad for the citrus trees and, sheltered as so many of them were in narrow valleys of old worked-out stone quarries, they were either ruined by rain or plundered.

One of the curiosities of the siege was the fact that among the imported goods so urgently required in the cargo ships was tinned fish — principally sardines and tunny, especially asked for indeed as being, 'the principal food of workmen'. It might have been thought that an island could supplement its rations by a little fishing; but no fishing boats could venture out and there were few enough afloat (most having been sunk at their moorings or destroyed in bombed buildings around the Marsa at the far end of Grand Harbour), and there were very few fish to be caught at any time. The Maltese islands, being situated on the submarine ridge separating the eastern from the western Mediterranean, have no fishing banks near, and the two best fish to be caught in the vicinity, the *lampuki* and the *dentici*, are both seasonal. Boat fishing by night was impossible, since a flare or acetylene lamp was needed to attract squid or flying fish. The water of the Mediterranean, in any case, is biologically exhausted and too saline ever to support fish like the great oceans. Except in a few places — and Malta is not one of them — the *frutti di mare* which rejoice the traveller are far from abundant, and the swordfish of the Messina Strait and the tunny which annually come close to the coast of Sicily to spawn do not venture this far south.[2]

Shortage of goat's milk led to increased demand for tinned milk, the sweetened condensed milk in particular being very popular with mothers for their children. (The wartime acquired taste for tinned milk never deserted the islanders and even many years later, when cows' milk was available as well as goats', many still preferred tinned milk in their tea or coffee.) The increasing shortage of local meat and the limited amounts of frozen meat available meant an even greater call for tinned meat — principally corned beef. Like most Mediterranean southerners the Maltese were never large meat eaters, but even so the shortage was so acute that no animal was safe unless guarded. A countryman going in his cart up steep Rinella Hill in Kalkara village during an air raid suffered the misfortune of his horse slipping and falling between the shafts. Being unable to get the horse to its feet and finding no one around, since the people were all in the shelters, he went home on foot to get one of his sons to help him. When they got back the road was still deserted, with the cart in the middle of it — but the horse had gone. He never expected to see it again between the shafts of any other cart.[3]

Throughout this period, with the airfields steadily deteriorating despite the incessant work put in on them by British soldiers and Maltese Pioneers, Malta still maintained its other important role as a posting station for aircraft flown from Britain to the Middle East. Night after night, landing often under incredible conditions, this steady traffic flowed through to build up vital reinforcements for the desert war. Not only fighting planes came this way, but all the time that 'merchant service' of the air, the British Overseas Aircraft Corporation, flew in unarmed planes bringing essential supplies to the island and taking out sick and wounded so as to relieve the pressure on the local hospitals. Air Vice-Marshal Lloyd, the air officer commanding in Malta at that time, had already signalled his superior in Cairo that the situation in Malta was becoming increasingly serious — continuous alerts, aircraft on the ground being damaged yet again while awaiting repair, and seventeen Wellingtons at that moment undergoing repair and therefore unserviceable for night bombing raids. The Hurricanes, as had always been known, were outclassed by the new Messerschmitts and, although they still fought on without respite, he had to report that the enemy was rapidly achieving air superiority. He made a most urgent request for some Spitfires. Almost at the same time Admiral Cunningham was reporting to the chiefs of staff that unless something could be done about the air situation over Malta, and the military situation in Cyrenaica improved, it would seem useless to try to pass a convoy through to Malta. The reply he received was that Malta was of such importance as an impediment to the enemy's supply line and as an air staging post to the Middle East that almost any steps were justified to hold it and that 'no consideration of risk to ships need deter you'.

Cunningham by this time had few enough ships to risk, but the combination of his signal and the Air Vice-Marshal's as well as the Governor's regular reports on island conditions were to have some effect. First of all, a change in the responsibility for Malta, which had previously been divided between the Governor, and the naval and air commanders-in-chief in the Middle East, now placed all the troops in Malta under the Commander-in-Chief, Middle East. This meant that all three commanders-in-chief now shared the responsibility for the island, thus ensuring a high degree of cooperation between the three services which was to be very clearly demonstrated in the matter of the next convoy that was run to the island. The second result of these urgent signals was that the Air Ministry at last allocated Spitfires to Malta. Force H in Gilbraltar, which still had no armoured-deck modern carrier capable of being risked within range of the Axis air forces, was nevertheless augmented by two old prewar carriers, the *Argus* and *Eagle*. On 7 March, from a position well clear of the central Mediterranean (slightly south-east of Mallorca), fifteen Spitfires were flown into the island. All arrived safely.

An eye witness remembered: 'They came in waggling their wings as if to say "Okay, boys, we're here".' The war-torn Hurricanes were up above to cover their landing, forcing away Messerschmitt intruder patrols. Their arrival of course had not passed unnoticed in Sicily, and that night all hell broke loose over the airfields. The

Maltese knew about their coming, probably long before the first shining distinctive shape of the world's most famous fighter was seen heading in from the sea over the island's cliffs. They had to wait three days before they first saw them go into action.

On 10 March the superiority that the Messerschmitts had held over the Hurricanes was established over them in their turn. Crowds were out in the streets and on the ramparts again, just as they had been in the early days, clapping and cheering at the dogfights overhead. Two Messerschmitts were shot down, there were two probables, and one damaged. Sixteen more Spitfires were flown in before the end of the month. But Field Marshal Kesselring had ordered his chief of staff, Marshal Deichmann, to commence the final all-out onslaught on the 20th. Everything was to be devoted to the suppression of Malta, regardless of cost in men or machines. Fliegerkorps X was to be diverted even from its duties in the eastern Mediterranean and the desert for this purpose. The hope that the Spitfires brought the islanders was temporary and illusive.

CHAPTER TWENTY-THREE

Convoy

On the very day that the deadline had been set by Kesselring for the all-out blitz to begin, a convoy sailed from Alexandria destined for Malta. There were three fast freighters, the *Clan Campbell* (knocked out of the February convoy by bomb damage), the *Pampas*, the Norwegian *Talabot*, and the battle-seasoned *Breconshire*, a ship that was by now a household name on the island. The anti-aircraft cruiser *Carlisle* and six destroyers formed the close escort, while Rear-Admiral Vian in *Cleopatra* together with two other light cruisers, *Dido* and *Euryalus*, and four destroyers provided the covering force. In advance of the convoy 'Hunt' class destroyers carried out an anti-submarine sweep westward towards Tobruk. This type of mass-produced, small destroyer with its six high-angle, four-inch guns housed in twin mountings, and equipped with Oerlikons and pom-poms, was the backbone of many a wartime convoy. In the Mediterranean, where anti-aircraft firepower was all important, they proved their worth over and over again.

As evidence of the close cooperation of the three services to facilitate the passage of these ships to the island, numerous diversions, feint attacks and bombing raids were carried out. The army made an advance to threaten enemy airfields in the desert, the Long-Range Desert Group raided landing grounds far back behind the Axis lines, while the R.A.F. attacked airfields in Crete and Cyrenaica to keep aircraft grounded. Fighter cover was provided as far out as possible over the Mediterranean, and the small port of Derna on the Benghazi bulge was attacked two nights running. These diversions all played their part in securing for the convoy and its covering force a most welcome and unusually trouble free passage through 'Bomb Alley', the area between Crete and Cyrenaica. One of the 'Hunt' class on the sweep ahead of the convoy was torpedoed and sunk by a U-boat in daylight on the 20th, but otherwise their progress towards Malta was undisturbed. It was not unobserved, however, for Junkers transport aircraft flying on a regular route between Crete and Cyrenaica inevitably spotted the undulant wakes of the merchantmen on the clear sea and the crisp wave patterns of the destroyers zigzagging around them. That was on the evening of the 21st.

Not long after midnight on 21-22 March the Malta submarine P36 on patrol off Taranto reported that destroyers and heavy ships were leaving the harbour. Admiral Iachino in his flagship *Littorio* — nine 15-inch guns and twelve six-inch guns — was putting to sea in company with two heavy 8-inch gun cruisers, *Gorizia* and *Trento*, the light cruiser *Bande Nere*, and four destroyers. They headed southward to intercept the convoy.

At 8 a.m. on the morning of the 22nd Vian was joined by the six-inch cruiser *Penelope* and the fleet destroyer *Legion* from Malta. His force was now complete and with the convoy and its close escort headed for Malta, about two-hundred and fifty miles distant — the Ionian Sea to the north and to the south the great gulf of Sirte that sweeps the Libyan shore. They were now beyond range of their fighter escort, heavy ships were out to intercept them, and air attacks might be expected to develop at any moment.

In earlier days Vian would certainly have received further sighting reports from air reconnaissance out of Malta — course, speed and composition of the enemy force at sea. It is evidence of the overwhelming wave that was at that moment engulfing the island that no aircraft could scramble into the sky to follow up the lone report of P36. The air attacks began at 9.30 a.m., Italian bombers coming in against the convoy and its escorts. These were carried out at long range and, deterred by the escorts' fire-power, were of no great concern, nor were similar high-level bombing attacks. It was later in the day that the Luftwaffe was to take over, and then the sporadic alarms of the morning would be quite forgotten. It was later reckoned that throughout that day one hundred and fifty aircraft in all came into action against the convoy.

Rear-Admiral Vian was more concerned about those heavy surface forces that must now be steaming hard to cut him off. He had already made known to his captains that, come what might, 'the convoy would proceed to Malta, even if surface forces made contact'. The pattern of any action that might follow had been long rehearsed, under various circumstances of wind and weather and the constitution of whatever force might oppose them. Hardly perceived as yet by those about to engage in what was tactically the most brilliant naval action of the Second World War, the wind and the weather were about to take a hand. Far away in the desert a *khamsin* was blowing — the dust clouds rising in front of it — a typical spring *khamsin* that would reach Malta as a strong south-east sirocco.

Shadowing aircraft had never left the ships out of sight throughout the day, and at 1.30 p.m. one of them dropped a line of flares across the path of the convoy. This could only be a signal to surface forces which must therefore be fairly close at hand. Forty minutes later

Euryalus reported four enemy ships in sight bearing north-east. They were earlier than Vian had expected but, according to the pre-arranged plan, the convoy under its close escort immediately turned away to the south-west, while Vian's covering force turned north to lay their smoke screen. 'It was blowing a strong breeze from the south-east, which was rapidly freshening, with a rough sea and moderate swell.'[1] The wind laid the smoke clean athwart the advance line of the Italian ships.

The four ships sighted were two destroyers and the two heavy cruisers — out of sight behind them were two more destroyers, the light cruiser *Bande Nere*, and then the *Littorio*. Vian headed his ships in five columns straight for the enemy, while the *Carlisle* and a Hunt class destroyer laid a smoke screen across the wake of the convoy. At a range of 30,000 yards the two Italian heavy cruisers opened fire, which Vian's ships of course were unable to return. The black oily smoke laid by his advancing ships now blew under the strengthening south-easterly steadily in the direction of Malta to the north-west, effectively screening the convoy. After fifteen minutes when his own ships were within range Vian opened fire and there was a brief exchange before the Italians turned away to the north-west. Signalling to the commander-in-chief 'Enemy driven off', he headed back towards the convoy which had by now come under heavy air attack from Junkers 88 and Stuka dive bombers. The Italian withdrawal had been in response to an order from Admiral Iachino — had the British precipitately followed they would have come under the guns of the *Littorio*.

Because of its salinity the Mediterranean sea 'gets up' quicker than any other, and the seas were already heavy, the small destroyers of the escort washing down as they plunged alongside the convoy, the gun crews soaked through as they fought their guns against the attacking aircraft, which in their turn were distracted by the breaking seas and the showers of spray that covered the ships. Even the director range-finders and the bridges of the cruisers, some forty feet above the sea, were seething with high-flung spume. They were in a better condition than the Italians, though, for they were capable of radar ranging, whereas the Italians only had optical range finders which were being obscured as they steamed at full speed to cut off the convoy. At 4.48 p.m. the whole force was in sight to the north-east and shortly afterwards Vian signalled the commander in chief that he was in contact with an enemy battleship, four cruisers and four destroyers. Even after all these years the feelings of Cunningham and his staff far away in Alexandria can be imagined — one broadside from the battleship was more than the firepower of all Vian's ships combined.[2] According to every canon of naval

156

warfare the covering force should be annihilated and the convoy and its lightly armed escorts picked off at leisure.

Vian moved out again towards the Italian ships, the thick smoke behind him rolling densely across the face of the sea — driven to the north-west and screening the opposing warships from one another. Whereas the Italians on the far side of it could not see their fall of shot neither could they risk emerging through the dark curtain for fear of what they might find on the other side. Iachino was rightly unwilling to hazard his heavy ships through a smoke screen, on the far side of which enemy destroyers were waiting. The British on the other hand, both destroyers and cruisers, could emerge briefly from the rolling smoke, fire their guns or torpedoes and then wheel back again into its protecting cover. They were at full risk during those brief moments when they were in view, and Vian's *Cleopatra* was hit on the bridge by a 6-inch shell and her sister-ship the *Euryalus* was near-missed by a 15-inch shell which peppered her with heavy splinters.

Admiral Iachino, wanting to get at the convoy without entering the smoke screen, had two options available. He could either circle around the smoke to leeward by continuing on his south-west course, or he could drive to windward and come round the smoke at the point where it was all the time thinning and clearing away. The wind was now almost gale force and, if he turned to windward to come round the smoke, his ships would have to batter at high speed into a damaging sea and at the end of it, with range finders blinded by spray and ships possibly having suffered weather damage, he might emerge to find a portion of the British waiting. He decided to keep his ships together in a body and work round the smoke screen to leeward from the west. Admiral Vian, however, having considered his counterpart's options, had come to the conclusion that the most seamanlike procedure would be to head windward and come round the smoke where it was failing. Accordingly he divided his cruisers and sent *Penelope* and *Euryalus* to keep an eye on the weather gauge.

At about 6 p.m. Admiral Iachino had almost reached the fraying edges of the smoke to the north-west and decided to stand boldly for the south where the convoy must lie. For nearly half an hour Captain Micklethwait and Captain Poland in command of the two fleet destroyer divisions, boldly moving out with their ships 'like a pack of snapping terriers', raced through the edge of the smoke to fire their torpedoes. At times they seemed to move through a forest of shell splashes as they closed to within 6,000 yards on their run-in, their 4.7 inch guns like toys against the 8-inch and 15-inch shells that were bursting around them. Two destroyers were badly damaged by near misses from the *Littorio* during this part of the action, one having her speed reduced to 16 knots, and the other being temporarily crippled;

but both managed later to reach Malta safely. *Penelope* and *Euryalus* raced back and rejoined the action and the cruisers also fired their torpedoes. There were no hits.[3] Yet the combination of the British destroyers closing to 6,000 yards to attack, a spread of torpedoes fired by the *Cleopatra* crossing the *Littorio's* bows, and a hit on his flagship by a 6-inch shell between his two after-turrets, caused Admiral Iachino to turn away. The wind was now gale force, night was falling, and without radar, the Italian force wisely disengaged and headed northwards. The Battle of Sirte was over.

The convoy, despite the many air attacks it had undergone throughout the day, was still unharmed and its four ships, dispersed under the orders of Captain Hutchinson of *Breconshire*, made their own way at full speed for Malta. Their close escort divided to cover each ship and went with them, while Admiral Vian's force returned to Alexandria to receive the welcome that it deserved. Sirte was a tactical and moral victory that, in its reduced state and with increasingly bad news from the Far East, provided a welcome tonic to the British fleet. The ships as they entered Alexandria harbour bore the marks not only of near misses from heavy calibre shells, but damage from the south-easterly through the teeth of which they had returned. Except for the two badly damaged destroyers that had gone on to Malta, they were all still functional.

The Italians, as they made for home, their morale in no way improved by the day's action, suffered even more severely from the south-easterly as it roared up astern of them into the Gulf of Taranto. Evidence that Iachino had been wise not to steam at full speed into it to gain the weather gauge during the action was provided by the damage that his ships now suffered from this quartering south-easterly. Two destroyers foundered, the *Littorio* shipped thousands of tons of water, and the cruiser *Bande Nere* was sufficiently damaged to require dockyard repair at Spezia.[4] As she was proceeding to this northern port, she was torpedoed and sunk by the submarine *Urge* out of Malta.

If the Italians had not achieved their objective in sinking the convoy they had nevertheless forced it to make a big detour to the south, and this was sufficient to prevent the scattered ships from being able to reach Malta at first light on 23 March as had been planned. Malta was now under the full weight of that onslaught which had started on the 20th and which, despite the weather, did not let up. As Air Vice-Marshal Lloyd put it: 'Every aeroplane in Sicily seemed to be flying round the island.' Despite a lowering dawn aircraft immediately appeared looking for the convoy and they soon found it. Labouring over the grey sea the ships kicked up masses of spray and their torn wakes made them easily visible. Their escorts' ammunition had been so depleted during the previous day's attacks that their reply to attacking planes had to be severely rationed to the planes which came in lowest and seemed most threatening. From dawn onwards all ships came under attack, the *Breconshire*, veteran of so many Malta runs, being hit in the engine room and completely disabled when only eight miles off the island. The Norwegian *Talabot* and the *Pampas*, each accompanied by a destroyer, passed through the breakwater into Grand Harbour between 9 and 10 a.m. Despite the fact that there was an almost continuous air raid in progress — dive bombers swooping, bomb splashes all around, fighters above engaged in combat — the people of Malta were out along the ramparts as the savaged ships came in. Both freighters had been near-missed many times and the *Pampas* had actually received two direct hits from bombs which failed to explode. The people stood and waved and cheered as they moved down the harbour. The fourth ship in the convoy, *Clan Campbell*, was destined never to see Malta. Hit and disabled in the previous February convoy, then towed to Tobruk and repaired in Alexandria, on this occasion she received the *coup de grâce* some twenty miles offshore. She had been under air attack since daylight and was sunk at 10.30 a.m. by a bomb in her engineroom. A Hunt class destroyer stood by her and saved many of the people aboard, but the fleet destroyer *Legion* (which had taken part in the torpedo attack on *Littorio* at 6000 yards) ran out of luck as she steamed to her rescue. Near-missed, she managed to reach Marsaxlokk where she was beached: three days later, having effected temporary repairs, she made her way to Grand Harbour where she was sunk in another dive-bombing raid.

The plight of *Breconshire* — a name that had become synonymous with Malta — was irremediable. All efforts to tow her to Grand Harbour were rendered hopeless by the weather and the depth of her damaged draught. Nearly wrecked on the shoal off Delimara Point in the south-east of the island, she was finally towed into Marsaxlokk where, after being hit yet again and set on fire, she finally rolled over and sank on 27 March. Part of her bottom remained exposed and some of her oil fuel was later saved by fitting valves to it.[5] The outnumbered Spitfires and Hurricanes operating from cratered and ceaselessly attacked airfields had not been able to save her, any more than they or the Malta barrage could save *Talabot* and *Pampas*. Over three hundred bombers and fighters were ordered down from Sicily to see that no ship remained out of the hard-fought convoy.

The *Illustrious* blitz had been more or less one short action directed against one ship, but now the island and its inhabitants reeled under incessant air attack. On the 26th *Talabot* was hit, fire broke out, and she had to be scuttled in Grand Harbour because of danger from ammunition aboard. *Pampas* was also hit and settled on the bottom, but only two of her holds remained unflooded. Apart from the oil fuel later salvaged from the *Breconshire*, only 5000 tons of cargo reached the island out of the original 26,000 tons. Despite the brilliant naval action in the Gulf of Sirte, despite the subsequent courageous battles to get the convoy through to the island, sea power had been defeated by air power.

CHAPTER TWENTY-FOUR

April '42

To effect the passage of three ships out of four to Malta at that time was in itself a supreme achievement. To lose the three ships under the island's protection — two of them in Grand Harbour itself — was intolerable. Any claim that the air force could still provide fighter cover was manifestly untrue. It was also quite clear that there was something disastrously wrong with the system for unloading ships. *Talabot* and *Pampas* had been berthed on 23 March, but it was not until the 26th that they were both sunk. Malta was basically a lighterage port; there were no unloading quays for deep draught ships, and even if there had been they would by now have been a heap of rubble spilled into the harbour. Merchant ships normally made fast to buoys out in the harbour and were then unloaded by dumb lighters towed out to them by harbour tugs. Many of the lighters had now been sunk or damaged as had the tugs, and one of the causes for the delay in moving the *Breconshire* had been the lack of seagoing tugs capable of getting out to her in the weather that was blowing. The efficient unloading methods evolved to deal with all later convoys was the result of the disaster of *Talabot* and *Pampas*, ships which had lain at anchor for nearly twelve hours before systematic unloading had begun at all.

It was clear that if Malta was to survive, a tighter grip needed to be taken on the whole organization of the island, and above all something had to be done to get more and more Spitfire replacements. This, as would be seen, was useless in itself unless the organization for their reception and protection (until battle-worthy and airborne) was as streamlined and improved as the harbour arrangements had to become. How many of the inhabitants of today's large cities, who unwillingly have to live with the acceptance — consciously or subconsciously — of the possibility of their nuclear devastation, can even comprehend, less than fifty years later, what the bombing of London was like in 1940? Uncomfortable thoughts are shuffled out of sight by most people in the same way as the tacit acceptance of their own mortality. How many of the inhabitants of modern cities, it is fair to ask, would even be able to endure — in their termite skyscrapers, totally dependent upon an oil-fuelled civilization — one month of heavy bombing at the level of that experienced by a city like London in 1940?

Malta occupied an area smaller than Greater London. During two months, March and April 1942, the tonnage of the bombs dropped on Malta was twice that dropped on London during the worst whole year of the blitz. In the first half of 1942 there fell such a rain of explosive on that small island that the survivors — children then, or young men and women — cannot even manage to reconstruct it in memory. 'The survivors', as Stewart Perowne wrote in 1968, 'are curiously reticent. Not that they are not willing to furnish any scrap of information which may be of use to a recorder. On the contrary, they will do all in their power to help him. But there is a psychological obstacle to be overcome. The time really is "lost", and it is a hard task to recover it. I feel that myself. After visiting a friend, and going over with him memories of the war, documents perhaps relating to his war duties, I come out into the bright sunlight of Malta at peace, hear the children at play, look down into Grand Harbour from which German and Italian tourists are coming up to admire and to purchase — I find it hard to realize that five minutes ago I was listening to tales of death and destruction, of ruin and survival in this same square, where the flowers grow and transistors howl.'[1]

This is because time really is lost. As T.S. Eliot put it: 'Between the idea/And the reality/Between the motion/And the Act/Falls the Shadow.'[2]

Facts, however little they can really convey, must make their statement. A computer age can recognize them, though not the emotion behind them. During March 1942 there were two-hundred and seventy-five air raids, ninety of them at night, and during April there were two-hundred and eighty-three, of which ninety-six were at night. Malta suffered one-hundred and fifty-four days of continual day and night bombing, whereas the longest number of consecutive days on which London was raided only amounted to fifty-seven. In the Coventry blitz (which gave a temporary verb to the language, 'to conventrate') it is reckoned that two-hundred and sixty tons of bombs were dropped. Six-thousand seven-hundred tons of bombs fell on the towns and installations around Grand Harbour during six weeks of March and April. In the latter month the airfields alone received twenty-seven times as great a weight of bombs as that which fell on Coventry in October 1940. In March 1942 Fliegerkorps II flew four-thousand, nine-hundred and twenty-seven sorties against the island but in April, when Fliegerkorps X also joined in the attack, nine-thousand, five-hundred and ninety-nine sorties were flown. Between 1 January 1942 and 24 July there was only *one* raidless period of twenty-four hours.

162

Except for those who had earlier moved out to the country or been evacuated (three-thousand people had gone to the sister island of Gozo early in the war) the shelter life became for months the norm for all the inhabitants of Valletta and the Three Cities around Grand Harbour. It was hardly surprising that under the crowded conditions and with growing malnutrition as the siege went on many health problems arose. Vitamin deficiency diseases increased, particularly pellagra and ulcerative stomatitis, and there were also cases of rickets and scurvy (something normally unheard of). Trachoma and other eye diseases, not uncommon in an island of dust and blinding light, became widespread. Every type of tuberculosis spread unchecked as might be expected in those living conditions, reaching a peak — along with everything else — during 1942. (Tuberculosis was also a major hazard for the communications personnel housed in the dank tunnels below Lascaris Bastion.) Typhoid, with all its complications, had been on the increase since the beginning of the war but was to reach epidemic proportions during the summer of 1942. Bacillary and amoebic dysentery were its attendants.

All this was inevitable in view of the sanitary problems encountered when masses of people were cooped up in such circumstances, with house drains out of action and main sewers badly damaged by bombing. The disposal of human excreta and household refuse remained a problem until well after the siege was over. In the main shelters water closets were installed whenever possible, although the pail system was generally used in houses and private shelters where water was unavailable. Refugee centres and public shelters could be kept under supervision by hygiene officers, and ablution rooms were organized and walls, floors and beds regularly sprayed with disinfectants and insecticides.

The typhoid epidemic of 1942 started through sewage escaping from fractured sewers due to bombing and infecting cultivated land, as well as through the use in some areas of crude sewage to irrigate the fields. Lice, fleas and bed bugs were common, but scabies was almost the worst medical plague. Benzyl benzoate for the treatment of scabies was often unattainable or at best in short supply and the mites spread throughout the island, even among those who were not shelter dwellers. Many developed septic sores from scratching, and the combination of acute hunger with the itching of scabies has been described by survivors as their most permanent memory of the siege.

All these factors, when combined with permanent nerve strain and anxiety, might have been expected to lead to a great increase in nervous breakdowns and mental illness. Contrary to the expectation of the psychiatrists this was not so, and the behaviour of the besieged

163

in Malta was a surprise to the practitioners of this somewhat ambiguous branch of medical science.

Before the opening of hostilities it was anticipated that the people would react to the horror and havoc of modern warfare in an exaggerated and abnormal manner. It was consequently forecast that the number of psychiatric casualties would be high and beds for 'cases of war neuroses and psychoses' were prepared in special wards at the Mental Hospital at Attard. Subsequent experience, however, showed that this precaution was unnecessary because the factors that were regarded as being precipitants of mental illness did not produce the expected baleful effects on the population. Indeed anxiety for one's personal safety, sudden bereavements, the disruption of family life and the presence of material discomforts and food privation did not react unfavourable on the mental health of the population. Panic and hysteria were absent. A most remarkable feature was the fact that admission to the mental hospital fell to 138 in 1942 from the pre-war figure of 169 in 1939.[3]

As was found in other bombed cities during the war, the inhabitants of this besieged island adjusted themselves to the increased hazards of living. They had been, in the horticultural term 'hardened off' by the first months of the Italian bombing so that, when the Germans really unleashed the full fury of modern war, they were already resistant. (It is a matter for speculation as to what might have been the effect if the Luftwaffe had arrived in force in the summer of 1940.) It is a curious fact, which has been remarked on before, that although the Germans did infinitely the greatest harm to the island and its life the deepest hatred of the people was always directed against the Italians. The Germans were perhaps too remote and too unknown a quantity, whereas the Italians had broken some familiar bond? In general, people lived only for the day and a deep-rooted Mediterranean fatalism, older by far even than the Catholic Church, underlay a superficial reckless gaiety that all newcomers to the scene remarked upon.

Wartime love affairs were not uncommon, and in the atmosphere of 'Carpe Diem' that prevailed it would have been strangely abnormal if they had not been. Yet, in so old-fashioned a society, strictly controlled by an authoritarian Church, they were far fewer than might have been expected or than were usual in, say, a bombed city in western Europe. For one thing privacy was almost unobtainable, and for another poor diet, physical fatigue and sleepless nights under bombardment were hardly conducive to sexual desire. Contraceptives were unknown in so strongly Catholic a society, except to those who had deliberately or accidentally fallen outside of it, and these — except at the level of Strait Street girls — were comparatively few. The Maltese are a handsome race, and the young women — before pregnancies, a starch diet, and a hot climate have swollen them into images of the Mother Goddess — are exceptionally beautiful. They had a good motive to want to marry (the operative word) British servicemen, because this would bring a guaranteed marriage allowance and, later, a family allowance, benefits unknown in their own society. Such marriages were rejected as far as possible by the British authorities because they knew from peacetime experience how few of them lasted. Within a year or two in servicemen's married quarters back in unfamiliar, grey and rainy Britain the wives sought the warmth of their island again, their family and familiar surroundings, and departed together with the children. Being Catholic, there could be no question of divorce.

In Maltese society at every level the strictest of distinction was made between 'good' and 'bad' women, the latter being socially ostracized and if of working class stock more or less driven into prostitution. Naturally endemic in any sea port prostitution had been well known in Malta for many centuries and indeed even as early as 1565 special arrangements were made to transport the island's prostitutes to Sicily before the siege began. A British submarine captain, arriving in the island for the first time in 1942 and naturally ignorant of the prevailing social distinctions, expressed some wonder at the lack of shoreside romance: 'Surprisingly, perhaps, there was little fraternising between the lads and the local beauties, although one or two, after filling themselves with lunatic's broth in a boiled-oil shop did use their rations for a purpose regulations never intended. In the main, however, *l'amour* was kept on a vicarious level by watching highly professional clinches on the ten-year-old films shown at the local cinema.'[4]

By April 1942 the submarines on Manoel Island hardly got ashore at all, in the sense of into Malta itself or Valletta. The island's airfields were so badly damaged that on some occasions not a single plane could get into the air and often six fighters, at the most, were all that were airworthy. To Kesselring it naturally seemed that the first part of his operational plan had been achieved and the second — the destruction of all naval ships and harbour installations — could now be attended to. The defence of the island for nearly two months rested almost entirely on the guns; the British Royal Artillery and the Royal Malta Artillery being stretched as never before by raiders whose confidence was such that for a time they seemed to ignore the losses that they were daily sustaining.

165

Manoel Island, the submarine base, was obviously the principal target and, far from being able to find girls ashore or get drunk in 'boiled-oil' shops, more often than not the crews of the submarines were compelled either to stay on Manoel Island or aboard their submarines, lying submerged in the harbour. To come in from long days on patrol, having been in action and probably depth-charged on more than one occasion, and then to find that far from there being any rest or recreation one was likely to be confined to an islet under constant bombing attack or serving a duty spell in one's 'boat' lying on the bottom and constantly shaken by exploding bombs was not conducive to a high state of morale. Now was the time when those submarine pens, cut deep into the rock of Marsamuscetto (which had often been discussed before the war, though nothing had ever been done about them), would have served their purpose. Later, when Fortress Europe came under attack, Hitler was to see that such bomb-proof submarine pens were built for the U-boats, but then the Germans had the advantage of all the technology and labour force of Europe behind them. The submarines *Unbeaten* and *P36* were both badly damaged while lying submerged off Manoel Island, their crews managing to escape off the bottom. The mine-laying submarine *Pandora*, fortunately after she had delivered her essential supplies, was caught on the surface and sunk by two direct hits. The *P39*, badly damaged by a near miss, was towed round to the dockyard for repair, where she was blown apart by a bomb exploding underneath her. A Greek submarine operating out of Malta was also sunk by bombing and the Polish *Sokol* so badly damaged that she had to be sent to Gibraltar for repair. It was during April that it became known that Wanklyn and his legendary *Upholder* had been lost with all hands, and a fortnight later her sister ship the *Urge* was mined and sank off the island.

The mining by aircraft and E-boats had now reached such proportions that Malta was surrounded by every known type of mine and was practically unapproachable. So long as a passage could be swept through these minefields Captain Simpson, under whose direction the 10th Flotilla had achieved its astonishing record, had been very unwilling to withdraw his vessels. He had pointed out that the 10th Flotilla was all that was left able to take offensive action against the enemy's supply lines, and that it 'was the only remaining means of preventing the enemy from bombarding Malta by heavy surface forces. . . .' By the end of April, however, he was forced to agree to withdrawal because the few minesweepers left in Malta (all damaged) could no longer cope with keeping the approaches clear. It was high time. The submarine crews were getting practically no rest between patrols, servicing the boats was almost impossible, and the current losses from mines and bombing could no longer be sustained.

Early in May, when the last of the submarines had withdrawn, Malta was undeniably on its own. The surface ships had begun to leave after the March convoy when it had become apparent that no corner of Grand Harbour was safe from air attack, the barrage notwithstanding. The cruiser *Aurora* and the Hunt class destroyer *Avon Vale*, both rapidly patched up from bomb damage, sailed for Gibraltar. The destroyer *Gallant* was so crippled that she could not be moved and was laid up alongside a quay to be cannibalized for spares, fittings and metal. The destroyer *Kingston*, overturned by bombing while in dry dock, was later towed round to St Paul's Bay and used as a blockship in the channel between St Paul's Island and the mainland.

The only ship left in Malta from Force K, the cruiser *Penelope*, survived in an almost miraculous fashion — damaged and under repair in drydock, she was attacked time and time again, as *Illustrious* had been. Firing her twin 4-inch guns while in dock (to the extent of wearing them out by the expenditure of six-thousand, five-hundred rounds in two weeks) she was patched up and patched up again. Finally she managed to slip away on the night of 28 April and reach Gibraltar. Nicknamed HMS *Pepperpot* for the hundreds of wooden plugs that sprouted from splinter holes in her hull, *Penelope* had earned her battle honours and, curiously enough, in the same place as a predecessor of her name. In 1799 the frigate *Penelope*, one of Nelson's blockading squadron off Valletta, had shot away the main and mizzen topmasts of the 80-gun battleship *Guillaume Tell*, thus leading to the capture of this last French survivor of the Battle of the Nile.

'April is the cruellest month. . . .' The poet's words, untrue in Malta throughout all previous centuries, were accurate indeed that year. Wild flowers might still be found on the rocky uplands, but everywhere else there was no spring. A pall of dust and smoke compound of pulverized buildings, exploding dumps, gunfire, burning planes and collapsing walls hung over the whole island. Whatever wind was prevailing, a huge yellow dust cloud could always be seen moving away on the lee side of Malta. Sullying the sea, it wavered and turned slowly like a giant spinning top about to fall.

CHAPTER TWENTY-FIVE

A Volcano In Eruption

In the summer of 1565 Francisco Balbi di Correggio had written: '... the island was like a volcano spouting fire. When all of the guns fired simultaneously, the noise and the concussion were such that it seemed as if the end of the world was coming. To show you just how terrible was the volume of noise, it could be clearly heard in Syracuse and even in Catania, one hundred and twenty miles from Malta'. The concatenation of the guns and the bombs, both by day and night, in the spring and the summer of 1942 sounded like a permanent thunderstorm rolling away to the south of Sicily. The disruption of the air fields and the state of the few remaining aircraft was such that there were a number of days in April during which no fighters at all were airborne in the face of the attackers from Sicily.

'For two months during Malta's long air siege, it was anti-aircraft guns alone which bore the brunt of the attack.' British gunners together with some 4000 Maltese were ceaselessly engaged at heavy, light and machine-gun posts all over the island, from the airfields and main defences around Valletta and Grand Harbour to outposts on the coast and Corradino Heights overlooking the Marsa. In February the heavy guns had to be rationed to only three rounds per raid (firing pointer shots to indicate to the other gunners the direction of the approaching aircraft) and even the invaluable all-purpose Bofors guns had to be restricted so that no more than fifty per cent could be in action at any one time — always excluding those protecting any ships in harbour or specially sited for airfield defence.

By mid April the situation was so bad (and no convoy could be expected) that both light and heavy anti-aircraft guns were limited to fifteen rounds per gun per day. The choice of target out of the dozens presented during a typical raid had to be chosen with the greatest care before a single round was fired. For the fighters that got aloft and were either damaged or had run out of ammunition a special 'safe area' was established over Ta Qali airfield below Mdina: as soon as a Hurricane or Spitfire came in sight low over this area it was given full coverage by the guns massed around. As the attack switched from the airfields, when it became apparent that they were almost neutralized, the brunt was borne by Manoel Island

and Grand Harbour. Until the submarines themselves were withdrawn, their base naturally became the main target for attack.

.. it was the Battle of the Guns. There was no gun position more bombed or in a more exposed position than that on Manoel Island. I remember once seeing an intensive attack put in against this gun position which protected the submarine base. The bombs were dropped with great accuracy, and a thousand-pounder scored a direct hit on one of the guns. But even as it burst and the whole area seemed to be covered with black smoke I saw four red flashes burst through the haze. It was the last flash of the gun that was hit, but the other three carried on without cessation or hesitation until the attack was over.[1]

During April one-hundred and two enemy aircraft were certified destroyed by the guns, and about half this number by fighter aircraft. On 10 April Kesselring wrote: 'The aerial attack on Malta has, I feel, eliminated Malta as a naval base ... I intend to carry on with the attack until 20 April.'

Only one thing, it was felt, could enable the island to carry on any longer and that was the delivery of more Spitfires. Air Vice-Marshal Lloyd wrote: 'Malta's need is for Spitfires, Spitfires, and yet more Spitfires.' He sent a distinguished pilot, Wing-Commander Gracie, back to Britain to tell the authorities at first hand what the situation was like. Emphasis has earlier been laid on the difficulty of enabling people to understand the conditions of the siege nearly half a century later, but the fact that it needed a fighter pilot straight from the battlefield to explain to the authorities in London (even though they were in the heart of the war themselves) illustrates the almost unimaginable conditions in Malta. The fruit of all this pressure, and of Governor Dobbie's ceaseless signals to draw attention to the situation, was a signal sent by Winston Churchill to President Roosevelt. Spitfires were indeed available in Britain, but there were no British carriers seaworthy at that moment with the capability of carrying and flying them off. Churchill wrote: 'Air attack on Malta is very heavy. There are now in Sicily about 400 German and 200 Italian fighters and bombers.... Would you be willing to allow your carrier *Wasp* to do one of these [air ferry] trips, provided details are satisfactorily agreed between the Naval Staffs? With her broad lifts, capacity and length we estimate that *Wasp* could take fifty or more Spitfires ...' Roosevelt signalled back: 'Admiral King will advise Admiral Poland that *Wasp* is at your disposal as you request.' This was a good example of the top level accord between Churchill and Roosevelt, and evidence that the latter must have applied the full weight of presidential authority to his request — for Admiral Ernest J. King USN had no great love of the British. As Cunningham was to write later about events in North Africa: 'King always had a rooted antipathy to placing United States forces under British command....' Furthermore, this operation involving *Wasp* meant that British planes would be flying off a US aircraft carrier, and the *Wasp* herself would be the first American warship to enter the European theatre of war on what amounted to a combat mission. Early in April she sailed up the Clyde and preparations went ahead for embarking forty-seven Spitfires. On 14 April the *Wasp* with her precious cargo and her escort sailed south for Gibraltar.

On 15 April King George VI made the unique gesture of awarding the George Cross to the island of Malta, the highest honour, equivalent to the Victoria Cross in military terms, that was his to bestow. The King's citation was announced by the Governor: 'To honour her brave people I award the George Cross to the island fortress of Malta, to bear witness to a heroism and devotion that will long be famous in history. George R.I.'

Medals, which can seem to have little meaning in peacetime — except in the market place — possess in times of war a special aura and, even to the most cynical or disparaging, their statement remains clear: 'I was there — at the sharp end.' This acknowledgement by the King, and therefore by millions of others who heard of it, that the fight being put up by their island was indeed understood and appreciated did at that moment have an appreciable effect on morale.[2] Many are enduring in battle, some are cowardly, a few outstandingly brave, but only a handful of the few ever receive any ackowledgement. After that earlier Great Siege: 'Honours were showered upon Grand Master La Valette by all the kingdoms of Europe. Philip II sent him a jewelled sword and poniard, the hilts of enamelled gold set with pearls and facetted diamonds. *Plus quam valor valet Valette* ran the punning device.' But this was the first time that the Maltese people had ever received a medal.

On 19 April the USS *Wasp* was moving through the Mediterranean to her flying-off position south-east of Mallorca, and at dawn next day the first of her Malta bound Spitfires climbed into the sky and headed for the island. Unattacked and apparently unobserved, *Wasp* turned back for Gibraltar. Out of forty-seven planes that had been embarked forty-six were to reach Malta safely. Unfortunately, unlike *Wasp*, they had been observed.

Since the recollections of one of these pilots, Flt Lt D. Barnham, must echo those of many others who made similar flights during the war, it must stand for all.

The clouds have disappeared now. Empty sea stretches in all directions; but soon a disturbance of colour on the horizon grows steadily nearer. From navigational logic it's just where I expected it to be. We change formation as two islands, like autumn leaves floating in the water, grow larger and larger. The steep cliffs of the smaller and nearer, which must be Gozo with Malta lying beyond it, rush towards us. White walls crinkle a hilltop. The small fields are yellow. Blue water in front of my propeller and, as we cross the channel between the two islands, I can see waves breaking on the sunlit rocks ahead. Then we are leaping inland over the island of Malta.[3]

One after another the planes, upon which so many hopes were based, came in to land — and one after another they were destroyed. When they had left the *Wasp* American Martlet fighters had circled the air above the carrier, giving protection in that far-off part of the sea very distant from the war, but when they came to touch down in the heart of the volcano there was hardly a plane in the sky to cover them. Picked up by German radar on Sicily they were no more than fat pigeons to be seized on the ground by the swarm of fighters, fighter-bombers and dive-bombers that now descended. On that first day over three-hundred planes flew missions down from Sicily. Within seventy-two hours, out of those Spitfires which had been asked for, begged for, and prayed for, not a single one was airworthy. Most had been destroyed on the ground within an hour or so of touching down.

The causes of this disaster were several, but principally it was the condition to which the airfields had been reduced after more than two months of almost continuous bombing. Stone bays, or pens, in which to park an aircraft the moment that it had landed, were broken down, runways were heavily cratered, anti-aircraft defences were overwhelmed, and crash tenders and petrol bowsers destroyed. There was the added fact that repair facilities were inadequate, technicians worked off their feet, and workshops themselves bombed out of existence. Furthermore, although the ground crews and repair specialists were familiar enough with Hurricanes after years of working on them and were expert at cannibalizing crashed machines and using the spares, or even fabricating their own from bits and pieces of scrap, they were more or less completely untrained in the Spitfire. As the Air Officer Commanding wrote later: ' . . . I also wanted at least 200 spare engines. We couldn't run to an aircraft factory for help (the few Hurricane spares we had were useless), and the only answer was another convoy by sea. . . .' A successful operation had ended in total failure, and it was not difficult for those outside the battlefield to point to a great similarity between this new disaster and the one that had befallen the March convoy. On both occasions the supplies had reached the island, but all or nearly all had been immediately lost through the inability of the recipients to protect them, or to get either safely 'unloaded'. The fact was that everything on the island — communications, fuel supplies, transport, essential stores — was breaking down or worn out. Malta had become to a great degree what was implied by the term often used for individuals in those days — 'bomb-happy'. Akin to the state known as shell shock in the trenches of the First World War, it was not so much a failure of nerve as a deadening of nerve, almost an indifference, and indeed an inability to concentrate effectively. Starvation rations, lack of sleep and permanent tension through bombing was quite often coupled with deafness resulting from bomb blast or gun fire. Both the garrison and the islanders were more or less reduced to a zombie-like state: work was still somehow carried out, but lacking the energy that comes with physical health and the drive and initiative that comes from the same source.

The destruction of the Spitfires and the daily evidence that Malta was offering almost no opposition, but was lying supine under the raids, gave Field Marshal Kesselring good reason to think that his objective was attained. The submarines had been withdrawn from the island, the bomber squadron had long gone (the British could not even protect their airfields), no surface ships had been in evidence for many weeks — Malta could therefore be termed 'neutralized'. Demands were being made on him for the transfer of some of Luftflotte II to the Russian front (now opening again after a winter which had savagely surprised the Germans) and more planes were also needed in the desert where Rommel's operation 'Theseus' was scheduled to begin towards the end of May. Convoys were passing easily through to North Africa and reserves of fuel and armour were building up, now that no submarines, surface ships, bombers or torpedo aircraft operated out of Malta.

After success in the desert operation 'Hercules' could take place, but already it had begun to look as if it would not be needed. Yet, if Kesselring was confident enough, there were some doubts, particularly among the Italians, that the island was as harmless as it appeared. They feared its recuperative powers and, judging from the activities of the anti-aircraft guns and searchlights during their night raids, they reckoned that it was still far from safe to risk an invasion. They could hardly believe the propaganda of their own radio at the time of the award of the George Cross: 'This is but one more preposterous deception by the British Government. Had not our unfortunate Maltese brethren been under the heel of British domination, which is being forced on them under the threat of guns and bayonets, we have no doubt as to how the Maltese would behave.' They remembered the reception that their Maltese brothers had accorded their surface forces off Valletta, and they feared that iron-bound rocky coast.

At the very moment when for every possible reason it seemed as if the island would be unable to hold out for much longer, inexplicably — to the defenders — the pressure began to ease. 'One afternoon when the sirens went, instead of low-flying Junkers, five "Black Crows" — as the gunners called the multi-engined Italian bombers — appeared. They flew at an immense height in precise formation, just as they had flown before the Luftwaffe took over. The Germans had had to transfer some of their strength to other fronts; they also needed time for resting and servicing their aircraft. On 29 April there were two-hundred and twenty sorties against the island; on 30 April there were only sixty-eight. These attacks were directed mainly against stores, lines of communication and civilian targets.'[4]

Throughout all these weeks the army had been working along with civil defence and in every variety of activity to try and keep the island operational. Among their many tasks had been constant labour on the airfields; the boring, frightening and repetitive work of filling in bomb craters, rebuilding aircraft pens around the fields, and helping the gunners to patch up the defences of their heavily bombed positions on the perimeter. They, along with the Maltese Pioneers, were the maids of all work of the island and now their efforts were to be especially devoted to ensuring that the next delivery of Spitfires did not meet the same fate as the last. Along the Safi strip, a dispersal air lane designed to take aircraft between Luqa and the airfield at Hal Far (largely built by the army), at Luqa itself, and Hal Far and Ta Qali, the soldiers worked day and night shifts repairing damage and building new dispersal pens. Together with the air force ground staff they had to see that each one of these was a completely self-contained unit, where a Spitfire recently arrived could be made one hundred per cent ready for combat within a matter of minutes. Wing-Commander Gracie, who had been sent back to London to explain the immediate need for fighters on the island and who had himself flown the first Spitfire off *Wasp*, was in charge of the reception committee preparing for the next arrivals.

The easing of the air offensive happened at just the right time for the defenders — a reminder, perhaps, to all who are engaged in besieging a fortress that the time to slacken one's fire is not five minutes to midnight, nor midnight itself, but five past. (Kesselring, through force of circumstances perhaps, had made exactly the same mistake as had Mustapha Pasha in September 1565 when 'the daily

173

slackening of the Turkish fire . . . had raised the defenders' spirits at a moment when all had been resigned to death.') Although no one could have foretold it during the hot summer of starvation that lay ahead — the worst months as they were to seem to many of the whole war — the tide had lipped as far up the rock as it would ever go. It would hang there for a long time, seemingly irreversible before its slow retreat would be noticed by the survivors, whose handholds on the slippery rock would seem at that time to become daily more tenuous — even as an outside observer could see that they were saved.

CHAPTER TWENTY-SIX

A Change of Balance

It was a spring of many changes. The first and greatest was the one that was hardly observed by most — that slight relaxation of the Luftwaffe bombing of the island. The second, and one felt by all, was the departure early in April of Admiral Cunningham to Washington, to head the Admiralty delegation there and to be the representative of the First Sea Lord on the Combined Chiefs of Staff committee. No more suitable man could have been chosen for this all important post in Anglo-American cooperation which was to lead to the winning of the war. Cunningham himself was loath to go, particularly since he was leaving the Mediterranean at a time when his fleet was practically non existent.

Like Nelson he was 'an old Mediterranean man', and he had fought, usually with an outnumbered fleet, a sequence of battles that put him in the same class as his great predecessor — and he had also conducted a whole maritime strategy that the latter had never been called on to do. He had known this sea since the First World War as a young commander in destroyers, had served in it in many capacities between the wars, and had established himself in the past three years as the greatest fighting admiral that Britain had had since the victor of the Battle of the Nile. A quiet Scot, with a bourgeois domestic life, he was in many ways the antithesis of his famous predecessor, but it is certain that if anyone had benefitted by reading Southey's *Life of Nelson* it was he and not his Italian opponents. Apart from being an extremely skilful seaman, he was conversant with modern techniques but had avoided the trap of becoming enmeshed in technicalities. An able administrator, he was also more than able at coping with the politico-strategical problems that engaged so much of the time of a modern commander-in-chief. Like Nelson himself (and many other great commanders as far back as Drake) he had learned the business of war in small ships when young, but he had not become imprisoned within that panache of youth and had evolved into one of the most mature and great sea captains of all time. He had known Malta in his youth, middle years, and as commander-in-chief, and one of his last messages before relinquishing his command was directed to the Vice-Admiral Malta.

The record has been magnificent, and I heartily thank every officer and man who has taken part, not forgetting those who have had the less spectacular, but none the less exacting task of maintaining and bringing back into action our ships and aircraft to the discomfiture of the enemy. . . . The very extent of the success of the forces based on Malta has led to a ceaseless battering of the fortress, but one has only to think of the air effort that the enemy is diverting to this purpose to realise that this is but another of the services that Malta is rendering.[1]

He was succeeded by Admiral Sir Henry Harwood, the victor of the Battle of the River Plate, a dogged commander whose persistency would be tested to the utmost in the coming months. Curiously enough, although Cunningham suspected that he would probably never see the Mediterranean again, he was to return some seven months later to find that the tide had indeed turned. This great reversal of affairs had been largely brought about by himself and the men who served under him in the hard and sometimes seemingly hopeless years from 1940-42.

The third main change, and one of profound importance to everyone in Malta, was when General Sir William Dobbie relinquished his position as Governor of the island to General the Viscount Gort, VC on 8 May.[2] Until then Lord Gort had been the Governor of Gibraltar and prior to that he was the general who had managed to salvage the army during the desperate days of Dunkirk. The Cromwellian general who in his farewell address to the people of Malta, after thanking them for all their kindness to him and his family during recent years, had commended them to 'put your trust in Almighty God and seek to honour Him in all your ways', was relieved by a general who, if also God-fearing, was of markedly aggressive stamp. General Dobbie was not only physically ill but he was as worn out as the island: he had been there since the beginning and he had been in many people's eyes the embodiment of the same virtues that had once been displayed by the great La Valette. His involvement with the people had been total, as many accounts confirm, and it was to some extent this identification with the sufferings of the ordinary Maltese that had exhausted him. His successor, coming from Gibraltar (that other British fortress which had endured a famous eighteenth century siege), arrived comparatively fresh upon a worn-out garrison and people much in need of reinvigoration. His reputation as a fighting man was confirmed by an array of medals that few could ever match. The holder of Britain's highest award, the Victoria Cross (from the First World War), the Distinguished Service Order, the Military Cross, and nine Mentions

176

in Despatches, John Standish Surtees Prendergast Vereker, sixth Viscount Gort, arrived at the nadir of the island's fortunes. By his example and simple decency Dobbie had held the morale of the island together through the worst of times, whereas Gort, arriving just before the up-turn began, was with the aid of his fiery and self-disciplined nature to see it to the moment when the pale light in the east had become recognisable as the dawn. Dobbie was not to know as he left that, within twenty-four hours, a successful mission by the USS *Wasp* and HMS *Eagle* would have delivered sixty-one Spitfires to the island — Spitfires that were not destroyed on landing and that begun to turn the balance in favour of Malta's survival. The depression, afflicting the whole island from servicemen to the inhabitants of remote villages, that had followed upon the loss of *Wasp's* first Spitfires was lifted on 9 May. From 1 a.m. onwards sixty-one Spitfires, out of sixty-four which had been embarked, flew in from the two carriers lying invisible far to the west. A typical May morning in that part of the sea, cool, but with some dew presaging temperatures in the seventies at midday, heralded their arrival — an engine sound now familiar, recognized as friendly, coming in over the cliffs from the sea. This time there were no mistakes, no incompetence due to fatigue, and no unpreparedness due to 'bomb-happy' exhaustion.

The turn-around of the Spitfires was accomplished in six minutes in some cases on 9 May, so thoroughly rehearsed were the arrangements. When the enemy came to bomb them on the ground, he was met and attacked by them in the air. The infantry contributed essential manpower to carry out this plan. Each Spitfire was met and directed by a runner to a dispersal pen, which was a self-supporting unit. Owing to the shortage of petrol bowsers and the number of aircraft to be refuelled simultaneously, a supply of petrol was put in tins for refuelling by hand. These tins, together with oil, glycol, and ammunition, were waiting in each pen. Two airmen, assisted by soldiers, fell upon each Spitfire as it reached the pen. The moment their work was done a Malta pilot took over the machine, though in some cases newly arrived pilots went straight into action.[3]

Throughout that day the pilots, ground crews, and relief pilots lived in their pens. Food and drink were brought to them, while army despatch riders and signalmen maintained communications between the widely dispersed aircraft. So fast was the turn round that many of the Messerschmitt 109s which had taken off from Sicily the moment that the presence of the British aircraft had been detected, found not sitting pigeons as before but alert hawks already circling in the sky above them. One of the pilots later described how after arriving at Ta Qali: 'I immediately removed my kit, and the machine was rearmed and refuelled, I landed during a raid and four 109s tried to shoot me up. Soon after landing the airfield was bombed but without much damage done.' During that day there were nine air raids, but the results were very different from before. By nightfall eight enemy planes had been confirmed destroyed and eight 'probables' as well as many others reported heading for Sicily damaged. The same pilot concluded his memories of that first day: 'The tempo of life here is just indescribable. The morale of all is magnificent — pilots, ground crews and army, but it is certainly tough. The bombing is continuous on and off all day ... living conditions, sleep, food and all the ordinary standards of life have gone by the board. It all makes the Battle of Britain and fighter sweeps seem like child's play in comparison, but it is certainly history in the making, and nowhere is there aerial warfare to compare with this.'

Everything built up to a climax with the arrival at dawn the following day of the fast minelayer HMS *Welshman* from Gibraltar. Lord Gort, bringing fresh enthusiasm and initiative from the top, the Spitfires bringing hope at a moment when it had become thin indeed, and *Welshman* bringing the back-up to the Spitfires (ammunition, spare engines, spare aircrews, many other small essentials as well as several tons of mail for the garrison) had all arrived at more or less the same time. The combination acted somewhat like a booster shot in the arm to a patient who was hovering between life and death.

Something else that *Welshman* brought with her for use over the harbour when ships were unloading was a consignment of chemical smoke-making compound. Drums of this, generating a white haze (so thick that some of the attacking pilots later reported 'fog over Grand Harbour'), were in use within a short time of her arrival. As with the Spitfires, so with *Welshman*, there was to be no repetition of the *Talabot* and *Pampas* disaster. Army teams were ready waiting at her berth before the ship had even entered harbour and unloading by crane and human chain began the moment that her lines were ashore. (A jetty had been specially cleared for her reception in French Creek and a dense anti-aircraft barrage — 'a cone of steel' — had been designed to cover the whole area.) When the inevitable raids developed — the heaviest coming shortly before 11 a.m. with twenty Stukas and ten Junkers 88s escorted by Messerschmitt fighters — the three services were all in a combined operation at the same moment. The army gunners took over, as it were, from the army stevedoring parties, *Welshman*'s crew were at their guns, and the RAF in their Hurricanes and Spitfires were in the sky above. The attacking planes were forced to bomb more or less blind through the smoke, yet even so *Welshman* received a near miss and large lumps of her unloading jetty were blown onto the ship. By luck or (as the devout would have said) through the power of prayer, the ship was never hit during her day in harbour — a day in which all her stores were safely unloaded and swiftly transported by prearranged routes to safety. That same evening, preceded by the last operational minesweeper in Malta, HMS *Welshman* left for Gibraltar, damaged from her fourteen-hour stay in the most dangerous harbour in the world, but with her mission accomplished and still able to steam at over thirty knots. During the course of the day's air battles, in which Spitfires flew one-hundred and ten sorties and the Hurricanes fifteen, fifteen of the attackers were destroyed by aircraft and eight by the guns, with many probables for the loss of three Spitfires.

When the *Welshman* left Grand Harbour she had refuelled, but she had only taken aboard three-hundred tons of oil, her captain reckoning that this would be enough with what he already had to see him back to the western end of the Mediterranean. There were then only two-thousand tons remaining in the island's underground bunkers. The shortage of oil — like the shortage of food — was not something that could be alleviated by the upsurge in morale that had followed the past two days. Unless a large convoy could be brought into the island before the end of June Kesselring's optimism (on 10 May he had reported to Berlin 'the neutralization of Malta is complete') would be justified. Starvation by food and oil shortage would accomplish what the sustained blitz of the past three months had failed to do.

In an island like Malta, the pattern of events can often be seen more accurately than in the greater world because it is a microcosm. They present, as in a test tube to the trained observer's eye, evidence of what may be expected under given conditions on a world-wide scale. In 1942 Malta exemplified the plight of an oil-dependent society when it is cut off from its essential source of energy. Even the crane, the one survivor on that jetty, which had unloaded *Welshman* was dependent on power generated by oil. Most of the island's water wells could no longer be pumped because of shortage of oil fuel; other public utilities were also powered by oil. The constant power cuts in electricity were not only caused by cables being destroyed by bombing but by the rationing of oil fuel. This in its turn effected the electric power necessary for hospitals. Many of these had suffered in the bombing, and the toll of the war was being increasingly felt in the shortage of almost everything that surgeons and nursing staff needed — even when not working in dreadful conditions with too many patients to every ward. Public transport had long been reduced to a

179

mockery. Service transport had been severely rationed (one of Lord Gort's messages to the community was to take a bicycle instead of his official car when on his rounds of Valletta), and the whole island was coming to a halt. Such tugs and small powered craft as remained unsunk needed oil fuel to carry out necessary harbour work, as did minesweepers (when there was more than one operational). Without minesweepers no convoy could get into the harbour, and the escorts that might accompany any convoy would need refuelling before making their way back to Alexandria or Gibraltar.

The Malta war diary, which states that subsequent to the arrival of the Spitfires, 'such casualties were inflicted on the enemy that daylight raiding was brought to an abrupt end' erred as gravely in its optimism as did Field Marshal Kesselring in his. Although daylight raids did indeed decrease, particularly those on Grand Harbour (where there was almost nothing left to bomb), the conditions of the people during the month of May were in many respects worse than in March or April. Hunger and disease were by now taking their toll (although no one died directly of starvation). The Communal Feeding Kitchens (later renamed *Victory Kitchens*), the first of which had been established in January, grew in numbers until in May there were some forty of them in twenty-three different localities. These provided for all who were registered with them either 'one hot dish consisting of meat and vegetable stew' or a meatless soup. The former (kawlata) cost 6d, while minestra (vegetable soup with no meat) cost 3d. This was the only meal of the day, and might be taken either at midday or in the evening. Many of those without homes or without cooking facilities, as well as the unemployed or the unemployable, made regular use of these kitchens, although the quality and the quantity of the food were always a major source of complaint. Subscribers to the Victory Kitchens had to register for them every week: by mid May they were feeding 4000 but by the end of the year over 170,000 were registered with them. This was not so much a tribute to their organization or their cooking, but to 'the gradual depletion of the stocks available in the Black Market ... and the fact that available supplies which could be legitimately obtained were gradually reduced.'[4] Ships like *Welshman* and her sister ship *Manxman* which made their high-powered dashes to the island and mine-laying submarines converted to cargo-carrying did not bring food — except small bulk cargoes like powdered milk — but ammunition, petrol for the fighters, spare parts for the fighters and indeed essentials for the weapons of war. Without the latter Malta would undoubtedly have been invaded, but without a convoy with food the people would starve.

Plans for Operation 'Hercules' had not been put aside, but merely held over until Rommel should have successfully completed his attack in the desert. Ultra, which kept General Auchinleck in Egypt acquainted with Rommel's intentions, reported also the steady arrival of his armour. The German armour, as was seen when the campaign finally opened, even though numerically less than the British, was superior in firepower and in desert worthiness. After 'Theseus' would come 'Hercules', and reconnaissance aircraft out of Malta reported that fresh airstrips were being laid out near Gerbini airfield in Sicily. As the three bomber airfields already in existence seemed adequate for the planes available, and as this new activity was observed at about the time that the Luftwaffe had begun to withdraw some of their planes, only one interpretation was possible. These new fields were not, as had been first assumed, satellite airfields for the existing bomber force but were designed to accommodate a large number of gliders and their towing planes for an air-borne invasion. Troops were already in training up at Livorno in the north of Italy, where some features of the coastline resembled those of Malta, and plans were well advanced for the transport of German and Italian troops by German naval landing craft as a follow up to the airborne attack. An armoured unit of captured tanks from the Russian front had been set aside for the operation, three Italian parachute battalions were ready and would soon be joined by a German parachute division; the invasion would involve about 35,000 troops. Given the fact that the British no longer had any surface ships or submarines or bombers in the island, and had no battleships or aircraft carriers at Alexandria, it should indeed be possible for the Italian navy to provide adequate cover during the first phase of the operation.

The arrival of the Spitfires on 9 May, followed by further Spitfire reinforcements on 18 May, somewhat altered the picture. But the planning for it and the allocation of men and materials did not cease for some months to come. It was rather like Operation 'Sealion', the projected invasion of Britain itself — so attractive was the idea in certain quarters that it was hard to relinquish it. For the government of Malta, for the service chiefs, for every serviceman, and for every civilian, it remained a nightmare that would take a long time to dispel. Their fears were soon intensified by the success of Rommel's spring attack in the desert.

CHAPTER TWENTY-SEVEN

Bread of Adversity

Even in the quiet places where there had been a spring that year it was over by May. It was always over before the end of the month, when the thermometer would begin its steady climb up to a plateau of the nineties (in the shade) where it rested until mid or late September. No one looked forward to the summer. The war was now eternal. There were children born, just before or at the beginning of it, who could remember nothing but the shelter life, the sound of guns and bombs, their mothers' protective arms when dust fell shaking from the roof, and the smell of humanity crowded together.

All depended now not on Malta but on the battle that was about to break out in the desert some hundreds of miles to the south. Under permanent daily attack, the island had ceased to exert its pressure on the decisive area, which must inevitably explode. Refuelled, re-equipped, rested, the Italo-German armies now faced with confidence the British defensive line drawn up from Gazala to Bir Hacheim. Rommel was well aware that the Eighth Army had also had time to rearm and prepare an offensive, and he was determined to get his blow in first. His previous advance, designed as no more than a 'spoiling measure', had won him a lot of ground and he now aimed for Tobruk. Convoys to Tripoli and Benghazi were running almost unmolested, except by submarines from Alexandria, and a recent reorganization, whereby the German navy had taken responsibility for the shipment of supplies eastward to the small port of Derna, had resulted in such an improvement that he felt his confidence soar. The Luftwaffe together with the Regia Aeronautica had complete air superiority over the desert and over the sea itself, while Malta was apparently eliminated as a menace to his continuing sea supplies. His aim was not to attack the British forces head on, but to move around them to the south, encircling them and cutting them off from their supply lines.

On 26 May the Battle of Gazala, as it came to be known, opened with Rommel's forces making their expected move and being anticipated. The far end of the British line at Bir Hacheim down in the desert held firm against a superior force, the Free French conducting a superb defence. From the very beginning, however, the superiority of the German tanks showed itself — better protected, more heavily gunned, and in the final analysis more desert worthy than the British armour — it was they that turned the scale. The battle that had begun on Rommel's initiative was one which Churchill had been pressing General Auchinleck to open ever since February, while Auchinleck had constantly argued that his forces were not yet ready and not yet sufficiently well equipped to take the initiative. Churchill's insistence on an early engagement in the desert was largely prompted by his concern about Malta, for he was well aware that the island could not hold out much longer unless it was revictualled, refuelled, and ammunitioned. So long as Cyrenaica, and especially the threatening Benghazi bulge with its airstrips controlling the eastern passage to Malta, was in Axis hands there was no chance of getting such a convoy through from Alexandria. Pressured by delegates sent out by the prime minister, Auchinleck had held out for a date in mid June or at the very least the end of May, but in the event he had been forestalled by Rommel's advance. Auchinleck was proved right that the British forces were not yet fitted to match the German, but what at the time seemed the greatest of disasters turned out in the long run to be the saving not only of Malta but of the whole British war effort in the desert.

Four weeks after the battle had begun Rommel, having switched his tactics from the attempt at encirclement, had struck north and the German armour, brilliantly used by a master of warfare, had broken through and opened a passage to Tobruk. On 20 June he launched a massive assault on the garrison using every element of his bomber force, from high level Italian Capronis to Junkers 88s and Stukas employed for what they had originally been designed — heavy artillery in front of an infantry advance. Tobruk, so long a thorn in the side of the Axis forces and so long a besieged companion to which Malta had looked with affectionate regard, fell the following day. Poor local command, poor morale among the garrison, these and many other charges were later made as the reason for the collapse of this all important fortress. One fact remains inescapable — if it had been defended as Malta had been for so many months Tobruk would not have fallen as it did.

Rommel, ever an optimist, was overjoyed by this success which seemed to open the way into Egypt. The British army was in retreat to take up new positions on the Egyptian frontier, and it seemed that with the marked superiority of his armour — as shown in the recent battles — he only needed to punch a hole through the demoralized line ahead of him and the great prize was won. Rommel's ebullient nature was well enough known to the German High Command, and it was for this reason that General Paulus had been sent to North Africa in April 1941, shortly after Rommel's arrival, to formulate a strategy known and acceptable to Berlin. (It was the transmission of this strategy on a Luftwaffe cypher being read in Bletchley Park which had enabled the British at that time to plan a counteroffensive against Rommel's first moves.) Now, within a month, Rommel had achieved the whole object of operation 'Theseus', and his well justified satisfaction was crowned by immediate promotion to field marshal. Hitler also felt the backwash of this triumph, coming as it did at a moment when the war in Russia had entered a longer, more drawn-out phase than he had anticipated, and when the bomber raids on Germany were beginning to remind the conquerors of Europe that Britain was still unconquered. This sparkling shower of rockets from the desert war could not help but increase his regard for a general who had always been one of his closest adherents.

Rommel had many material factors to back his triumph — vast quantities of captured stores, ranging from thousands of tons of provisions, to nearly 1500 tons of petrol, whole ammunition dumps, and thousands of serviceable vehicles. (If Malta had ever been captured, there would have been exploding dumps all over the island, with nothing left for the victors.) In view of this sudden accession to his supplies, Rommel felt that all restrictions on his movements should be lifted and that the 5 May directive of the Italian *Comando Supremo* (to whom all Axis forces in the desert were subject) should be set aside. This would have held him back from any further advance and would have transferred the whole Italo-German war effort in the Mediterranean to operation 'Hercules' — the invasion of Malta. But, standing in shattered Tobruk, looking at the battered waterfront made famous in so many war photographs, at the blue harbour, beautiful despite its shattered wrecks, the prisoners of war filing past in their thousands, and his own Afrika Korps *soldaten* triumphant around him, Rommel felt with Brutus:

> There is a tide in the affairs of men
> Which, taken at the flood, leads on to fortune;
> ... On such a full sea are we now afloat;
> And we must take the current when it serves,
> Or lose our ventures.

More prosaically, but with the same enthusiasm shining through, he happily by-passed Rome and communicated direct with the German Supreme Command: 'The morale and condition of the troops, the quantity of stores captured and the present weakness of the enemy make it possible for us to thrust onwards into the heart of Egypt. Therefore request that the Duce be prevailed upon to remove the present restrictions on my movement and that all troops now under my command be placed at my disposal to continue the offensive.'

Hitler was at once disposed to agree with his new field-marshal. He too felt the run of the tide, and it seemed to dispose of the awkward matter of invading Malta — something about which he had always felt uneasy. At the German Supreme Command it seems to have been agreed that 'with the capture of Tobruk the situation is completely changed. The conquest of Malta is no longer necessary.' Although it was still at times discussed, the invasion of Malta was dropped for ever.

There was still a great deal of argument from the Italians that operation 'Hercules' should be pursued: they knew very well that the supply line was fully stretched (because of the previous heavy losses of their merchant marine) even with Malta apparently suppressed. Rommel was now at the far end of a long desert route, and even with Tobruk available as an unloading port, they were not optimistic — unless of course he should sweep into Egypt within a matter of weeks. Mussolini, however, was seized by the drama of the moment (and also perhaps by the happy fact that his forces would not be called upon to fulfil their obligations in operation 'Hercules'). While Hitler, with his indifferent health improved by this good news, was already turning back to his preoccupation with the iron realities of Russia, Il Duce saw a vision that exceeded any other in his operatic life. Verdi's *Aida* had first been performed in Cairo in December 1871, but he envisaged a production that for massive ensemble, richness of production, and magnificence of local colour should transcend even that master's imaginings. At the end of June he flew to Derna, a white charger following in another aircraft, to await the moment 'when he should make his triumphal entry into the Land of the Pharoahs'.

The fall of Tobruk, which Churchill wrote 'was one of the hardest blows of the entire war', was to prove in the end a turning point because it saved Malta. At the time, of course, it could not be seen as anything but a disaster, which it would indeed have been if Rommel had been able to pursue his precipitate advance. With his head-quarters now at Sidi Barrani, inside the borders of Egypt and with Alexandria only about two-hundred miles away, Rommel was unquenchable in his enthusiasm, as Kesselring and the Italian Marshal Cavallero (very much concerned in the Italian planning for the Malta invasion) found him when they arrived for a conference. What concerned Cavallero particularly was the length of the Axis supply line, while the British at El Alamein had a short supply line and were already regrouping in strength. Despite the fact that he had been able to pass Mersa Matruh, Rommel was soon to find that he was faced with a strong defence line and a resolute enemy.

At El Alamein, only sixty miles from Alexandria, with the glittering prize of the great harbour and city within his grasp, he was held. While Mussolini still dreamed of a triumphant entry into Alexandria and then Cairo, and the ebullient young field-marshal seemed to hold the rich prize of the Nile Delta and the ribbon of the Suez Canal within his hands, General Auchinleck was able to hold him and launch provocative counter-attacks. As one of those working at Bletchley Park at the time wrote: 'It was Ultra which enabled General Auchinleck in North Africa to fight Rommel and his Afrika Korps like an elusive boxer, bobbing up where Rommel least expected him.... It was Auchinleck's skill that brought Rommel to a standstill at the very gateway to Egypt.'[1] An additional factor in the exhaustion of the Axis armies at this moment was that Malta, knocked unconscious as had been thought, struggled to its feet. The addition of yet further Spitfires to the island's arsenal meant that the weight of air attack from Sicily which had been believed sufficient to keep the island suppressed was not enough.[2] Before the end of June Marshall Cavallero was forced to ask for a transfer of planes from North Africa to Sicily to maintain the assault. Rommel's inability to crack the British defensive line at Alamein early in July was partly due to the fact that he no longer had air superiority in the desert.

One of Dobbie's last actions in Malta had been to send a signal to the War Office concerning the island's food, ammunition and fuel situation. It had not changed for the better over the ensuing weeks and, combined with the disastrous news from the desert of the fall of Tobruk and therefore the unlikelihood of any further convoys getting through, his successor Lord Gort knew how slight were Malta's chances of survival. Before he had arrived to take over as governor, he had had time to digest Dobbie's account of the supply position:

(a) Wheat and Flour. No material cuts seem possible as these are staple foods. Present stocks will, with care, last until early June.

(b) Fodder. Issues already inadequate were recently cut; stocks will now last until end of July.

(c) Minor foodstuffs. Meat stocks are entirely exhausted. Most other stocks will last until June.

(d) White oils. Aviation fuel till mid August; benzine until mid June; kerosene till early July.

(e) Black oils. We have only 920 tons of diesel oil (5 weeks' supply) and 2,000 tons of furnace oil, all of which will be needed for fuelling HM ships now in dock. The black oil position is thus becoming precarious, and very urgent action appears necessary to restore it.

(f) Coal. Welsh coal will last only until end of May ... other grades until mid June.

(g) Ammunition. Consumption of ack-ack ammunition has greatly increased in the recent heavy raids ... and we have only 1½ months stocks left....

Dobbie had requested a convoy not later than mid May and had been informed that there was no chance at all of a convoy during that month. More Spitfires arrived, flown in from carriers in the western Mediterranean, but Gort, familiar within a day or two of the actuality of dust and dereliction and near starvation by which he was surrounded, knew that only a substantial convoy could save the island. Churchill, who had written to the chiefs of staff, 'We are absolutely bound to save Malta', remained determined on this whatever might befall. He had known the island's essential importance from the very beginning of the war, and despite all his other myriad preoccupations, he never faltered in his determination. Like Cunningham, he had always realized the role which it could also play — in the uncertain future — in any assault on Hitler's Europe.

Not one convoy, but two, were planned for mid June — the earliest date by which suitable merchantment and warships could be gathered at both ends of the sea. This was to be the most massive effort yet, with seven merchantment escorted by a battleship, two carriers, cruisers and destroyers from Gibraltar (Operation Harpoon), and no less than eleven merchantmen with seven cruisers and twenty-eight destroyers from Alexandria (Operation Vigorous). At the same time, profiting by the cover provided for the Harpoon convoy, the minelayer *Welshman* with her specialized stores would slide through from the west. The convoy from the Alexandria end could have no capital ships since none were available due to the demands of the Eastern fleet, and its only 'heavy cover' was provided by the old *Centurion*, for a long time a wireless-controlled fleet target ship and now mocked up to look like a new battleship. (It was hoped that she would at least draw much of the attention of the bombers.)[3] Since Malta was by now almost entirely 'mined in', and there could be no certainty as to how many of her own minesweepers would be seaworthy to sweep in the convoys, four fleet minesweepers together with six minesweeping motor launches sailed with the Gibraltar convoy. It was only the latter, Operation Harpoon, that got any ships at all through to Grand Harbour.

At this time, just prior to Rommel's advance in the desert, the

Italian navy with its capital ships and heavy cruisers dominated the central Mediterranean while the Luftwaffe dominated the skies. It was to be expected that the convoy from Alexandria would meet with heavy bombing in the area between Crete and the Benghazi bulge but the appearance of the Italian battle fleet, with two new battleships the *Littorio* and the *Vittorio Veneto* together with two heavy cruisers, two light cruisers and twelve destroyers, was beyond the fighting capacity of the Alexandria covering force. On 15 June both this convoy and its screen were ordered back to Alexandria. So the whole of this, the largest convoy, never reached Malta. The convoy from the west fared slightly better. Even though its passage involved an action in the Skerki channel between British destroyers and a force of Italian cruisers, two merchant ships, *Orari* and *Troilus* (as well as *Welshman*), managed to reach the island and unload.[4]

The threat posed by the Italian battleships had been sufficient to turn the scales in the eastern part of the convoy, but it was the weight of air attack that really prevented any of the ships from being ventured through to Malta. Most of the escorts had fired off so many shells that they were practically without ammunition, while the toll taken by the bombers included four merchantmen sunk, and two merchantmen damaged. The escort, which also underwent submarine attacks, had three cruisers damaged, three destroyers sunk, two corvettes damaged and one torpedo boat sunk. The cold statistics for Operation Vigorous from Alexandria reveal at the end: 'Tonnage of Cargoes landed — NIL'. Harpoon from Gibraltar had four merchantmen sunk (including the American oiler *Kentucky*, the most important ship in the convoy), one merchantman damaged, two cruisers damaged, one destroyer sunk, and one destroyer damaged. If it had not been for *Orari* and *Troilus* reaching Grand Harbour and being promptly unloaded of some 20,000 tons of flour and ammunition (an appropriately divided package) the island must have fallen — for no other convoy could possibly be put together until August.

The Italians rightly claimed the turning back of the convoy from Alexandria as a signal naval victory. So indeed it was, in the sense that the threat of their battle fleet out of Taranto had been the final blow which had determined Admiral Harwood to recall the convoy and its escort. The debit side was one Italian heavy cruiser torpedoed by an aircraft out of Malta (later sunk by the submarine *Umbra*) and *Littorio* hit by one bomb and one torpedo. Invisible as yet on that debit sheet was something which would prove of immense importance in the future. The operation of the Italian fleet against the western convoy, and the battlefleet against the eastern, had reduced their oil reserves to such a degree that they would never again be able

188

to take the sea in force. Hitler's optimism about the great oil fields of Russia coming within his grasp were to be disappointed, and from then on the oil fields of eastern Europe would be called upon as never before to fuel the German war machine (to the exclusion of the Italians).

The sight of *Welshman* and the two merchantmen unloading in Grand Harbour could not ease the acute sense of desperation that rapidly spread throughout the whole island. No one could, or did, conceal the news that two convoys had been destined for their relief, and that this was all that had been fought through. True, it was better than March when nothing arrived at all — but this was now June and the two terrible months of April and May lay like a great weight on everyone's heart. The loss of *Kentucky* meant that the oil and kerosene situation was acutely serious. Fortunately it was now summer and, despite the sufferings that the sun brought, it meant that heating was relatively unimportant and that the damp, disease-ridden shelter life could be somewhat put aside. The fact that the two ships which had unloaded had contained a cargo divided between flour and ammunition did at least mean that the island could eat and fight for a little longer.

General Gort and the Deputy Governor of the island, Sir Edward Jackson (known to all since he had been in his post since the very beginning), both broadcast to the islanders. They made no attempt at concealment for, contrary to Italian propaganda, these were not a submissive people 'held down by British bayonets' but equal and enduring partners — and it was their own island that they were defending. Gort could promise them nothing but 'further privations', and Jackson elaborated: 'We received about 15,000 tons of stores from the two ships which arrived. That is something, and certainly a help, but it is a very small part of what we had hoped for.' He went on to tell them that there would unavoidably be further restrictions in the rations and he concluded: 'Our security depends, more than anything else, on the time for which our bread will last.'

It had come down to that, as it had always done in all sieges throughout history — bread.

CHAPTER TWENTY-EIGHT

Heat of the Day

Malta is always a dusty island. Just as all singular places on the planet invariably have a distinctive smell (all can supply their own memories) so Malta's smell on the sea air to the visitor by boat is dry, old, and dusty. Even in places as remote as the Mnajdra temples on the western coast, when the sun flares over an empty sea as the watcher waits for the green flash at sunset, the scent is very old — older somehow than the sands of Egypt. Those who knew it in the summer of 1942 all recorded the same overwhelming impression — the dust. The thousands of powdered dwellings, the bombed-out airstrips and the torn roads contributed to the perpetual feel of it on the skin. Even the harbour — its surface foul from sunken ships and oil fuel — was powdered with dust. The quaysides eddied with it, scraps of old dirty paper blowing on every errant puff of wind, and broken doorways opened like sightless eyes upon the ruin of fallen roofs, old lost lives, sad fragments like a wheel from a broken toy, torn wallpaper rustling in a sundried corner — and dust. It was in the food, on the surface of the water in an old enamelled drinking mug and it gritted between the teeth over the rough torn piece of bread, valued now as no one could ever remember valuing bread before. And with the dust, the flies. Eye diseases were of course on the increase, and the dust exacerbated the sores where scabies sufferers had been unable to stop scratching. So dry did the island seem that it might have been thought that it was impossible for mosquitoes to breed. Yet the *nemus* was everywhere — zithering out of bomb craters, out of dead houses where excrement lay, from broken water pipes and the beehived-shaped cisterns shattered beneath old ruins. Not only house flies and blue-bottles, mosquitoes, and gnats exulted, but sandflies (productive of a short but high fever and a long slow recovery rate) seemed to thrive on war. Indeed, was not the great Prince of Darkness known from millennia before as 'Lord of Flies' and 'Lord of Dung'? Like most Roman Catholics the Maltese were not familiar with the Old Testament, but there must have been some among the priesthood who recalled the mysterious words of the preacher in *Ecclesiastes*, suggesting that they were living in the days 'when they shall be afraid of that which is high, and fears shall be in the way, and the almond tree shall flourish, and the grasshopper shall be a burden, and desire shall fail: because man goeth to his long home, and the mourners go about the streets.'

Valletta, that perfect example of a planned capital and fortress combined, was a ruin. The city, which Sir Walter Scott had described as 'quite like a dream' and of which Disraeli had said that it 'equals in its noble architecture, if it even does not excel, any capital in Europe', had been devastated in the terrible raids of April. The narrow streets were blocked with rubble — fast though demolition squads and soldiers laboured to clear them — and the destruction of this famous city and its suburb Floriana could only be put down to spite on the part of the attackers, many of whom naturally preferred to drop their bombs on these noble streets rather than face the hell of Grand Harbour — whose installations and ships were their real target. The ancient university, the *Sacra Infirmeria* (the great Hospital of the Knights, one of the first ever built in Europe), the famous palace, St John's co-cathedral (a monument to the Age of Chivalry), all were hit, as well as six of the auberges (the magnificent palaces of the various Tongues of the Knights), and inevitably a number of fine baroque churches. The Victorian Opera House, redolent of upper class splendour and display, was destroyed along with much of the squalid but vivid Manderaggio area of the poor.

It was noticeable that the fury of the onslaught on the island's capital increased in ratio as the attacks on the dockyard areas and the airfields began to lessen. Like the 'Baedeker raids' carried out on Britain in the later stages of the war, the destruction of Valletta was largely prompted by the fury of frustration.

Everywhere one looked [wrote Weldon] one could see nothing but desolation and rubble. In particular was this so if one walked to the top of the ramparts and looked down some of the streets. It was then that one realized the extent of the damage. Malta's buildings are made of very solid blocks of stone and it takes a direct hit to destroy a house. The traveller arriving at Valletta might, at first, think that the damage was comparatively slight, but let him just walk to one high vantage point and look down and he will see that almost every building is nothing but an empty shell. That alone will show the intensity of the bombing. It was estimated at one time that there were a million five hundred thousand tons of debris in Valletta and Floriana alone. In the whole island over fifteen thousand buildings had been destroyed, amongst them seventy churches, eighteen convents or monasteries, twenty-two schools, eight hospitals, ten theatres....[1]

In this fly-blown, dust-ridden landscape, a southern hell such as Dante Alighieri hardly envisaged, the scale of human suffering was different from that found in other cities under attack during the Second World War. This was because, although the casualties were far less than might have been expected due to the nature of the island, the condition of being shelter bound was almost without end. Days, weeks, months and even years passed in which men, women and children (particularly the last two) were forced to spend so large a part of their lives underground — undernourished and often in ill health. A Reuter correspondent in Malta, who took shelter in one of the beehive-shaped cisterns beneath Valletta during a major raid, described with the vividness of a newcomer a situation which had become familiar to the inhabitants:

... the air was filled with the crash of masonry and the uncanny swirl of blast. The building above was hit. Clouds of dust penetrated the shelter, smothering and half-choking the shelterers with dust, mostly women with babies and young children. Some of the children were terrified and cried, but their mothers open-eyed and stupefied, calmly dipped their handkerchiefs in a pail of water kept in the shelter for the purpose and put them over the mouths and noses of the babies. Then hugging their youngest to their bosom they muttered a silent prayer.... After a short lull another wave of bombers came over. The lights in the shelter flickered and the blast lifted the skirts of women and children as it swept through. One of the next stick of bombs brought down more of the buildings overhead. A shower of masonry and debris burst in through the emergency exit — immediately followed by a dark cloud of dust and cordite, which spread throughout the shelter until none could see the other. Mothers looked up expecting to see the dome of the well give way. All were temporarily deafened by the noise. In this unreal scene figures only faintly visible through the pall of dust moved as if in a trance.[2]

Over the whole island indeed the great Florentine might have seen, carved deep in the limestone rock, the words of his vision:

> Per me si va nella città dolente,
> Per me si va nell'eterno dolore,
> Per me si va tra la perduta gente ...
> Lasciate ogni speranza, voi ch'entrate.

But hope was the one thing that they did not lose. Something else which emerged quite decisively from the war and which, as has been seen, was a matter of some surprise to the psychiatrists, was the ability of people to withstand situations of great peril, pain, suffering and terror, without succumbing to what are termed 'nervous break-downs'. Such indeed appear to be more common under the daily stresses of peacetime, or of the condition known as 'peace' in the great industrial communities of the west. The incidence of break-down among African or Asian people or among peasant communi-ties in general has never been properly studied for obvious reasons. Among the physically softer, better fed, more self-indulgent citizens of the world one expects — probably quite rightly — that the least endurance will be found. In this matter the people of Malta's performance in those days was different from great cities like London and Berlin since they were required to endure for a far longer time, and on rations that were about half of those available to the citizens of London for instance. The temperance and frugality common among Mediterranean peoples had been bred into them by centuries of being required to exist on very little. It was these qualities, among others, which enabled the besieged to survive under conditions which, one has reason to think, the inhabitants of modern cities could not endure.

The great French historian Fernand Braudel has pointed out an important distinction between Mediterranean man and the norther-ner: 'The truth is that the Mediterranean has struggled against a fundamental poverty, aggravated but not entirely accounted for by circumstances. It affords a precarious living, in spite of its apparent or real advantages. It is easy to be deceived by its famous charm and beauty.... In fact, Mediterranean man gains his daily bread by painful effort. Great tracts of land remain uncultivated and of little use. The land that does yield food is almost everywhere subject to biennial crop rotation that rules out any great productivity.... There is one visible sign of this poverty: the frugality that has never failed to impress the northerner.'[3]

This frugality, which had amused British soldiers and sailors in Malta in days of peace, continued to amaze them — and other observers — during the war. It is significant that in the many British firsthand accounts of life in Malta during the siege an almost constant theme is the shortage of food and drink. The Maltese accounts, however, tend to refer to the subject only when it became — as in July and August 1942 — a matter of near starvation. On 20 June the Government had to announce cuts that Sir Edward Jackson described over the radio as 'a far greater privation than any other ... a far greater hardship than any of you have had to bear hitherto'. Among the rations for a family of five were four tins of corned beef, four tins of fish and four boxes of matches *per month*. The daily bread ration per person was fixed at 3/8ths of a ratal (under 14 ounces). The daily calory intake was now 1,500 (as compared with 3,000, regarded as a daily minimum for a man 'leading a moderately active life'.)

After the failure of the June convoys to bring in more than two ships to the island's relief the calculations of the Government were that on the present reduced rations the island could just last out until the end of August. Its fighting capacity was immensely improved by the arrival of the Spitfires, resulting in the decline in bombing raids, particularly during the day. By mid July the minesweepers had managed to clear the entrance channel to the island so that before the month was out the submarines were able to return. The first to arrive was the *Unbroken*, shortly to be followed by the *Ultimatum* and the *United*, until there were nine in all operating from the island. August, the first month in which the revived underwater route became available again for the fortress to hit back at the besiegers, was marked by the sinking of over 40,000 tons of shipping on Rommel's supply route. All this was of course to the good as far as the war effort was concerned, but it did not alter the fact that Malta would starve to death unless a supply convoy could get through.

The air raids while continuing were noticeably fewer, and to the astonishment and relief of the people a number of raid-free nights occurred during July. At the same time, Beaufort torpedo bombers together with Beaufighters joined the island's forces in a new striking capacity. The diversion of some of the Luftwaffe from the desert to renew the assault on Malta did not meet with the success expected, and in the first ten days of July over one hundred enemy aircraft were shot down. Unknown to the besieged the long term prospects for the whole Mediterranean war looked better than they had ever done before; but, even if they had known, it could have done nothing to alleviate their condition. For them it was enough if one day succeeded another in this moon landscape of dust and deprivation where even the slackening of the bomber offensive had as yet meant very little. But the signs on the horizon were so favourable that, for those in the know and capable of taking a long-term view of things, the outlook for Malta was brighter than it had been for nearly a year. This was always provided that a convoy could be fought through to keep the people and the garrison alive.

First of all, Rommel was held in the desert. His troops were themselves suffering from water and food rationing, ammunition and petrol were short, and his advance was firmly contained at the Alamein position. At the same time the British, with their short lines of communications, were growing stronger almost daily and their air force, reinforced by new types of aircraft from the United States, was not only achieving parity with the Luftwaffe but would soon be dominant. Far away from the wasteland of July in Malta the Anglo-American agreement was reached in the middle of that month laying plans for the invasion of French North Africa in October, to be combined with a great offensive in the desert by a massively reinforced British army equipped with American Sherman tanks and 105mm self-propelled guns.

On 2 August Lord Alanbrooke stopped off at Malta on his way through to Egypt. He was determined to tell Lord Gort of the imminent events that would make all the difference to Malta and his role as the island's leader. He knew, as he put it, that Gort was in a depressed state and suspected that 'his depression had been increased by the fact that he insisted on living on the reduced standard of rations prevailing in the Island, in spite of the fact that he was doing twice as much physical and mental work as any other member of the garrison.'[4] So, early in August, Malta's governor learned that the whole Mediterranean situation would be changed by October, but he could communicate this to no one else — and he still had to try and ensure that his command would last beyond the end of August. He knew by now that a convoy of exceptional size was planned for the middle of that month.

During July two minelaying submarines, *Parthia* and the *Clyde*, reached Malta with their essential stores, while the *Welshman* made another of her lightning dashes from Gibraltar. Fifty-nine more Spitfires, ferried to a flying-off position by *Eagle* in two expeditions, reached the island safely. Almost imperceptibly the balance was changing. But this could not be felt by those who manned the guns or looked out from the windows of their stone cottages over the hot and barren cactus land of July and August.

CHAPTER TWENTY-NINE

Preparations

Once the build up of Spitfires on the island had been achieved the whole situation was irrevocably changed. It was something that the Luftwaffe had been wise to try and prevent, but it was the success of the new reception arrangements (more important than almost anything else during this crucial period) that ensured the new climate of confidence. Air Vice-Marshal Lloyd, who had seen the island through its worst days and into the new era when fighter protection was once again assured within the flying limits of Malta, relinquished his command in mid July and handed over to Air Vice-Marshal Sir Keith Park. The latter, even with his experience from commanding a well known fighter group during the Battle of Britain, had been forewarned that activities over Malta made even that famous conflict seem comparatively simple. The whole of his new command was an airfield in the front line, with practically no rest and recuperation areas available and no cessation from the sound of battle when the raiders approached their restricted target. He had, however, a slow and steady build up of the fighter aircraft which could cope more than adequately with the Messerschmitt, and this enabled him to alter the whole basis on which the island's defence was planned. No longer was Malta in the state of being able to do no more than desperately defend itself with overworked pilots and undergunned and over-worked planes; it was now possible to take the offensive. The fighters would lead the way, with the new bombers and torpedo carriers that were reaching the island, for the offensive that would shatter the Axis shipping route to North Africa. Since intelligence confirmed that Luftwaffe squadrons had been withdrawn for service in Russia, and since the brief offensive at the end of July had been easily contained, now was the time to put the attackers from Sicily on the defensive. It was sweet revenge for what the island of Malta had suffered over the past six months and more. Rather than waiting for the raiders to come — all that had been possible when there had sometimes been no more than six airworthy fighters for the defence — they were now to be met far out from the island. Improved radar, and training in its use by experts out from Britain, played its part in what amounted to the counter puncher going on the offensive.

In a Special Order of the Day Air Vice-Marshal Park acknowledged the debt to the past but instilled the new outlook for the future.

During the blitz in the spring, the enemy was so vastly superior in strength that our day fighters were practically forced on the defensive. Under these conditions it was inevitable that Royal Air Force personnel on the ground and civilians should undergo severe bombing daily.... Our day fighter strength has during June and July been greatly increased, and the enemy's superiority in numbers has long since dwindled. The time has now arrived for our Spitfire squadrons to put an end to the bombing of our airfields by daylight.[1]

Aggressive tactics became the keynote, the Spitfires sweeping skywards as soon as a tremor on the radar screens indicated activity over Sicily. The squadron at stand-by had to be off the ground within two minutes, the squadron at immediate readiness within three minutes, and the squadron at readiness within five minutes. The Regia Aeronautica rarely came by daylight over the angry beehive to the south, and the obsolescent Stukas (still deadly on the Russian front) had given place to the Junkers 88s which themselves, without heavy fighter escorts, could no longer triumphantly ride the Maltese sky. The enemy to the north, baking on the sun-scorched summer airfields of Sicily, could only venture fighter sweeps over that southern rock and, fighter against fighter, they no longer had that almost contemptuously hard edge which they'd had before over patched up Hurricanes and exhausted pilots.

Aware of the large convoy that was being planned, and aware that it would be months before the passage to the island could be rendered in any degree safe for convoys, the Air Vice-Marshal cautioned his crews against easy optimism. 'All fighter formations are warned that the enemy will probably reintroduce bomber formations whenever there is an important operation in the Malta area. Because our Spitfires, using the forward plan of interception, have recently stopped daylight raids does not mean that only fighter sweeps are likely to be encountered over or near Malta in the future.'[2] He knew that in mid August the Axis would switch every available plane to attacking a convoy on which the island entirely depended for survival.

Nearly four centuries before, towards the end of the long hot summer of 1565, the defenders of Malta had noticed that the assaults against them were beginning to lose their ferocity and there were even signs that some of the troops were having to be driven to the attack. Something similar had been noticed over Malta during 1942; the reluctance of the Regia Aeronautica had been noticed so long as not to be worth comment. Even the Luftwaffe fighters which now came down on gadfly raids, dropping a few bombs and strafing, were a far cry from those who in earlier months had almost leisurely cruised low over the island, let alone he who had 'flown his gage' down Grand Harbour at the beginning. An increased use of anti-personnel bombs revealed some desperation on the part of the attackers. The new tactics of engaging the enemy over the sea meant that many more pilots were coming down by parachute off the island and Malta's Air-Sea Rescue Service in their highspeed boats were constantly on call from their base at Kalafrana in the south. Injured German aircrew in Mtarfa Hospital began to outnumber the soldiers and airmen of the defenders, and a great change in their morale was noted from the easy selfconfidence of the springtime attackers. One gunner from a Junker 88, echoing as it were some earlier Turk, later said of Malta: 'We were always being driven to it.'

As in the unhappy occupied Europe of the New Order so in besieged Malta, which was fighting against being brought within that fold, only one thing thrived during the war, the Black Market. In London, in Paris, in Berlin, in Rome, and equally here, the natural cupidity of man could not be erased, and the same circumstances which brought out the qualities of heroism, self-sacrifice and abnegation produced a black market in everything. Because supply ceases demand does not cease, and when the demand is not so much for luxuries but for all the basics of life, the competition to supply it increases in ratio to the price that can be obtained. Malta, dependent on imports for every form of manufactured goods, lacked everything from clothing to razor blades and soap. Second-hand clothing, clothes stolen from bombed houses, old shoes, belts, shirts, linen of every kind, there was not a thing of the most ordinary household use that had not acquired under siege conditions a value far beyond normal comprehension. Naturally, the real black market existed in food, from any form of meat (as rare as might have been caviare in peacetime) to bread, eggs, and even vegetables. The result of a government policy of buying up a large part of the green vegetables, onions and potatoes for use by the Victory Kitchens, the services and the hospitals meant that little was left over for the private suppliers, the *pitkali* who sold from baskets or carts direct to the public. The foundations of many small fortunes were inevitably laid by farmers large and small in Malta and Gozo during the siege, but particularly during the desperate summer of 1942 when starvation was very close and the island was only a few weeks away from surrender. Jail sentences, heavy fines, increased jail sentences, heavier fines, nothing could possibly extirpate the root of this trouble which stemmed from the desire to survive.

In Pwales valley to the north of Malta, and especially in Gozo, farmers thrived on visits by night from *pitkali* and individual citizens eager to make some money or to keep their families alive and healthy. Daytime ferries from Gozo could be inspected, but by night individual boats, making their way across to Malta from the agricultural and relatively untouched island to the north, formed a steady chain of private enterprise that no public authority could possibly break. Archbishop Caruana himself might denounce the black marketeers over the radio, but there are few who will not face the possible future penalties for sin rather than accept the real and imminent danger of starvation. Among the interminable catalogue of shortages, but one which meant a great deal to the thousands of servicemen on the island, was the absence of any beer, due to lack of fuel to maintain the breweries in working capacity. Minimal perhaps compared with solid food, beer had nevertheless remained the one luxury of the day, and there had been little enough of it even when it had been available. Many months before, the normal exercises and marches undertaken by the troops to keep them fit had been discontinued, and in their place were now instituted compulsory rest periods or, as they were known, 'sleep parades'. To conserve their energy for their duties, as well as not to make them more hungry than they already were, the troops were required to lie down and rest at set times.

By July 1942 the Germans were right when they said, '*Malta ist sturmreif*' (ripe for attack), but by then Operazione C3, Operation Hercules, had been called off and the organization almost entirely disbanded. Furthermore the island's capacity to strike back as well as to attack locally had been immensely increased not only by the replenishment of Spitfires but by the return of the bombers and submarines. The minesweepers which had come through from the Gibraltar convoy in June had been able to carry out sweeping duties under protective air cover during the day (although E-boats still made their minelaying runs by night) and the battle against the island's waters being completely mined was to carry on for many months. The swept channel to Grand Harbour required never ending attention — for it was only down that passage that relief ships could reach the island on the day when the anticipated convoy fought its way through. All were interdependent under the conditions of the siege in a way that would never be comprehended in peacetime life, but which was visible and tangible in a locked-in island. From fighter pilot to the officer in charge of the minesweeping party on the afterdeck of a motorlaunch or minesweeper, from gun crew in St Elmo to decoder in the tunnels behind Lascaris Bastion, from water pumping station mechanic to air-raid warden, through all the gamut of life (women having babies in underground delivery centres, to the old, breathing the last familiar dusty air as the priest bent over them) Malta was a microcosm of the world, a world continuously at war.

To keep the island alive until such time as the survivors on this Promethean rock could receive substantial help the minelaying submarines from Alexandria continued to bring in such essential small bulk cargoes as were needed — medical stores, kerosene, bags of mail, powdered milk, armour-piercing shells, and petrol. The *Cachalot*, the *Porpoise*, the *Rorqual*, the *Osiris* and the *Urge* were among those which kept this slender lifeline open while the preparations went ahead for a major relief. This was something which it would be impossible to conceal once it had entered the Mediterranean, and against which every available aircraft, submarine, surface ship and destructive device would be hurled.

Operation 'Pedestal' was planned to pass a large convoy through from the Gibraltar end of the sea. The experience of the 'Vigorous' convoy from the eastern end in June had shown that, so long as all the coast to the south (as well as Crete to the north) was in Axis hands, it was impossible to run a convoy from Alexandria. The assembly of a large convoy — fourteen ships in all were to be made available — almost inevitably meant that it would be sighted passing through the Straits of Gibraltar, and once into the Mediterranean it would soon be found. The acceptance of grave losses from air attack was understood from the first, and the possibility that the Italians, under pressure from the Germans, would make some move with their fleet had always to be considered.

A heavier fleet escort than usual must therefore be provided, with battleships to cover the voyage as far as the Skerki Channel and an escort of modern cruisers and destroyers through to Malta.

The heavy escort was to be provided by the two sister ships, *Nelson* and *Rodney*, each of 34,000 tons with nine 16-inch guns, and twelve 6-inch secondary armament. Vice-Admiral Sir Neville Syfret, a South African, flew his flag in *Nelson*, being the flag officer in command of what was called Force Z. With him would go an aircraft carrier squadron under Rear Admiral Lyster, carrying his flag in the new *Indomitable*, together with the 1939-built *Victorious* and the old *Eagle*. Forty-six Hurricanes, ten Martlets and sixteen Fulmars aboard the carriers would provide fighter cover. With this main escort would be the three fast, 5.25 inch anti-aircraft cruisers, *Charybdis*, *Phoebe* and *Sirius* and fourteen destroyers. As close escort to the merchantmen were the heavy cruiser *Nigeria* (Rear Admiral

Burrough) together with the similar *Kenya* and *Manchester*, and the anti-aircraft cruiser *Cairo*. Designated Force X, it would be their task together with eleven destroyers to cover the convoy through to Malta after Force Z had turned back at the Skerki Narrows. Separate from main operation 'Pedestal', but designed to take place at the same time, the carrier *Furious* with a destroyer escort was to fly off thirty-eight Spitfires as reinforcements for Malta. As back up to the fleet there were two fleet oilers with a corvette escort, a deep-sea rescue tug and another salvage vessel. All in all, it was the largest naval operation ever set in motion until that time in the Mediterranean.

Thirteen of the fast modern merchantmen which formed the *raison d'être* of this armada carried the usual mixed cargo for Malta — flour, ammuniton and petrol in cans. This combination of food fuel and war fuel was a direct reflection of the island's needs and requirements — but no one on board any ship could have the comfortable feeling that they carried harmless goods alone, since all were almost equally burdened with a highly-explosive mixture on the most dangerous convoy run in the world. The fourteenth ship, *Ohio*, was a large tanker, pure and simple, a new ship from the Texaco Oil Company. She had been loaned for the occasion to the British, was manned by British seamen and commanded by Captain Mason of the Eagle Oil & Shipping Company. American owned and also American manned were two general cargo ships, *Santa Elisa* and *Almeria Lykes*. The remainder comprized some of the finest and fastest British merchantmen then afloat. *Port Chalmers* headed the list, in which the Convoy Commodore, Commander Venables RN, flew his broad pennant, followed by *Wairangi*, *Waimarama* and *Empire Hope* of the Shaw Savill Line, *Brisbane Star* and *Melbourne Star*, of the Blue Star Line, *Dorset* of the Federal Steam Navigation Co., *Rochester Castle* of the Union Castle Line, *Deucalion* of the Blue Funnel Line, *Glenorchy* of the Glen Line, and *Clan Ferguson* of the Clan Line.[3]

Although no attempt was to be made to pass a second convoy through from the eastern end of the sea a cover plan was devized whereby Admiral Harwood would mount a dummy operation from Alexandria in company with Admiral Vian from Haifa. A total of five cruisers, fifteen destroyers and five merchantmen would sail as if bound for Malta, and then on their second night out disperse and turn back. It was hoped that this would tie down some of the enemy and possibly cause dissension among the Italian navy as to the choice of targets. Meanwhile Air Vice Marshal Park in Malta was to hold in readiness a torpedo-bombing force in case the Italian fleet might be tempted to leave Taranto, the rest of his air forces, including over one-hundred and thirty fighters, being kept for support of the convoy. Six British submarines from Malta would be on patrol west of the island in case the Italian fleet should try to interfere in the region of Pantellaria, while two were on patrol to the north of Sicily.

Even if intercepted radio messages had not given them an inkling that a large British operation was afoot in the western Mediterranean any sensible Italian staff officer could have foretold that Malta must soon receive a convoy or surrender. German and Italian bombers, dive bombers and torpedo planes were assembled on the airfields of Sicily and Sardinia along with fighter aircraft and reconnaissance planes. In all, some seven-hundred aircraft were put on duty as reception committee for this convoy once it came within range. Eighteen Italian submarines were on patrol, one off Malta itself, eleven in the Narrows, and six spread between Algiers and the Balearic Islands. Three German U-boats were also stationed in this approach area where the whole body of the escorting fleet might be expected. Off Cape Bon in Tunisia E-boats and Italian MTBs were to lie in wait, while in the same area a new minefield had been laid where the British might not expect one, since it was part of a swept channel that had previously been kept clear for Axis convoys running to Tripoli. Three heavy and three light cruisers together with ten destroyers were held in waiting to intercept the convoy south of Sicily.

Operation 'Pedestal' was scheduled to start with the assembly of the convoy off the mouth of the Clyde on 2 August 1942. Upon it Malta would stand or fall, and upon it directly and indirectly depended the fate of millions.

CHAPTER THIRTY

Nine Days to Santa Maria

The convoy moved south through the Bay of Biscay in three parallel columns. They had been told their destination on the first morning at sea and from then on they had not been surprised at the degree to which the convoy was put through its paces. The gun crews aboard the merchantmen, composed of Royal Naval and Maritime Regiment gunners manning the anti-aircraft weaponry, were aware that ships had more than doubled their normal wartime quota — several Oerlikons where one or two were normally sufficient, and heavier AA guns as well as machine guns and rockets. They were endlessly at exercises. The ships themselves were also regularly engaged in tactical manoeuvres — altering formation, reducing and increasing speed, and making emergency turns. On either side of them went their constant escort companions and astern the heavyweight shoulders of the great ships rose and fell as they headed south.

On 6 August, when the convoy was well on its way and other units of the fleet were standing by at Gibraltar or on passage to join them from Freetown in West Africa, a great many more people went to church in Malta than was normal. Special prayers were offered to Our Lady, as well as to Saint Paul, premier patron saint of the island, while other local saints of special devotion in different parishes were also remembered. A few days earlier the Archbishop had sent a circular to all parish priests, ordering a novena to be said in preparation for the feast of 'the Assumption of the Blessed Virgin Mary, Mother of God, into Heaven'. 15 August, the Feast of the Assumption, is normally a major *festa* of the summer months — that season of fireworks, illuminated churches, gaudy stalls selling ice creams, almond and honey *helwa*, Turkish delight, images of saints, fruit, pile upon pile of coloured sweets, and iced lemon and orange drinks — all under bright electric bulbs or hissing kerosene flares. Since seven parishes in Malta and one in Gozo are dedicated to Santa Marija this is one of the most widely celebrated summer *festas*, but there had not been, nor could there be, any outdoor festivities once the war had broken over the island. The order from the Archbishop for a special novena to be said for the nine days prior to the Feast of the Assumption on the 15th conveyed not only the gravity of the hour but suggested something unusual — some hoped

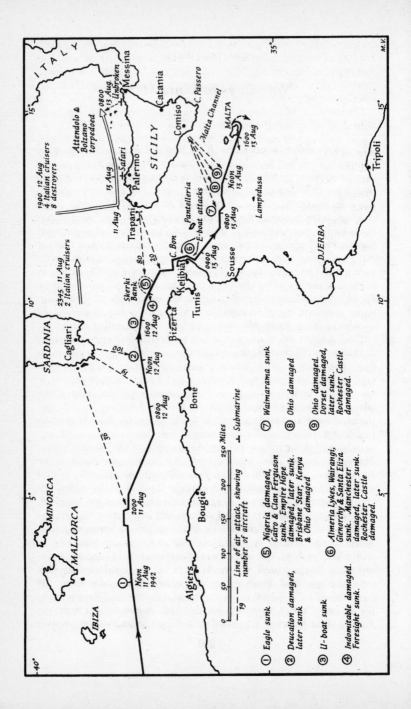

ITALY

Messina
0800 13 Aug. Unbroken

Attendolo & Bolzano torpedoed

1900 12 Aug. 4 Italian cruisers 8 destroyers

13 Aug. ✠ Safari

Palermo

Catania

Comiso

C. Passero

SICILY

11 Aug.

Trapani

2345 11 Aug. 2 Italian cruisers

80

20

Sherki Bank

④

⑤

C. Bon

Kelibia

Pantelleria

E-boat attacks ⑥

⑦

0800 13 Aug.

⑧ Noon 13 Aug.

⑨

Malta Channel

MALTA

1600 13 Aug.

Lampedusa

③

1600 12 Aug.

Bizerta

Tunis

0400 13 Aug.

Sousse

DJERBA

Tripoli

SARDINIA

Cagliari

001

② Noon 12 Aug.

19

36

0800 12 Aug.

2000 11 Aug.

Bone

Bougie

MINORCA

MALLORCA

IBIZA

① Noon 11 Aug. 1942

Algiers

0   50   100   150   200   250 Miles

19 — — — Line of air attack, showing number of aircraft

✠ Submarine

① Eagle sunk

② Deucalion damaged, later sunk

③ U-boat sunk

④ Indomitable damaged. Foresight sunk.

⑤ Nigeria damaged, Cairo & Clan Ferguson sunk. Empire Hope damaged, later sunk. Brisbane Star, Kenya & Ohio damaged.

⑥ Almeria Lykes, Wairangi, Glenorchy & Santa Eliza sunk. Manchester damaged, later sunk. Rochester Castle damaged.

⑦ Waimarama sunk

⑧ Ohio damaged

⑨ Ohio damaged. Dorset damaged, later sunk. Rochester Castle damaged.

M.V.

for form of deliverance perhaps? The faithful were requested in their prayers to ask that 'God the merciful may shorten the time of this scourge and grant us His help. . . .' Their children were exhorted to receive Holy Communion and on Santa Marija Day itself all the faithful were recommended to do the same.

On the night of 10 August the convoy was entering the Straits of Gibraltar — the weather fair, though foggy as so often in that area. There could never have been any concealment of the passage of so large a convoy, even if some of the fishing vessels in the straits had not had Axis agents aboard them, even if plain language communications between carrier-borne aircraft had not been inevitable in earlier routine practices and even if there had not been an Italian naval agent in Ceuta across the straits from Gibraltar. Questions were later asked in the House of Commons about bad security over the destination of the convoy, but security involving so many items that had to be handled by so many dockers and involving so many ships was always an impossibility. Any large convoy at that time bound for the Mediterranean could only be bound for Malta.

On the morning of 11 August the whole convoy with its many escorts, its two battleships and its three aircraft carriers, was steaming through the Mediterranean, the fourteen merchantmen in the centre now in four parallel columns. Early that morning, some sixty miles south of Ibiza in the Balearic Islands, they had been sighted, ineffectively attacked, and reported by the Italian submarine *Uarsciek*. The entire waiting line of submarines, the torpedo boats hundreds of miles away, the bombers and the torpedo bombers, and the Italian fleet units had all stiffened for action. Among those waiting in the line ahead was Lieutenant Rosenbaum of the U73, an old Mediterranean hand who had nearly lost his boat in a bombing attack off Tobruk on a previous occasion and who was now in his patrol position off Algiers. Alerted by the steady thrumming sound of the advancing convoy, he skilfully evaded the outriders of the fleet, diving beneath the destroyers (profiting possibly by one of those cold layers that were the bane of Mediterranean sonar operators.)[1] Lieutenant Rosenbaum now manoeuvred himself into a firing position. He had before him one of the very targets that the U boats had been specifically ordered to try for, an aircraft carrier; he had already identified her as *Eagle*. He fired at a range of five-hundred yards and his full spread of four torpedoes, set to run at twenty foot, hit the old veteran along her port side.

In less than eight minutes *Eagle* had sunk, some two-hundred men going down with her. U73, taking advantage of the confusion as destroyers raced to pick up survivors, made her escape as skilfully as she had made her kill. The convoy executed an emergency ninety degree turn as gravely as if on a fleet exercise while destroyers depth-charged all those errant echoes that occur on such occasions. Four of the *Eagle*'s fighters which were in the air at the time landed safely on the two other carriers, but so early in the operation, and long before the need for them had been felt, some twenty-five per cent of the air cover had been lost.

The convoy and its escort were now steaming on their inevitable line of advance expected by the waiting submarines. Throughout that afternoon, while the destroyers worried away at contacts, with erratic pillars from depth charges foaming against the picture-postcard blue of the sky and sea, the convoy made seventeen emergency turns. Torpedo tracks were seen, but there were no further repetitions of that submarine commander's dream, the death of an aircraft carrier. Others lay in wait for them as they neared the Narrows, but the submarines that had been spread to the north of Algiers had nothing further to record in their log books.

The ships were now edging up into the shadow line that spread out concentrically from the airfields of Sardinia, coming within range of bomber and torpedo bomber. During the afternoon high reconnaissance came over, just to confirm the convoy's course and composition; only the heavy anti-aircraft guns of the *Nelson* and *Rodney* opening up on these spotter aircraft that were out of range of all lesser calibres. They made it back again untouched to Cagliari and Decimomammu while the ships surged on through the stillness and heat, where sky and sea merged in the northerner's dream of the Mediterranean. At dusk, when the fighters were being struck down below for the night, the raiders came in to hit them — Heinkel torpedo planes and Junkers 88 dive bombers. They had to fight their way through circles of firepower — destroyers spread around, cruisers, the carriers and the battleships — an immense storm of metal that tested the nerves even of seasoned pilots. The convoy made an emergency turn, torpedoes tracked vivid through the phosphorescent sea, bombs erupted against the darkening water, and the roar and the whine combined with flak startled the darkness in the east where they were heading. The Evening Star was effaced by tracer and four planes came down burning into the sea. The ships ploughed on again — no casualties. That night Beauforts out of Malta struck against the airfields on Sardinia. Shadowing aircraft stayed with the ships throughout the dark hours, reporting their course and speed, never leaving them, so that they could be effectively met at dawn. But at 6 a.m. Martlet fighters swept up off *Indomitable* and cut two of the shadowers out of the sky. Wednesday, 12 August (far back in some never-never land the opening of the grouse-shooting season) was certain to prove a noisy one on these moors of gently undulating sea, for the convoy was now only about seventy miles south of Sardinia. If it had not been for the bombers from Malta who had destroyed planes, hangars and fuel dumps in their base airfields, the first attacks would have been heavier. As it was, eight Junkers 88s were shot down in the first raid just after 9 a.m. by Hurricanes and Martlets already up to greet them. This reception aloft was matched by the gunfire below and such planes as did break through dropped their bombs ineffectually before heading for safety in the north.

The morning was full of U boat alarms, one apparently determined attack being put down by two destroyers working in conjunction on the port side of the screen. All waited for what was surely being prepared for them, the really big raid of the day, the *grande battue* of the 12th. It had indeed been carefully prepared, involving over one-hundred aircraft of various types as well as a number of new weapons. High noon and the August sun blazing over a sea wrinkled only by the ships' passage saw the five waves of the main attack from the Sardinian airfields launch themselves against the convoy. The first move was made by ten Savoia bombers escorted by Macchi fighters and fighter bombers, and was designed to break up the convoy formation by an ingenious new weapon, the 'motobomba'. The 'motobomba' was a torpedo dropped on a parachute and designed to run in a circle or on an eccentric course, and would have been hazardous indeed to a convoy in formation if dropped only a short distance ahead. But in this case, the Savoias and their escorting fighters were detected well in advance, the convoy's Martlets and Hurricanes were vectored in their direction and the convoy itself, as soon as the descending parachutes were observed, executed a ninety degree turn. It thus neatly sidestepped the weird torpedoes. Fighter bombers which had accompanied the first wave (designed to distract the outer screen of the destroyers) were again met by carrier fighters and the attack, alarming only because of its mysterious weaponry, petered out.

The second part consisted of over forty torpedo planes, approaching in two groups, one from each side of the convoy — a convoy which in theory should have already been disrupted and suffering casualties from the 'motobombas'. The attacking planes were met far out by Hurricanes and Martlets, causing them to drop their torpedoes at ineffectively long range, while those which approached further met the full firepower of the fleet — including immense air-bursts like thunderclaps from the 16-inch guns of the *Rodney*. During this hurricane of shot and shell over a tranquil sea the convoy faultlessly executed two emergency turns, and such torpedoes as came within range passed harmlessly by.

207

As the torpedo bombers were retiring, the first German attack developed with a formation of dive-bombers attacking the *Nelson* and the *Rodney*. Both giant ships were narrowly missed, but their 14-inch armour plate was impervious to fragmented bombs while the anti-aircraft cruiser *Cairo*, also near-missed, emerged with disciplined guns shouting through the pinnacles of spray. The dive bombers achieved a success on one of the merchantment, *Deucalion*, which was leading the port wing of the convoy. Hit by one bomb, which passed right through the ship, she was so severely damaged by other near misses that she fell behind the convoy and, escorted by a destroyer, turned towards the North African shore. Dive-bombed again later in the day, she was still under way at dusk (hoping to reach Malta on her own) when she was found by torpedo planes. One hit was sufficient to touch off the petrol and kerosene aboard her. Hardly had the crew abandoned ship than *Deucalion*, veteran of a previous Malta convoy, blew up with an ear-shattering explosion — the first of the convoy to be lost, and a sinister portent of the night to come.

Italian ingenuity in the meantime had tried again where direct action had failed, and a pilotless plane, loaded with explosive, had been launched against the fleet under radio control from a Cant seaplane.[2] Intended for one of the capital ships, its control malfunctioned and it carried on over the sea to reach the land and explode in North Africa. Last, but almost most successful of the day's surprises, were two Reggione fighters (much resembling Hurricanes) which followed in some Hurricanes as they were landing on *Victorious*. Accepted as friendly by the gunners, each dropped a large bomb. One just missed the bows, but the other fell square on the flight deck, where it would have done immense damage had it penetrated and almost as much if it had exploded among the parked planes. To the general astonishment on board and the justified anger of the pilot, it fragmented without exploding, the carrier steaming on unharmed.

Throughout the long hot afternoon, as the convoy and its escort drew nearer to the Sicilian narrows, one submarine alarm succeeded another. There were so many reports of contacts that eventually Rear-Admiral Burrough ordered the convoy escort to drop routine depth charges every half hour on either side of the convoy to discourage prowlers. Real enough, however, was a torpedo track seen at 4.40 p.m., followed by a periscope sighting; in the ensuing depth charge attack the Italian submarine *Emo* was damaged but managed to escape. On the other side of the convoy, and almost at the same time, the Italian *Cobalto* was forced to the surface by depth charges, and then rammed by the destroyer *Ithuriel*. Her survivors were taken prisoner.

Throughout all the blinding day, when the proverbial egg would have sizzled on any exposed metal surface, every member of every ship's company, whether carrier, destroyer, battleship or merchant-man, had been ceaselessly at action stations. Submarines could retire to reconsider another attack position, the bombers could withdraw and be replaced by other planes with fresh pilots, but the carrier pilots like the gun crews, the sonar ratings, the stokers and the entire complement of convoy and escort had to remain per-manently at their posts. Tired and blistered by heat, the armada turned at last towards the Skerki Channel, the beginning of the approaches through the concentric rings of the inferno at the heart of which lay the island.

So far the fleet had lost *Eagle*, while *Ithuriel* with damaged bows had retired to Gilbraltar, and the convoy had lost *Deucalion*. *Victorious* had been hit but not seriously and many other ships had received near misses but suffered only slight damage. Even allowing for the fine defence put up by the carrier-borne aircraft and the accurate gunnery of the fleet, it had to be conceded that, in view of the weight of attack thrown at them, they had been lucky so far. The great testing ground lay ahead, as they came within range of the Luftwaffe airfields in Sicily and the narrows where submarines were bound to lie in wait, and undoubtedly E boats, and probably the dangers of an attack by surface ships from Sicily. It was at this point, as the evening came down, that Force Z, the battleships and carriers and other units, must leave and turn back to the west. But before that could happen there came one last daylight raid of Stukas coupled with torpedo bombers fresh from Sicily that gave a bitter foretaste of the future. The raid was not unexpected for radar and reconnaiss-ance aircraft had for some time been reporting planes gathering around the edges of the convoy, visible here and there, then thicken-ing — waiting.

When they were perfectly coordinated, a combined attack by Savoia torpedo bombers and Stuka dive bombers overwhelmed the defences and broke through — to achieve the first major air success of the whole operation. As in that earlier convoy to Malta, when Fliegerkorps X had effectively cripped HMS *Illustrious*, so now amid the general maelstrom of Savoias attacking with torpedoes, fighters peeling off in defence of their bombers, and the thunder of the fleet's anti-aircraft guns, a group of Stukas dropped down in perfect sequence, taking *Indomitable* as their target.

No two accounts of confused actions between sea fleets and air fleets ever agree, for the good reason that everyone concerned is totally concentrating within his own sphere of action. For each there is only one particular cone of light and noise and danger that exists.

The historian's distant eye, examining the information, can piece together no more than flecks of colour, as when a *pointilliste* painting is seen too close up to coalesce into a coherent whole. *Victorious*, receiving several near misses, was hit by three bombs on her flight deck and flared with petrol fires; aircraft were burning and her after lift was out of action. She could no longer receive her own aircraft when they needed to return from the air battle and they had to be redirected to the *Indomitable*, now over burdened with aircraft and the only carrier left operational out of the three that had set out from Gibraltar. No other ships were put out of action by the Stukas, but the screening destroyers lost one of their number to the torpedo bombers as *Foresight*, her whole stern blown away, shuddered to a halt. With her motive power gone and too damaged to be towed, she had to be sunk as the convoy moved on.

The raid ended towards dusk and Force Z had come to the end of its protective role. Admiral Syfret was well aware, as he turned back to the west, that the worst lay ahead for the Malta bound convoy. His heavy ships, those powerful pieces on the great chessboard, had been ventured as far as possible; he left Admiral Burrough with his three cruisers and twelve destroyers in possession of a convoy out of which only one merchantship had been lost so far.

As the convoy prepared to enter the Skerki Channel, that narrow passage of deep water between invisible sandbars (a place ideal for the skilful submariner to lurk since sonar transmissions were confused by the irregularity of the bottom) they had to change formation and become a long double line. Well drilled though they were, it was inevitable that this major changeover for convoy and escort led to some degree of loss in their organized progression. At 7.45 p.m. the first ship to enter the channel, at the head of the port column of ships, was the cruiser *Nigeria*, Admiral Burrough's flagship. A minute later the anti-aircraft cruiser *Cairo*, leading the starboard column, followed her in. Behind them the others, closing up into their two columns, followed their leaders over the darkening calm sea, where Lieutenant Renato Ferrini of the submarine *Axim* had already noted: 'It is flat calm [and] the feather of the periscope is conspicuous even at minimum speed.' At 7.55 p.m. he fired his full spread of four torpedos from the bow tubes. At almost the same moment another Italian submarine, *Dessie*, had also fired. Within a few minutes the darkening waters were lit by brilliant flashes and split by the thunderous roar as *Nigeria* was hit amidships. *Cairo* was hit aft and had her screws blown away, while the convoy's only tanker, *Ohio*, was hit amidships.

In a moment all coherence of convoy and escort was lost. *Ohio* came to a temporary halt, thus causing *Empire Hope* behind her to go hard astern in order to avoid collision. Other ships were turning independently to comb torpedo tracks while those maids of all work, the destroyers, were racing to give help — and adding to the confusion. The fact that the two column leaders, the *Nigeria* and *Cairo*, were torpedoed was bad enough, but the fact that *Nigeria* was Admiral Burrough's flagship meant a temporary loss of control. *Cairo* was also the only specifically anti-aircraft cruiser in the escort, while she and *Nigeria* were the only two ships fitted with fighter-direction equipment for controlling fighter aircraft from Malta. Against the flames and sounds of rending metal, shouts and agitated figures visible here and there in leaping fires and the drumming roar of *Nigeria* blowing off steam, the well timed last aircraft raid of the day came in out of the east. They had the disordered convoy silhouetted against the pale afterglow of the vanished sun. The carrier fighters had been struck down aboard *Victorious* which was well on her way back to Gibraltar. To add to the confusion, during the attack by Junkers 88s and Savoia torpedo bombers, a formation of long-range Beaufighters arrived from Malta, only to receive an irregular and irrational fire from the ships. ('If it flies, shoot it!')

Lieutenant Puccini in the submarine *Alagi* now put in an appearance and fired his bow torpedoes 'at a cruiser' — undoubtedly hitting *Kenya* and possibly a merchantman at the same time. Certainly, during this combined submarine and air attack, *Kenya* was hit in the bows, narrowly escaping two other torpedoes, while *Brisbane Star* and *Clan Ferguson*, both hit either by submarine or aerial torpedoes, came lurching to a halt. The ammunition on the latter went up with a shattering roar and she disappeared. *Empire Hope*, hit by one of the dive bombers, caught fire and had to be abandoned. *Nigeria*, it was soon established, was so badly damaged that she would only be a liability if she continued with the convoy, so Admiral Burrough was reluctantly forced to transfer his flag to the destroyer *Ashanti* while his cruiser limped back westwards to Gibraltar. At the same time Captain Russell in *Kenya*, not knowing what had happened to the admiral, signalled that he had taken command. After his own ship was hit in the bows but it was established that she could still maintain a fair speed, he hastened to the head of the convoy, even as Admiral Burrough was transferring to *Ashanti* to take over again. Some time after Lieutenant Puccini had made his attack and disengaged to settle on the bottom, he decided to surface again to see if he could establish what all the random explosions and high-speed propeller noises he had heard above him signified. At 9.13 p.m. he came up, looked around and noted: 'The horizon between bearing 180° and 240° is a continuous line of flame from the burning, sinking ships' and a little later: 'A burning ship blows up.'

Ohio meanwhile, which had come to a stop with a great hole torn in her side, had by fine seamanship been got under way again and, with bulkheads shored up, was making her way slowly after the convoy. *Brisbane Star* had also got under way but her master, realizing he could not catch up, had turned to hug the Tunisian coast in the hope that he could make his way independently to Malta. (This was something he finally managed to do, in an epic voyage distinguished even in a convoy that had enough such epics to keep sea writers busy for years.) Cohesion had now left Force X, as some masters made their way alone or accompanied by one or other of the destroyers, while only one small body was still sailing as a group. This consisted of two fleet destroyers with their minesweeping sweeps streamed (it was still thought that some of the losses might have been due to mines) followed by the two cruisers *Kenya* and *Manchester* and two merchantmen, *Glenorchy* and the American *Almeria Lykes*.

After the aircraft and the submarines it was the turn of the fast motor torpedo boats, the E boats, which had been waiting quietly, their engines stopped, lolling on the easy swell off the great bulk of Cape Bon. It was ideal weather for their work, and no young lieutenant in command of one of those powerful boats could have imagined a more perfect night for a convoy attack. As the ships began to draw close (it was a moonless night but bright with stars), the hunters, invisible against the dark loom of the land, one by one began to spring into attack. The quick cough of the engines starting was followed by that dark and powerful roar as their engines hurled them towards the oncoming ships. Two Italian boats sprang towards the cruiser *Manchester*, and two torpedoes left her immobilized — to be scuttled the following day. Everywhere now the night began to be lit by tracer fire, an occasional searchlight beam, harsh cracks from the ships' main armament, the old-fashioned hammering sound of pom-poms, spraying crackle from Oerlikons, and the intermittent tracer and stammering of Italian Breda all purpose guns. This was indeed revenge for so many ships sunk by the British in the Cape Bon area. The American *Almeria Lykes* went down, most of her crew being taken off by one of the destroyers. *Glenorchy* was hit and the crew, all except the master, abandoned ship. (She sank the next day, Captain Leslie going down with her.) E-boats also claimed *Wairangi* while the American *Santa Elisa*, damaged by bombing the previous day, now succumbed to a torpedo that set fire to her cased petrol which then ran into her ammunition, which in its turn exploded.

Rochester Castle which had made as many as eleven emergency turns to evade attacking E boats finally ran out of luck and was hit by a torpedo forward. Fortunately the bulkheads held and she was able to stay with the surviving ships as, almost all order lost, the survivors plodded east towards the dawn.

It was a dawn for which they prayed — and at the same time they feared. All the flash and the roar and the scattering of fire and shells and the inexplicable explosions of the night were so much the worse for occurring in the Middle Watch, the graveyard watch, where darkness, tiredness and confusion added to simple human fear. But with the dawn they could expect the bombers. Although they knew they were within range of some kind of long range protection from Malta, they knew that they were too far away for secure fighter cover. They had also seen how, even under an umbrella of fighters from the fleet, nothing could stop a determined torpedo plane or dive bomber.

Admiral Burrough aboard the *Ashanti* had a further grim preoccupation at dawn on 13 August. He had heard from Malta the previous evening that a reconnaissance aircraft had reported six cruisers and eleven destroyers steaming south through the Tyrrhenian Sea. Although he had been reinforced from Force Z by two destroyers and a light cruiser, *Charybdis*, he was otherwise left with only the damaged *Kenya* and seven destroyers should the Italians decide to complete the destruction of the convoy. There was not much of it. Astern of him trailed *Melbourne Star* and *Waimarama*, then the damaged and most important ship of all, *Ohio*, and behind her again *Dorset* and *Port Chalmers*. He was not to know that in the waters of Tunisia to the south *Brisbane Star* was fighting her solitary battle to reach the island. Nor was he to know that the threat posed by the Italian cruisers had vanished.

CHAPTER THIRTY-ONE

Miraculous Relief

During the night of the 12th-13th, while the convoy had been fighting and sinking off Cape Bon, the Italian cruisers had indeed been heading to round the north-western point of Sicily to intervene on the following day. Their destination obvious, their course and position observed, Malta had despatched Wellington bombers to illuminate them with flares and attack during the night. Although none of the Italian ships were hit, their naval command was concerned since, their position being known, they would certainly be attacked by torpedo bombers from Malta at daybreak. They were further confused by signals that they picked up from the British planes (deliberately made in plain language) which suggested that Liberator bombers were also being despatched to attack the cruisers. All this, coupled with the fact that the Regia Aeronautica, under pressure from Kesselring to provide every plane for the destruction of the convoy, had informed the navy that no fighters would be available for the protection of their ships during daylight hours, led to the recall of the cruiser squadron. While they were retiring to the north on the morning of 13 August they were intercepted by Lieutenant Mars in the submarine *Unbroken* in the vicinity of the Lipari Islands. Two of them were torpedoed, a heavy and a light cruiser being so badly damaged that they were never repaired to take any further part in the war.

If Admiral Burrough could have been spared this worry, nothing could spare him and the ships under his protection from the weight of air attack that was soon to fall on them. They were some two-hundred miles from Malta, south-east of the Italian island of Pantellaria, and they had no means of communicating with the Beaufighters from Malta when they did arrive nor of directing them since both the cruisers with VHF direction sets had been lost. At 8 a.m. the first wave of Junkers 88s came in, and *Waimarama* received a direct hit. She disintegrated with an ear-splitting roar and the sea around her ran like a steel furnace with flaming aviation spirit. *Melbourne Star* following close astern of her was deluged with flaming debris, fire and giant pieces of iron raining down all over her. Engulfed in flames, her own paintwork burning, her boats turning to torches, *Melbourne Star* steamed through the explosion while over thirty of her crew, convinced that it was their own ship that had blown up, leaped over the side. Most of them, together with two or three tragically-burned survivors who had been hurled from the exploding *Waimarama*, were rescued from the blazing sea by the destroyer *Ledbury*. *Ohio*, next in line behind the *Melbourne Star*, was also showered with burning fragments, starting a fire in her deck cargo of kerosene, which her crew fought with superhuman fervour — for no one expects much future in a tanker that has already been torpedoed and is now on fire.

Ohio was inevitably the main target for the next wave of dive-bombers. Although they missed her some of her forward plating was buckled while, to add to the damage, part of one of the planes which had been hit by gunfire crashed aboard. *Rochester Castle* also received a near miss and caught fire, but the fire was brought under control and, although heavily laden from the tons of water rolling about inside her, managed to struggle on. *Dorset* was left crippled while *Ohio*, straddled again by half a dozen bombs (Stukas were attacking on this occasion), finally ground to a halt. Admiral Burrough sent the destroyers *Bramham* and *Penn* to stand by the two vessels. In the roar of the attacks, crash of guns, thunder of exploding bombs and bursting boom of water falling aboard the ships from near misses, there was no time to remember that it was the thirteenth of the month. . . . *Port Chalmers*, the Convoy Commodore's flagship, which had hitherto come unscathed through bombing raids and torpedo attacks, nearly came to an end when one of her paravanes (mine-cutting devices streamed from each bow) suddenly began to vibrate in a sinister manner. This happened shortly after a further attack by Italian torpedo planes, operating at long range and some of them launching 'motobombas'. When the ship was stopped to investigate and the starboard paravane hoisted out of the water, it was seen that they had 'caught' a torpedo. There was only one thing to do — lower it into the sea again, back away, and then slip the paravane when a suitable distance had intervened. As *Port Chalmers* eased away astern from the taut, thrumming wire there was a huge explosion (probably when the torpedo at the end touched bottom) and the ship shook as a fountain of water burst off her bows. No real damage done and she rejoined what was left of the convoy. There was now only *Port Chalmers* herself, *Rochester Castle* and *Melbourne Star* left in the main body, *Ohio* far behind with a destroyer standing by, and *Dorset* also immobilized with another destroyer at hand. The Hunt Class *Ledbury* had been sent back to look for the cruiser *Manchester* (it was not known that she had been sunk) and after a fruitless search she too was later to stand by *Ohio*.

The small group of three merchantmen with their escorts and the cruiser *Kenya* (which had suffered an engine-room fire after another dive-bombing attack) were now all within the cover of the short range Spitfires from Malta. The minesweeping squadron from Malta came out to meet them and Admiral Burrough could withdraw to Gibraltar with what was left of his Force X, handing over his remaining charges to the island's protection. *Ohio* still wallowed uneasily some seventy miles away, the *Dorset* singled out in another dive-bombing raid had, despite the gunfire of the protecting *Bramham*, been hit by a stick of bombs and gone down. Far away, almost forgotten, *Brisbane Star*, after outwitting the French authorities in Tunisia and playing hide-and-seek with a U-boat, was still making progress. She had yet to make her solitary dash from the Tunisian shallows to Malta by night, hoping that the island's protecting aircraft would remember her existence on the following morning, before the enemy found her.

In what seems, from a suitable distance, the comfortable eighteenth century, the great jurist, Sir William Blackstone had written: 'The Royal Navy of England hath ever been its greatest defence and ornament; it is its ancient and natural strength; the floating bulwark of the island.' It was to the limestone bulwark of another island that the minesweeper and motorlaunches now preceded the three survivors of Operation 'Pedestal'. At 6 p.m., under an evening sky when Fort St Angelo glowed like a ruby against the light, one by one *Melbourne Star*, *Rochester Castle* and *Port Chalmers* came through the breakwater, past the ancient forts into the stained and devastated harbour. This time there was no panache. These were indeed survivors and though, as always, the people were there in their thousands wildly waving and cheering, this time there was something different in those voices that echoed round the ramparts. A large convoy had been expected, the radio had been full of it, and everyone knew that only a large convoy could save them. But there were only these ships whose very metal looked tired, their paintwork blistered, one was so low in the water that it was a wonder she'd made it at all. All were scarred with torn metal, bullet holes and sides savaged by bomb splinters. And there was no tanker. Everyone knew that there had to be a tanker — oil was as important as bread. The Governor, Lord Gort, was there to salute them — and there was even a small band playing. Santa Marija! Yes, the convoy had arrived. But only three ships — and there was no tanker.

At about the time that they made for their unloading berths, where soldiers and dockers waited, where transport was ready the moment that lines could be got ashore, *Dorset* sank. At the same time three destroyers *Penn*, *Bramham* and *Ledbury* were all standing by the crippled *Ohio*. They had just got way on her, so delicate and

216

precarious a movement of her shattered and torn sides that it seemed like a breath on the water. And then another raid developed. One bomb fell under the tanker's stern and yet another went down into her engine room where it exploded. For the second time *Ohio*'s crew were taken off. It seemed impossible that the ship could live.

Throughout the night the stores streamed ashore into Malta, the transport moving off by specially-allocated routes to storage dumps far from danger. But no raids had developed over this convoy once it had reached the harbour. The cover of Spitfires above the island had been complete (four-hundred and seven sorties by Spitfires and Beaufighters had been flown as soon as the convoy came within range) and the only sound of aircraft engines overhead was friendly. Some crew members from the ships went ashore only to find no bars, no cafés, no signs of life. They had been used to coming into battered ports in Britain, where at least there was always some form of entertainment; pubs certainly, with beer — even if no spirits and cigarettes. This was like landing on the moon. They had not previously understood what the word 'siege' meant. When they went back to their ships (those of them who were not found berths ashore) they would not be disturbed by the clatter of machinery, the trampling of feet, the creek and groan of winches unloading, unloading, unloading. Covered in oil and sea salt, dirty in dirty clothes, they slept out their nightmares far beyond the reach of dreams.

The still August weather, with hardly a cat's paw of wind stirring the sea, remained friendly to *Ohio* throughout the night. While her own exhausted crew lay where they dropped, heads pillowed on lifebelts in the attendant ships, the officers and men of *Penn* and the Malta minesweeper *Rye*, later joined by *Bramham* and *Ledbury*, struggled with the interminable problem of trying to tow a vessel that under any normal conditions would have been sunk. By the morning they had her moving again, *Penn* lashed alongside, *Rye* towing from ahead, and *Ledbury* acting as stern tug to try and keep her pointed in the direction of Malta. Captain D.W. Mason, the ship's master, who had been without sleep for the past three days and nights, reported that he thought *Ohio* might last a further twelve hours. She had less than three feet of freeboard and was slowly settling by the head, but he now had three destroyers, two minesweepers and a number of motor launches around him. They were producing sufficient power to move the ship and keep her from sinking — but, as he had estimated, not for very long.

The same night that had seen the great tanker slowly come to life had also been kind to Captain Riley in *Brisbane Star*. He had managed to lose his shadowing U boat in the Tunisian shallows at dusk and had headed north for Malta, making between five and nine knots, as much as could be expected since the bows had been blown open in the torpedo attack off the Skerki Bank on the night of the 12th. When he raised the old lion skin of the island in the daylight hours of the 14th, with a circle of Spitfires perpetually renewing itself over his head, and when his ship came in through the breakwater pushing an awkward sea ahead where her shored-up forward bulkhead did duty as a bow, there were almost as many tears as cheers among the crowds. The torn ship seemed like a monument to the whole convoy. Although well down by the head, and with her forward holds flooded, most of *Brisbane Star*'s cargo was intact. Unloading began immediately.

That same morning *Ohio* with her cluster of ships around her (the whole curious pattern of them spread like a broken flower head on the sea) was pushing slowly with eccentric wake in the direction of Malta. It was then that she received her last and nearly mortal blow. Despite the Spitfire patrols Junkers 88s made a final determined effort to deny the island that oil, more important than ever now that for sure some bread had got through in the other ships. The Luftwaffe's dive-bomber pilots were brave and determined as ever, accepting the fire put up by the *Ohio* herself and her watchdogs of destroyers and minesweepers, but inevitably when the Spitfires got among them their attacks were broken up. Three of the bombers still got through, although only one of them came close enough to all but sink the ship. His thousand pound bomb landed just off her stern, the explosion buckling her plates, and causing her to heave forward on a great wave, and parting the tow. The saga of *Ohio* has been often told[1] and in particular of her last twenty-four hour fight, avoiding minefields while destroyers and shore batteries put down submarines lying in wait for her, and of how finally she came round the south of the island. Countrymen and women, gunners and children watched with nail-biting tension what seemed like a raft of ships struggle along the island's coastline. The Great Siege of 1565 had never witnessed anything as desperate and strange as those last miles of *Ohio* when Malta's hopes were suspended, so it seemed, on a bubble of air (or a prayer). For it was on 15 August, the very day of the Festa of Santa Marija, that the last and most valuable of the ships struggled into Grand Harbour. Torpedoed, bombed, with parts of a bomber still on her deck, she was nursed down the harbour to be berthed alongside the sunken auxiliary tanker *Plumleaf* at Parlatorio Wharf. Her cargo was intact but, even as she was berthed, she began to settle on the bottom. Her decks had been almost awash for a long time. It had been a very close thing.

CHAPTER THIRTY-TWO

'We Shall Never Take You!'

The arrival of the four merchant ships, damaged though they were, and the survival of the tanker *Ohio* did indeed ensure the salvation of the island. It did not mean the end of the siege. The ultimate result of the expensive Operation Pedestal was to enable Malta to stay in the war. For the high price of nine merchant ships sunk, one aircraft carrier, two cruisers and a destroyer sunk, and one aircraft carrier, two cruisers and one destroyer damaged, the Royal Navy and the Merchant Navy had indeed saved Malta — but only just. Some 32,000 tons of general cargo had reached Grand Harbour together with petrol, oil fuel, kerosene and diesel fuel — enough to give the island about ten weeks more life beyond the existing stocks of only a few weeks. It was immediately recognized by the Axis command that 'the supplies which got through in this last convoy have assured an effective resistance by the island for some time to come.'

No further attempts to neutralize Malta were contemplated, at least for the present; the Regia Aeronautica and the Luftwaffe were diverted to the defence of their own convoys to their forces in North Africa. Operation 'Pedestal', though tactically disastrous, was transformed by its participants into what proved a strategic triumph, wrung out of appalling losses by the endurance, courage and seamanship of the masters and crews of merchant and naval ships alike. As always, Shakespeare had summed it all up centuries before: 'Out of this nettle, danger, we pluck this flower, safety.'

After the relief of 1565 Balbi had described in his diary how the soldiers and sailors went ashore, 'to see the enormous damage to our battlements. These were so ruined that even the oldest veterans were astonished.' This was to be the reaction of all the many thousands who came to Malta in the later years of the Second World War.[1] A further entry in Balbi's diary was unfortunately not to prove true for the survivors of 1942: 'Now that the fleet has arrived, all of us who had been in the siege ate well, for there were supplies enough for all, even though they were costly.' He adds, though, what was certainly true enough of this occasion also: ' . . . during the siege, a fowl had cost two ducats (and even at that price they were rare to come by), while an egg had cost one *real* and a half.

As for the other luxuries, I do not bother to mention them for they could not be obtained for any sum of money.'

About the only improvement in food supplies that occurred after the arrival of the August convoy in 1942 was that the bread ration for males between 16 and 60 was slightly raised. During 1942 infant mortality, normally low in the island, significantly increased while for the first time since records had been kept in Malta the population declined by nearly 2000.

The principal effect of the Santa Marija convoy (as it is called to this day) was a great uplift of the spirits, coupled with the morale-boosting knowledge that they had all been as near to the end as could be faced by men and yet still endured. For several months they would still be dependent upon essential stocks being maintained by the steady turnover of fast minelayers like *Manxman* and of minelaying submarines, chuntering in at night — but on nights that nowadays as often as not were raidless. From the moment they saw the shield of Spitfires shining over the battered hulls as they entered Grand Harbour and then that no air attacks had developed during the unloading of these five prayed for ships, a wave of confidence had surged through the watching thousands — to be communicated to others all over the island. Hunger had not gone away, but the knowledge that ships could now arrive and be protected meant that more ships would come in due course, and the will to endure was sustained.

The island of Malta was a legend now in the world, but it had been a legend in this sea long before. During the sixteenth century, after that first great siege, its example had been held up to the Greeks of the Aegean, who were at that time suffering severely under the ravages of the Ottoman Turks. Someone in Cyprus (at least the ballad is attributed to that island) had first framed the words designed to give men hope:

> Malta of gold, Malta of silver, Malta of precious metal,
> We shall never take you!
> No, not even if you were as soft as a gourd,
> Not even if you were only protected by an onion skin!'
> And from her ramparts a voice replied:
> 'I am she who has decimated the galleys of the Turk
> And all the warriors of Constantinople and Galata'[2]

The words were true once again, only they spoke now to the whole free world.

The evidence of the convoy was soon to be seen in the increased activity of the island, an activity that was swiftly reflected by

Rommel's calls for reinforcements and help at the end of his long supply line in Egypt. It was not so difficult for him to obtain men, for these were ferried across to North Africa in regular flights by Junkers 52 transport planes, but petrol above all, and then tanks, guns, armoured cars and every form of transport could only come by that same old sea route, threatened once again (and now as never before) by that island in the middle of the Middle Sea. Mussolini had long returned to Italy, disappointed of his Napoleonic triumph in Egypt, and the much diminished Italian merchant fleet was again called upon to run the gauntlet from air and sea exercised by the submarines, bombers and torpedo planes of Malta. It was now the turn of the German field marshal in the desert to lament 'the frightful hardships in the heat and desolation of our positions'.

Submarines and torpedo-carrying Beauforts escorted by Beaufighters were now unleashed upon that supply line at the end of which the harassed Axis forces were scarcely able to cope with the spoiling attacks launched by the British desert army, which was all the time building up for a great offensive towards the end of the year.[3] It was no longer a question of 'How many days to Cairo?' but of whether Rommel could even hold his enemy's attack when it came. His own supplies were not only being sunk on the sea route but destroyed on the coastal roads. He complained of how 'the RAF had shifted the main weight of its activity to our lines of communication between the African ports and the front, where they were shooting up our transport columns and sinking one barge and coastal vessel after another.'

At the same time the British with their relatively secure supply line were beginning to profit by the immense American industrial expansion; new guns, tanks, and aircraft arriving regularly by sea in Egypt. Meanwhile the bulk of German arms and armaments were being eaten up by the Russian campaign, and what reached the Axis armies in the desert was only a trickle by the time it had survived the crossing past revived Malta and into the desert ports and onto the roads regularly harassed by the RAF. The route by the western coast of Greece through the Ionian Sea was no longer safe for Axis transports since the long range Beauforts and Beaufighters were able to reach them. Merchant ships had to be diverted through the Corinth Canal down through the Aegean past Crete on their tortuous route. Rommel by this time was a sick man and would have been replaced — at his own request — if a suitable Panzer general could have been found. There was none available and so, beset by worry and ill health, he continued at his post. His sanguine nature had — somewhat naturally — led him to feel after the fall of Tobruk that Egypt was within his grasp. It was an understandable dream that had beckoned him, but he had known the reality early in 1941 when he had told Berlin: 'Without Malta, the Axis will end by losing control of North Africa.'

That control was finally lost in October 1942 at Alamein: largely contributory to the British victory and the Axis defeat was the toll that had been taken over those summer and autumn months by the aircraft and submarines operating from Malta. Transport after transport had gone down, and tankers — as important to Rommel's army as *Ohio* had been to Malta — sank blazing into the sea before torpedoes and bombs. Yet the island which dealt out this savagery was itself once again on the verge of starvation. Despite the continuance of the stringent rationing (the slight alleviation in the bread issue was soon found to have been a mistake) there was at the time of the breakthrough following upon El Alamein less than two weeks food to feed the garrison and the islanders, while the petrol supply was so low that there was under one week left for offensive operations by the aircraft. To ensure that they flew and the submarines continued in their patrols Malta had been taken even further to the limit of 'the target date' (the date for surrender) than in August, when the Santa Marija convoy had arrived.

On 11 October at a time of the greatest shortages and starvations in the island Field Marshal Kesselring, in a last desperate bid to paralyse Malta and take the pressure off the Axis armies in the desert, managed to assemble some three-hundred German and Italian bombers in Sicily for a further onslaught. This meant transferring some aircraft from North Africa, which in itself weakened the defence of Rommel's forces. Although the total number of aircraft mustered at the Sicilian airfields, including fighters, was something like six-hundred, Malta could now put up one-hundred Spitfires and a number of Beaufighters in its defence. The raids were among the heaviest of the whole war and the number of civilian casualties in the island was also heavy because the bomber formations, broken up by the British fighters, inevitably dropped their loads over civilian areas rather than on military targets, now heavily protected by anti-aircraft guns that were no longer rationed as they had been in the terrible days of the spring.

In many ways [wrote Colonel Weldon in his memoirs of the siege] this last onslaught must have been the severest trial of all to the Maltese. It came after a long period of comparative inactivity by day when, perhaps, they might have been forgiven for thinking that the days of sudden and violent death had departed and gone. As it was, the full force of this attack struck them when they were almost at the lowest level of their powers of physical resistance.

222

The prolonged starvation had begun to leave its mark and it is much easier to be brave if one has a full stomach.[4]

The townships of Qormi, Tarxien and Rabat (outside the old capital Mdina) all suffered badly in these raids and it was noticed — as some evidence of the attackers' desperation — that a large amount of anti-personnel bombs as well as incendiaries were dropped by high-flying bombers. The first killed some harmless civilians and the second, as the Italians had found out during the first days of the war, had little or no effect on limestone houses that were as enduring as the island itself.

The principal aim of this nine-day renewed attack was to damage the airfields and to submerge the island's striking power at a time when all important convoys were being sent through to enable the Afrika Korps and the Italian forces to withstand or counterattack the advancing British. It was a failure. The bomber losses were well over one-hundred to thirty defending fighters, many of whose pilots parachuted to safety. At the same time the air offensive against the Axis shipping route never faltered, and during this same month of October forty per cent of the supplies destined for Libya never reached there.

With the swing of the pendulum in the desert Malta, which had been so largely responsible for it, could itself expect to reap some reward. Operation *Stonehenge*, the passage of four merchantmen from Alexandria escorted by five cruisers and sixteen destroyers, took place in November. One old friend of Malta, the cruiser *Penelope*, was damaged in the course of it, but despite attacks by torpedo bombers, all four ships and their escort entered Grand Harbour safely. The last part of their passage had been run through a November gale — conditions in which three Spitfires were lost and the island took on its wintry aspect under lowering clouds. But when the clouds parted the sight of the first peaceful relief to reach Malta since the great siege had started more than two years before was revealed. There was the cruiser *Euryalus* with her Royal Marine band playing on the quarterdeck, the four undamaged merchantmen, the Hunt Class destroyers jinking around outside the breakwater, and the flashing wheel of fighters permanently overhead. The crowds that had cheered and waved bomb-battered arrivals even when Grand Harbour itself had been under heavy attack were now free to indulge in real rejoicing. Although it would be months before full rations could be restored and even more months before the physical effects of the past had worn off,[5] and even more years before — the war being over — the island could be restored to anything approaching its former state, yet the people knew at the sight of those four slabsided merchantmen unloading, untouched, in their harbour that the siege was really over. There would still be occasional air raids in 1943, when the island would see the gathering of the armada that was to overwhelm Sicily and begin the restoration of Europe, and true peace was some years ahead, but the island's longest and most devastating siege was raised.

Although the bells could not yet be rung, the people might still have echoed the words written by the arquebusier Balbi on 8 September 1565, when the bells of the conventual church of Saint Lawrence had sounded out once more over the shattered harbour: 'I do not believe that ever did music sound so sweet to human beings. It was three months since we had ever heard a bell which did not summon us to arms against the enemy. That morning, when they rang for Mass, it was at the same hour that we had grown used to expect the call to arms. All the more solemnly then, did we give thanks to the Lord God, and to His Blessed Mother, for the favours that They had poured upon us.'

Notes

CHAPTER ONE

A Distant Day

1   For information about the reception of Mussolini's declaration of war I am indebted to *Hitler's War* by David Irving (Hodder and Stoughton 1977) and in particular to the chapter 'The Warlord at the Western Front'.

2   Peter Elliott in *The Cross and the Ensign: A Naval History of Malta 1798-1979* (Patrick Stephens, Cambridge 1980) has much useful information about Malta in the inter-war years and its first preparations against aerial attack.

3   There are numerous accounts of the first day of Malta's air bombardment. Lt Col. H.E.C. Weldon R.A. in his *Drama in Malta* (printed BAOR 1946) recorded his impression from the point of view of a serving artillery officer — as well as much else in the subsequent siege. Joseph Attard in *The Battle of Malta* (William Kimber 1980) has given us his impressions of a young boy growing up during those years.

4   For the number of aircraft involved during these raids and similar information during the course of the siege I am indebted not only to the British records but to Mariano Gabriele's *Operazione C3: Malta* (Rome 1975). This book also contains detailed information about the preparations by the Italian military and navy for the abortive plan to capture the island, 'Operation Hercules'.

5   Casualty figures vary from one account to another. Stewart Perowne in *The Siege Within the Walls* (Hodder and Stoughton 1970) takes his figures from 'A young amateur statistician, Mr Michael Galea, [who] has compiled from official records a list of every single civilian victim from this first day until the last raid in April 1942. (The last alert was sounded on 28 August 1944).'

6   See my *The Great Siege: Malta 1565* (Hodder and Stoughton, 1961).

CHAPTER TWO

Islanded In Time

1   There are many books about every aspect of the Maltese archipelago, for the history of these small islands comprises the history of the Mediterranean. Among the most comprehensive is Brian Blouet's *The Story of Malta* (Faber and Faber 1967). *Malta* by Sir Harry Luke (Harrap 1960) presents a sympathetic picture of the island and its political and economic problems by one who was Lieutenant Governor of Malta from 1930-38.

2 P. Brydone, *A Tour through Sicily and Malta in a Series of Letters to William Beckford, Esq., of Somerly in Suffolk* (London 1773).

CHAPTER THREE

The Divided Sea

1 Here and where indicated throughout the quotations from Admiral Cunningham are taken from his autobiography: *A Sailor's Odyssey* by Admiral of the Fleet Viscount Cunningham of Hyndhope (Hutchinson 1951).
2 *Ibid.*
3 *Ibid.*
4 Francis Ebejer in his novel *Requiem for a Malta Fascist* (A.C. Aquilina, Malta, 1980) has vividly recaptured the atmosphere of the pre-war years and of the siege itself seen through the eyes of a young Maltese growing up under British colonial rule, the shadow of Mussolini, and the massive aerial bombardment.
5 Despatch of the Secretary of State for the Colonies on the Language Question, 16 August 1934.
6 Luke, *Malta*, has dealt at length not only with the language question but other social and political matters of the period.

CHAPTER FOUR

Thunder Afar

1 For this information I am indebted to Stewart Perowne's *The Siege Within the Walls* (Hodder and Stoughton, 1970). Mr Perowne, although not himself present during the siege, knew Malta well for many years, both before and after the war. His account is largely based on the reminiscences of friends and acquaintances whom he interviewed in later years.
2 Cunningham, *Sailor's Odyssey*.
3 This brief account of this action is based on Admiral Cunningham's despatch of 27.4.48 to the *London Gazette*.

CHAPTER FIVE

Parochial and Other Matters

1 A.E. Housman, 'Epitaph on an Army of Mercenaries'.
2 Brian Blouet in *The Story of Malta* writes: 'On the first day of the Italian campaign against Malta the Gladiators brought down an enemy aircraft, and although one of the four was quickly damaged beyond repair the remaining three continued to make

a considerable nuisance of themselves and were soon nicknamed Faith, Hope and Charity. . . . Some measure of the Gladiators' effectiveness is given by the fact that Italian airmen operational over Malta estimated the strength of the defending fighter force at 25! How many aircraft Faith, Hope and Charity accounted for is in doubt as in the hectic battle conditions it was rarely possible to confirm a kill. One Gladiator pilot was credited with six victories in one month and awarded the Distinguished Flying Cross early in June 1940.' The partially rebuilt skeleton of Faith (the only survivor) has been preserved in Malta, as have some of the arms and armour of the Knights who in their time had fought to preserve the island from invasion.

3 Cunningham, *Sailor's Odyssey*.
4 George Hogan, *Malta: The Triumphant Years* (Robert Hale, 1978).
5 Joseph Boissevain, *Saints and Fireworks: Religion and Politics in Rural Malta* (LSE Monographs, 1965).
6 Weldon, *Drama in Malta*.
7 Cunningham, *Sailor's Odyssey*.

CHAPTER SIX

The Germans Intervene

1 Joseph Micallef, *When Malta Stood Alone* (Malta 1981).
2 The one word *Is-Silġ* in Maltese serves to cover snow, hail and ice. Literally, *Ilma maghqud*, congealed or frozen water.
3 Ian Cameron, *Red Duster, White Ensign* (Muller 1959).
4 Cunningham, *Sailor's Odyssey*.

CHAPTER SEVEN

Full Fury

1 Weldon, *Drama in Malta*.
2 Cunningham, *Sailor's Odyssey*.
3 Joseph Attard, *The Battle of Malta* (William Kimber 1980). An invaluable account from an islander's point of view.
4 *Ibid.*
5 *Ibid.*
6 Weldon, *Drama in Malta*.
7 Quoted in Anon, *The Air Battle of Malta* (HMSO 1944).
8 *Ibid.*
9 Cameron, *Red Duster*.

CHAPTER EIGHT

Island, Desert and Sea

1 The full story of the Italian involvement in the war as far as it related to Malta, as well as the planning of the invasion that never happened, is to be found in *Operazione*

C3: Malta (Rome 1975), which is valuable in presenting the other side of the picture as well as that presented by the British and Maltese historians and diary writers.

2   Eric Brockman, *Last Bastion: Sketches of the Maltese Islands* (Malta 1975).

3   *The Times of Malta* was admirably edited throughout the siege by the remarkable Miss Mabel Strickland, OBE. The daughter of Lord Strickland, she profited by her father's perspicacity in seeing the necessity for deep air-raid shelters long before the war. Although his counsel had gone unheeded by the authorities at the time, he had provided for his own newspaper an almost bomb-proof headquarters carved out of the rock. The newspaper continued to be issued daily under Miss Strickland's direction throughout the war, even when most of Valletta lay in ruins round about.

4   Quoted by Micalleff in *When Malta Stood Alone.*

5   A full account of this action can be found in the *Battle of Cape Matapan* by Captain S.W.C. Pack as well as in the account given by Admiral Cunningham, *Sailor's Odyssey.*

CHAPTER NINE

Voices

1   The breaking of the Enigma cypher as first told in Group Captain Winterbotham's book — F.W. Winterbotham, *The Ultra Secret* (Weidenfeld and Nicholson 1974) — revealed one of the last great secrets of World War II. All previous histories have to be reviewed to some extent in the light of this revelation. Subsequent books enlarging upon the subject have included Peter Calvocoressi's *Top Secret Ultra* (Cassell 1980). The United States, being a more open society than the United Kingdom, claimed somewhat similar American successes in breaking Japanese cyphers before and after Pearl Harbour; these have long been public knowledge. The absence after so many years of a great deal of Ultra material in the Public Records Office in Britain has been commented upon by others.

2   The author spent some months of 1951 in his sailing boat in the old Boat Pound of the Knights of St John, where some of their galleys used to be housed. It lies between Fort St Angelo and the old city of Birgu (Vittoriosa). Opposite it, right under the towering rock on which St Angelo was built, lies the cave-like entrance to the tunnels that once housed the galley slaves, and later some of the World War II staff as described. To walk through these tunnels today is to walk with many ghosts.

3   Although the German paratroop invasion of Crete was known about in advance and General Freyberg was fully informed, it would seem that it was not so much an unwillingness to act upon Ultra that prevented a counter-attack at the right time as some military mishandling of the information. On the other hand, it was due to forewarning by Ultra of German intentions that no seaborne convoys ever reached the island and that the losses among the paratroopers were so heavy as to be unacceptable.

CHAPTER TEN

Spring '41

1   Despite post-war official histories much vivid information about RAF activities during the siege can be gained from *The Air Battle of Malta.*

2   In the notes on rationing in his book *When Malta Stood Alone* Joseph Micallef comments: 'Families of five or less were entitled to four boxes of matches; larger families were allowed six. Soap and coffee rations were more complicated: a single person was entitled to one bar of soap [rations were issued on the 6th and 21st of each month]; a family of four or less got two bars; families of five to eight persons got three bars. Families of three or less had a ration of ¼ rotolo of coffee.... [A rotolo is an old Maltese measure, still in use in the island, being the equivalent of 28 ounces.] In August 1941 lard, margarine and edible oil were also put on the ration card. The tapering scale was also applied to these items.'

Kerosene, used for cooking and lighting, was rationed on a weekly basis from May 1941. The kerosene carts which supplied the towns and villages were horse drawn, the distribution being under the supervision of the police. The rationing of kerosene caused more disputes than almost any other item, being particularly susceptible to bribery and black market operations. Tinned tuna fish and sardines, a daily fare of the working men, became increasingly scarce and again were bought up by the unscrupulous and sold at black market prices.

3   George Hogan, *Malta*.

CHAPTER ELEVEN

War and Weather

1   'X' is pronounced 'sh' in Maltese. The sirocco is also known as the 'rih isfel' — the 'wind from below' — i.e. from Africa. Seamen's refinements are 'xlokk lvant' — south-east sirocco — and 'xlokk punent' — south-west sirocco. The sirocco is most common in spring and autumn; the latter is the most unpleasant, being warmer and more humid. The respite that the Maltese found from aerial attack during the war when a heavy sirocco blew was also enjoyed by the garrison of Tobruk, where the wind was felt as the desert 'khamsin' which could completely obscure sky and sun with sand. Under this gritty blanket, unpleasant though it was, the soldiers, sailors and airmen knew at least that they would be spared the routine attention of the Stukas.

2   The identification of Malta and Gozo with 'Calypso's isles' was made by Byron in a poem during a visit in 1809. The game of identifying places mentioned in the wanderings of Odysseus was popular enough in classical times but the Maltese archipelago does not seem to have been proposed as the home of the goddess Calypso until the eighteenth and nineteenth centuries when the identification of places mentioned in classical literature was being pursued all over the Mediterranean, mainly for the edification of rich classically-educated travellers from the north. Modern guides usually show visitors the cave overlooking the sandy bay of Ramla on the north-east coast of Gozo as the home of Calypso, where she detained Odysseus for seven years. All such ascriptions are of course purely imaginative, and as good a case can be made out for a cave above Pwales valley with its ever-running stream on Malta's north-eastern coast.

3   Vice-Admiral Sir Wilbraham Ford was one of the main pillars of Malta's defence. His work overseeing the dockyard and particularly in getting so great a part of the engineering workshops sited in tunnels and safe from bombs did much to ensure Malta's efficiency in the darkest days of the siege.

4   Commander W.P. Carne was the fleet torpedo officer responsible for suggesting this method for dealing with Malta's magnetic mine problem. He later went on to

become captain of HMS *Coventry*, one of the famous anti-aircraft cruisers which saw more action, protecting both fleet and convoys in the Luftwaffe-dominated years to come, than almost any other ship.

CHAPTER TWELVE

In Another Island

1   It has sometimes been suggested that General Freyberg did not make the best use of Ultra during the campaign. There is little evidence one way or the other. The great error, leading to the loss of Crete, was the failure to send into Maleme airfield the two New Zealand battalions held in reserve at Canea. That the Royal Navy would never permit — at whatever loss to itself — any reinforcements to be landed by sea seems to have been something that the general did not understand. Had he had full confidence in the navy, he would have sent in the reserve battalions and held the airfield. In fact, no seaborne reinforcements reached the invaders until such time as the order to abandon Crete had been given and the last of the allied survivors were being taken off — an operation which totally engaged all of Cunningham's ships that were still seaworthy.

2   In the post-war years a number of books were naturally written about the Battle of Crete by survivors and others. One which gives the bitter taste of those days is the second volume of Evelyn Waugh's *Sword of Honour* trilogy, *Officers and Gentlemen* (first published Chapman and Hall 1955).

3   Cunningham, *Sailor's Odyssey*.

4   *Ibid*. A previous attempt to send *Glenroy* to Crete with reinforcements 22-23 May had been turned back on Cunningham's express command — in contradiction to orders emanating from the Admiralty. 'It appeared to be sheer murder to send her on,' he later wrote. Winston Churchill seems always to have been hypnotized by the Aegean Sea and to have been unlucky there — from the Dardanelles campaign of World War I onwards. As late as 1944, for no good reason except perhaps the hope of involving Turkey on the allied side, he initiated the unfortunate (and usually tacitly ignored) Dodecanese campaign in which a number of destroyers were sunk or badly damaged — operating once again in narrow waters without air cover and providing perfect targets for the by then almost obsolete Stuka. The writer was aboard HMS *Glenroy* in the first of these campaigns and in HMS *Exmoor* for the second.

CHAPTER THIRTEEN

The Besieged Strike Back

1   Quentin Hughes, *Fortress: Architecture and Military History in Malta* (Lund Humphries 1969).

2   A typical instance of such a raid is given by Eric Newby, *Love and War in the Appenines* (Pan Books & Collins 1971). In this case a raid on the aerodrome at Catania was the objective and the whole atmosphere of such an operation is well portrayed.

3   Donald Macintyre, *The Battle for the Mediterranean* (Batsford 1946).

CHAPTER FOURTEEN

The Hot Summer

1 The dramatic story of how *Sydney Star* managed to reach Malta on her own through every kind of hazard is told in Chapter Five of Ian Cameron's *Red Duster, White Ensign*, a book which recounts the exploits of the major convoys to the island and many of the individual actions which form part of that history.

2 Joseph Attard in *The Battle of Malta* states that a number of these expeditions were made for reconnaissance purposes and that Commander Moccagatta 'who was in charge of the Malta operation . . . said that the Italians had to rely on this type of reconnaissance because they could not find and they did not have a single spy on Malta.'

3 Quoted by Perowne in *The Siege Within the Walls*.

4 The siege of Fort St Elmo was a principal feature of the Great Siege of 1565, and the length of time that it took the Turkish forces to reduce the fortress was largely responsible for their ultimate defeat.

CHAPTER FIFTEEN

Aspects of War

1 George Hogan, *Malta*.

2 The quotation comes from 'A Chinese Sage' in *The Importance of Living* by Lin Yutang.

3 Francis Ebejer. *Requiem for a Malta Fascist*.

4 Whitworth Porter, *The History of the Knights of Malta* (London 1883).

5 Even between the citizens of the two main islands of the archipelago, Gozo and Malta, there exists some rivalry. Malta is basically dependent on the dockyards, shipping repairs, and light industry. Gozo is 'the market garden' of the islands. Tourism involving both islands has proved something of a levelling influence, but quite recently a Gozitan was still capable of remarking to the writer: 'That's the only thing that spoils the view.' He was pointing south across the blue strait at Malta, only three miles away.

CHAPTER SIXTEEN

The Fall of the Year

1 *The Air Battle of Malta*. (HMSO 1944) and Weldon, *Drama in Malta*.

2 S.W. Roskill, *The War at Sea* (HMSO 1956-1961).

CHAPTER SEVENTEEN

Individuals

1   Credit is indeed given in *British Intelligence in the Second World War*, Vol. III, Part I, ed. F.H. Hinsley (HMSO 1984) to the part played by Combined Operations pilotage parties to the invasion of Sicily. Even so, one distinguished review of this publication was headlined 'Bletchley's Victory'.

2   *The Air Battle of Malta* (HMSO 1944) has the following anecdote: 'While carrying out, unarmed, a low-level photographic reconnaissance of Bizerta in November 1942, Warburton was attacked and shot up by Me.109s. His aircraft was hit in the engine, oil tank and compass, and he was compelled to land at Bône. He made his way, via Algiers, to Gibraltar, where he collected a fighter [a Spitfire] which was awaiting delivery to Malta. While flying this machine back he encountered two Ju.88s in the Gulf of Tunis and attacked them. One he shot down, the other managed to escape into cloud. He then returned to his astonished colleagues who had already given him up as missing, having heard nothing of him for four days.' Later in the war Warburton was 'loaned' to the USAF for photographic missions after the big USAF daylight raids over Europe. In the course of his air force career he had earned two Distinguished Service Orders, and three Distinguished Flying Crosses. He disappeared finally under mysterious circumstances and it is right that his friend Group Captain Spooner should have the last word: 'Needless to say, he was flying an aircraft (an American one) that didn't belong to him. . . . Some profess to believe that he is still alive. Just as some believe that Lawrence of Arabia still lives. With such men, and there was much in common between them, anything is possible — anything other than the ordinary.' This and the quotation in text are from A. Spooner, *In Full Flight* (Macdonald 1965).

3   Joseph Attard, *The Battle of Malta*.

4   The following table shows quite clearly how, contrary to the general principle that ships are safer in convoy, this was not so in the exceptional circumstances prevailing in the Mediterranean in World War II.

	Set out for Malta	Sunk	Turned Back	Arrived
Aug. 1940–Aug. 1942				
Sailing in convoy	55	22	11	22
Sailing alone	31	9	1	21

The convoy system which operated so successfully elsewhere did not do so in the context of Malta because the movement of a large convoy was immediately known to the enemy and in the passage through the Narrows (dominated by enemy air as well as being mined) the odds were stacked against the convoy. Individual ships, on the other hand, especially if they were old and small and stuck to the edge of French territorial waters along the North African coast, making their final dash for Malta by night, had a good chance of getting through. See Cameron, *Red Duster, White Ensign*.

CHAPTER EIGHTEEN

Striking Force

1   The city of Valletta and the fortress architecture of Malta has been brilliantly dealt with in words and photographs by Professor Quentin Hughes, *Fortress*.

2   After the Great Siege of 1565 spies for the Ottomans quite often reported on the state of the island and its defences, as the Sultans succeeding Suleiman the Magnificent did not entirely despair of triumphing where he had failed. Well before the eighteenth century, however, the fortifications of Malta were so massive and so ingenious as to be quite beyond the besieging capability of any armies or navies of the time.

3   Letter quoted extensively in my *Mediterranean: Portrait of a Sea* (Hodder and Stoughton, 1971).

4   Spooner, *In Full Flight*.

5   Macintyre, *The Battle for the Mediterranean*. In Chapter Six the writer deals in detail with some of the worst Axis shipping casualties of this period.

CHAPTER NINETEEN

A Hard Winter

1   In the Great Siege of 1565 the Turkish High Command first made the mistake of concentrating all their efforts against Fort St Elmo, failing to observe that Fort St Angelo and the walled village of Birgu (Vittoriosa) behind it should have been the main objective and also that they should have severed the communications between Grand Harbour and the north of the island, including the old capital of Mdina. Unlike Kesselring, Dragut was unable to reverse these tactics for fear of loss of morale among the Ottoman troops. See my book *The Great Siege* (London and New York, 1961).

2   British and Maltese fought side by side at the gun positions; Maltese served throughout the war in the Mediterranean fleet; the Royal Malta Artillery received numerous awards for gallantry. As from February 1941 there was national service for all males between sixteen and sixty-five in the island and military service for those between eighteen and forty-one. The complaint of the Italian commander in charge of the small boat raid — that they did not have a single spy on the island — should be borne in mind in this context.

3   H.E.C. Weldon, *Drama in Malta*.

4   Vice-Admiral Sir Wilbraham Ford (knighted in 1942) had spent five years in Malta when he was relieved in 1942 by Vice-Admiral Sir Ralph Leatham. As Admiral Cunningham rightly said of him: 'It is no exaggeration to say that he was one of the mainstays of the defence of Malta....'

CHAPTER TWENTY

New Year 1942

1   One such prayer to the Virgin Mary, translated from Maltese, reads:

> O Maiden Lady of Victory,
> Queen of Heaven and Earth,
> Gather the bombs into your mantle
> And deliver us from the attack.

2   In post-war politics, prior to the island's Independence in 1964, some play was made by the Malta Labour Party with the argument — in favour of neutrality — that Malta's sufferings in World War II would never have occurred but for her being a British colony. But, given the moral approach of the German and Italian states at the time, is it conceivable that Maltese neutrality would have been respected? Such an ideal harbour, situated in the centre of the Mediterranean, would still have been fought over. Malta's geographical importance, which has also given it one of the highest standards of living in the depressed region of the Mediterranean, has always had to be paid for.

3   Hummel E. Siewert, *Il Mediterraneo* (Milan 1938). Siewert was also one of many who pointed out the proximity of Malta to Sicily, arguing that in the age of the aircraft Malta was untenable. This theory was one often adduced by RAF and army officers in Britain before the war which, despite the navy's protestations, led to the weak and unprepared state of the island when war did finally break out.

4   The whole area abounds in Homeric place names. The long-identified Scylla is the rock on the toe of Italy (opposite the whirlpool Charybdis on the Sicilian side of the Messina Straits) from which the legendary monster seized passing sailors. Italian journalists also sometimes referred to Malta as 'Medusa', not inappropriate since the Homeric Medusa turned people who looked upon her to stone. Also in modern Italian, *medusa* is the word for the poisonous jellyfish.

5   German books and articles dealing with Malta in World War II include: H.J. Nowarra's, *Geleitzug-Schlachten im Mittelmeer* (1978). Th. Weber, *Luftschlacht um Malta: Flugwehr un Technik* (1956). O. Möhlenbeck, *Ein Kampf gegan Malta und um Nordafrika* (1966). W. Warlimont, *Insel Malta in der Mittelmeer: Strategie des Zweiten Weltkriegs* (1958).

6   From a conversation with a Messerschmitt pilot in Mtarfa Hospital recorded in the diary of O. Ormrod, a Hurricane pilot who was himself killed over the island in April 1942.

7   Weldon, *Drama in Malta*.

CHAPTER TWENTY-ONE

Raids and Rain

1   Francisco Balbi di Correggio, *The Siege of Malta*. Trans. from the Spanish edition of 1569 by Ernle Bradford (Folio Society 1965).

2   Gray was a brave man, and his on the spot reports from Malta are as good as any that survive. George Hogan in *Malta: The Triumphant Years* has the following to say: 'He told the few of us who sometimes congregated near Fort St Elmo in Valletta of life in England, and brought over to us the feeling of home and the suffering there, too.' It was clear that he thought life in Malta and the interminable air raids were even worse — almost unendurable.

3   Hogan, *Ibid*.

4   Attard, *The Battle of Malta*.

5   Joseph Conrad, *Typhoon*.

6   Cunningham, *Sailor's Odyssey*.

CHAPTER TWENTY-TWO

Awaiting Invasion

1   Four-thousand tons of seed potatoes had normally been imported per annum. After the loss of this important cargo, substitute tuber were brought in from Cyprus but failed to germinate satisfactorily in Maltese soil.

2   In post-war years, during the reconstruction and redevelopment of the island, an attempt was made to start a commercial fishing industry using modern trawlers. The venture failed for, among other reasons, the salient one that the total unsuitability of the sea area had not been taken into consideration.

3   This story was still current in Kalkara when I lived in the village some years after the war.

CHAPTER TWENTY-THREE

Convoy

1   Cunningham, *Sailor's Odyssey*.

2   Too much should not be made of this. The British destroyers by their mobility and their diversity clearly had many advantages. One of the most surprising things about the day's action is the apparent inactivity of the Italian destroyers.

3   Under the circumstances — wind, weather, heavy sea, heavy fire — this may not appear surprising. The British torpedo control system, however, as compared with its gunnery control remained somewhat in the 'Jutland era' until late in the war.

4   The Italians certainly built the most beautiful looking warships of this period, but they were not comparable in seaworthiness to the British.

5   The last voyage of the *Breconshire* has been told in a number of accounts of the Malta convoys, notably by Ian Cameron in *Red Duster, White Ensign*.

CHAPTER TWENTY-FOUR

April '42

1   Perowne, *The Siege Within the Walls*.

2   T.S. Eliot, 'The Hollow Men' (from *Collected Poems 1909–1962*, Faber & Faber 1963).

3   Paul Cassar, *Medical History of Malta* (Wellcome Historical Medical Library, 1964).

4   Alastair Mars, *Unbroken: The Story of a Submarine* (Muller 1953). This, and the same author's *British Submarines at War 1939-1945* (William Kimber) gives a lively personal account of the submariner's life in the idiom of the times.

CHAPTER TWENTY-FIVE

A Volcano in Eruption

1 Weldon, *Drama in Malta*.
2 The medal itself was not officially presented until 13 September 1942, when Lord Gort who had succeeded General Dobbie as Governor handed it over to Sir George Borg, the Chief Justice of Malta, in a formal ceremony on Palace Square in Valletta. The silver cross was later displayed in the different villages throughout the island so that every citizen could see the tribute that had been paid to their courage in withstanding what Lord Gort termed 'the most concentrated bombing in the history of the world'. The medal and the citation are now displayed in the Palace in Valletta and a plaque on the wall outside records the citation.
3 D. Barnham, *One Man's Window* (William Kimber 1956).
4 *The Air Battle of Malta*.

CHAPTER TWENTY-SIX

A Change of Balance

1 Cunningham, *Sailor's Odyssey*.
2 Lord Gort arrived by Sunderland flying boat during the night of 7-8 May 1942, touching down off the Kalafrana seaplane base in the south of the island. He and General Dobbie, together with Malta's civic leaders and the Service Chiefs, met in a bomb-damaged building at the Fleet Air Arm base, where Lord Gort took the oath of office. 7 May was the Feast of our Lady of Pompeii, usually celebrated by the Maltese with offerings of roses. During the swearing-in ceremony a stick of bombs dropped near the building where the dignitaries were gathered. The whole situation was somewhat reminiscent of the last days of Pompeii. After the governorship of the island had been formally handed over General Dobbie and his family boarded the same Sunderland that had brought in his successor and flew off to Gibraltar. General Gort proceeded through the island through an air raid.
3 *The Air Battle of Malta*.
4 Micallef, *When Malta Stood Alone*. Mr Micallef presents many details of life under the siege which have escaped the attention of other writers more preoccupied with the war itself.

CHAPTER TWENTY-SEVEN

Bread of Adversity

1 Calvocoressi, *Top Ultra Secret*.
2 'In the period from 26 May to 27 July, Malta-based aircraft made 191 sorties of which 102 were directed against shipping at sea and sixty-two against ports and

bases. With the aid of air superiority Malta was regaining her position as an air/sea offensive base.' *The Air Battle of Malta.*

3 The *Centurion* certainly did attract the enemy, being the main object of attack and being hit a number of times. A W/T operator who was lent from HMS *Glenroy* to the *Centurion* for the duration of the convoy provided an illustration of something which the writer had hitherto thought to be an old wives' tale: he left the *Glenroy* with a normal crop of dark hair and returned to the ship after the convoy with a snow white thatch. All conceded that it was most interesting....

4 Both convoys were desperately hard fought — among the worst of all the Malta convoys, involving continuous bombing, submarine attacks, and even the intervention of surface forces. For full accounts see Donald Macintyre's *The Battle for the Mediterranean* and Ian Cameron's *Red Duster, White Ensign*. It is safe to say that if Rear-Admiral Vian, in command of the cruiser escort from Alexandria, had been left in sole control he would have fought as brilliantly as he had previously done in the Battle of Sirte. Certainly *some* of his merchant ships would have got through. The combined command ('remote control') exercised by the navy and the air force from Alexandria proved disastrous.

CHAPTER TWENTY-EIGHT

Heat of the Day

1 Weldon, *Drama in Malta.*
2 W. Beck, Reuter correspondent in Malta, quoted Micallef, *When Malta Stood Alone.*
3 Fernand Braudel, *The Mediterranean — and the Mediterranean World in the Age of Philip II*, trans. Sian Reynolds (Collins, London; Harper & Row, New York).
4 Field Marshal Lord Alanbrooke, *The Turn of the Tide* (Collins) Alanbrooke's impressions of the island which he toured briefly before flying on to Cairo confirm all the others: 'The destruction is inconceivable and reminds me of Ypres, Arras, Lens at their worst during the last war.' The salient difference was that a whole civilian population was *living* under these conditions.

CHAPTER TWENTY-NINE

Precautions

1 Anon, *The Air Battle of Malta.*
2 *Ibid.*
3 P. Elliott, *The Cross and the Ensign* (Cambridge 1980).

CHAPTER THIRTY

Nine Days to Santa Maria

1 The Mediterranean was a notoriously difficult area for the submarine detection device now called Sonar, but then known as Asdic after the British abbreviated name (it being a British invention). The high salinity, varying densities, and

occurence of curious layers of cold water which deflected the Asdic transmission were major factors in unreliability. This was also augmented by the presence in some parts of the sea of whales, which returned an echo that the nervous operators were likely to accept as submarines. The Mediterranean is not and never has been 'a whaling sea', but modern information suggests that a certain number of old bull whales 'retire' to its indulgent waters, usually accompanied by a small group of three or four cows. (Some human analogy seems obvious here.)

2 From these beginnings the Germans were later to develop a somewhat similar pilotless glider bomb that was first used effectively from a Junkers 88 against the Italian battleship *Roma* in September 1943 at the time of the Italian surrender. *Roma*, on her way to Malta, was a total loss.

CHAPTER THIRTY-ONE

Miraculous Relief

1 Apart from Captain Macintyre in *The Battle for the Mediterranean*, the story of this convoy has been told at length by Ian Cameron, *Red Duster, White Ensign* and as the central theme of Peter Shankland's and Anthony Hunter's *Malta Convoy* (Collins 1961). The latter, taking the saga of the *Ohio* in detail, gives a more accurate picture of just what such a convoy was like for those involved in it than many pages of official war histories.

CHAPTER THIRTY-TWO

'We Shall Never Take You'

1 In June 1943 King George VI visited Malta aboard the cruiser *Aurora*, familiar to the islanders from her days in Force K. He received a tumultuous welcome from the people, which Admiral Cunningham (now back in the Mediterranean as Allied Naval Commander of the Expeditionary Force in North Africa) described in his autobiography: 'The dense throngs of loyal Maltese, men, women and children, were wild with enthusiasm. I have never heard such cheering, and all the bells in the many churches started ringing when he landed. . . . It was the first time a Sovereign had landed in the island since 1911, and the effect on the inhabitants was tremendous. The visit produced one of the most spontaneous and genuine demonstrations of loyalty and affection that I have ever seen.' Malta was chosen as the site of Allied Headquarters for the invasion of Sicily (once again demonstrating its outstanding importance as a communications and intelligence centre). Apart from many other notables who visited over these months were Generals Eisenhower, Alexander and Montgomery. On 8 September 1943, anniversary of the end of the Great Siege of 1565, the Italian fleet set sail to Malta to surrender — the armistice with Italy having been concluded. On 11 September Admiral Cunningham was able to make the historic signal to the Admiralty: 'Be pleased to inform their Lordships that the Italian Battle fleet now lies at anchor under the guns of the fortress of Malta.' Early in 1945 Prime Minister Churchill and President Roosevelt both came to Malta, together with the many officers of their respective staffs, on

their way through to their fateful meeting with Stalin in the Crimea.

2 The song 'Malta of Gold' is quoted in Pernot's edition of Vendôme's *History of Malta and the War between the Knights and the Grand Turk* (Paris, 1910).

3 On 23 October 1942 the Battle of El Alamein began. On 8 November the Anglo-American assault forces landed in North Africa prior to the occupation of French Morocco, Algeria and Tunisia.

4 Weldon, *Drama in Malta*.

5 In December 1942 four convoys sailed into Malta without loss, and in this one month some 200,000 tons of stores of all kinds were brought ashore. It took a long time, however, for the physical damage caused by shortage of food and living conditions generally to be made good. The effects of malnutrition and its attendant diseases were further aggravated by a severe epidemic of poliomyelitis in November 1942, which did not cease until the beginning of June the following year.

Select Bibliography

Publications and documents from which specific quotations have been made in the text are referred to in the notes together with other relevant information.

General Historical Background
BALBI, F., *The Siege of Malta 1565*, trans from the Spanish, London 1965.
BLOUET, B., *The Story of Malta*, London 1967.
BOISSEVAIN, J., *Saints and Fireworks: Religion and Politics in Rural Malta*, London 1965.
BRAUDEL, F., *The Mediterranean — and the Mediterranean World in the Age of Philip II*, trans. Sian Reynolds, London 1972.
BRADFORD, E., *The Great Siege*, London 1961.
BROCKMAN, E., *Last Bastion: Sketches of the Maltese Islands*, Malta 1975.
BRYDONE, P., *A Tour through Sicily and Malta in a series of Letters to William Beckford Esq., of Somerly in Suffolk*, London 1773.
CASSAR, P., *Medical History of Malta*, Wellcome Historical Medical Library 1964.
ELLIOT, P., *The Cross and the Ensign*, Cambridge 1980.
HUGHES, Q., *Fortress: Architectural and Military History in Malta*, London 1969.
KININMONTH, C., *The Traveller's Guide to Malta*, London 1967.
LUKE, H., *Malta: An Account and an Appreciation*, London 1960.
PORTER, W., *The History of the Knights of Malta*, London 1883.
SIEWERT, H.E., *Il Mediterraneo*, Milan 1938.
VENDÔME, P., *History of Malta and the War between the Knights and the Grand Turk*, ed., H. Pernot, Paris 1910.

World War II

ADMIRALTY, *Mediterranean Pilot* Vol. I, 1951.
ALANBROOKE, LORD, *The Turn of the Tide*, London 1960.

ATTARD, J., *The Battle of Malta*, London 1980.

BRAGADIN, M.A., *The Italian Navy in World War II*, US Navy Institute 1957.

CALVOCORESSI, P., *Top Secret Ultra*, London 1980.

CAMERON, I., *Red Duster, White Ensign*, London 1959.

CHURCHILL, W.S., *The Second World War* — 6 vols, London 1948-54.

COCCHIA, ADMIRAL (AND OTHERS), *La Marina Italiana nella Seconda Guerra Mondiale*, Rome 1959.

CUNNINGHAM, LORD, *A Sailor's Odyssey*, London 1951.

EBEJER, F., *Requiem for a Malta Fascist*, Malta 1980.

GABRIELE, M., *Operazione C3: Malta*, Rome 1975.

HART, B.H. LIDDEL (ed.), *The Rommel Papers*, London 1965.

HAY, I., *The Unconquered Isle*, London 1944.

HINSLEY, F.H. (ed.), *British Intelligence in the Second World War*, Vol. III, HMSO 1984.

HMSO, *The Air Battle of Malta*, 1944.

— , *The Mediterranean Fleet*, 1944.

— , *The Mediterranean and the Middle East* — 5 vols.

HOGAN, G., *Malta: The Triumphant Years*, London 1978.

IRVING, D., *Hitler's War*, London 1977.

LLOYD, AIR MARSHAL SIR H., *Briefed to Attack*, London 1949.

MACINTYRE, D., *The Battle for the Mediterranean*, London 1964.

MARS, A., *British Submarines at War 1939-45*, London 1960.

— , *Unbroken: The Story of a Submarine*, London 1953.

MICALLEF, J., *When Malta Stood Alone*, Malta 1981.

MÖHLENBACK, O., *Ein Kampf gegan Malta und um Nordafrika*, 1966.

NOWARRA, H.J., *Geleitzung-Schlachten im Mittelmeer*, 1978.

OLIVER, R.L., *Malta at Bay*, London 1942.

— , *Malta Besieged*, London 1943.

PEROWNE, S., *The Siege Within The Walls*, London 1970.

PRESTON, A., *Navies of World War II*, London 1976.

ROSKILL, S.W., *The War at Sea* — 4 vols, HMSO 1956-61.

SHANKLAND, P. AND HUNTER, A., *Malta Convoy*, London 1961.

SPOONER, A., *In Full Flight*, London 1965.

TIMES OF MALTA, THE, 1940-3.

WARLIMONT, W., *Insel Malta in der Mittelmeer: Strategie des Zweiten Weltkriegs* 1958.

WEBER, T., *Luftschlacht un Malta: Flugwehr un Technik*, 1956.

WELDON, H.E.C., *Drama in Malta*, BAOR 1946.

WINTERBOTHAM, F.W., *The Ultra Secret*, London 1974.

Index

PEN & SWORD MILITARY CLASSICS

We hope that you have enjoyed your Pen and Sword Military Classic. The series is designed to give readers quality military history at affordable prices. Below is a list of the titles that are planned for 2003. Pen and Sword Classics are available from all good bookshops. If you would like to keep in touch with further developments in the series, including information on the Classics club, then please contact Pen and Sword at the address below.

2003 List

PEN AND SWORD BOOKS LTD

47 Church Street • Barnsley • South Yorkshire • S70 2AS

Tel: 01226 734555 • 734222

E-mail: enquiries@pen-and-sword.co.uk • **Website:** www.pen-and-sword.co.uk